Book design by Horst Blaich - Melbourne, Australia
Cover "Empire Comfort" leaving for Cyprus, April 1948
Cover photographs by courtesy of Richard O. Eppinger Private Collection

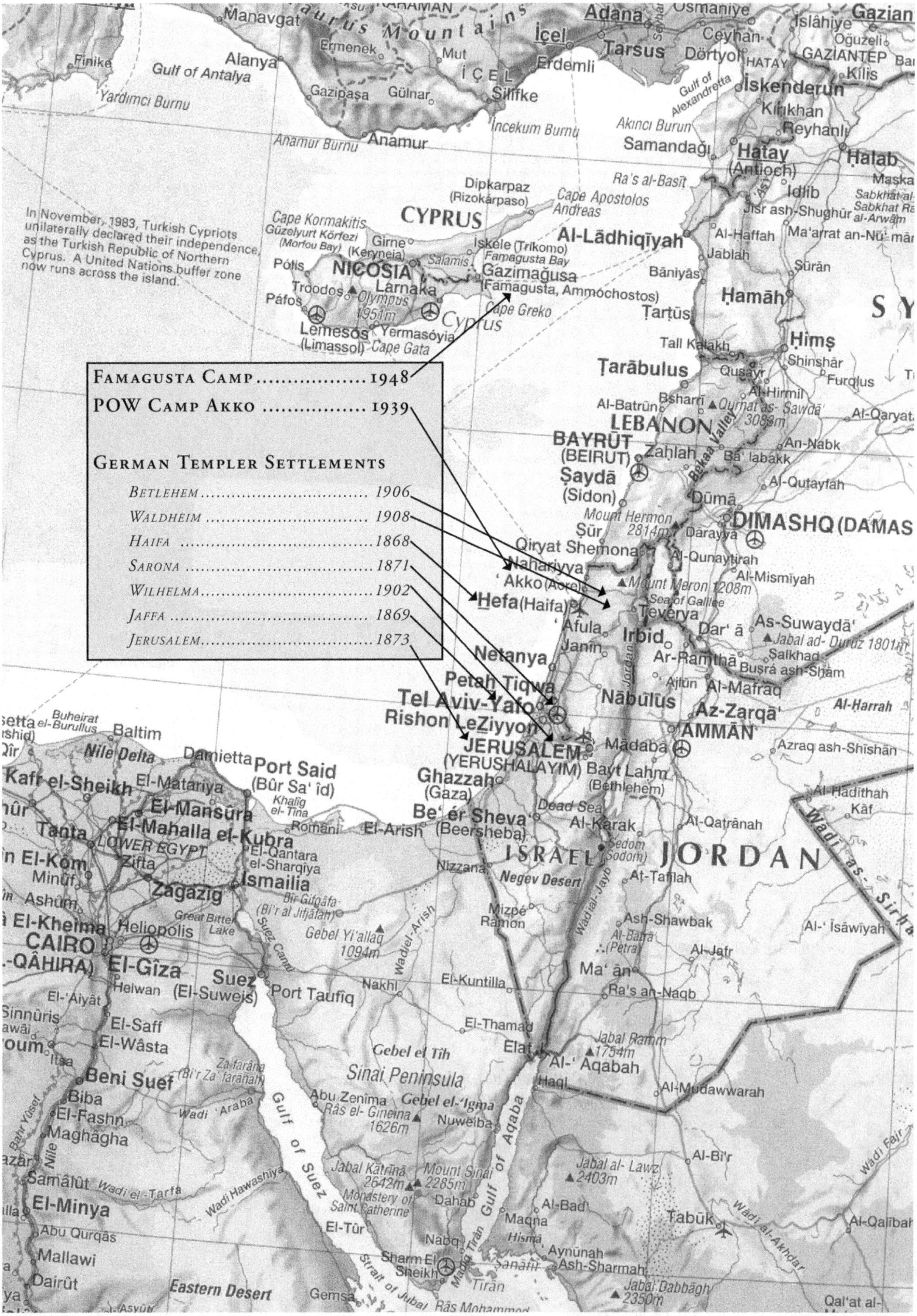
Famagusta Camp 1948
POW Camp Akko 1939
German Templer Settlements
Betlehem 1906
Waldheim 1908
Haifa 1868
Sarona 1871
Wilhelma 1902
Jaffa 1869
Jerusalem 1873
In November, 1983, Turkish Cypriots unilaterally declared their independence, as the Turkish Republic of Northern Cyprus. A United Nations buffer zone now runs across the island.
CYPRUS
NICOSIA
Larnaka
Gazimağusa
(Famagusta, Ammochostos)
Lemesós
(Limassol)
Taurus Mountains
Adana
Tarsus
İskenderun
Ḩalab
Al-Lādhiqīyah
Ḩamāh
Ḩimş
Ţarābulus
LEBANON
BAYRŪT
(BEIRUT)
Şaydā
(Sidon)
DIMASHQ (DAMAS
Qiryat Shemona
Nahariyya
Akko (Acre)
Hefa (Haifa)
Afula
Sea of Galilee
Teverya
Irbid
Netanya
Petah Tiqwa
Tel Aviv-Yafo
Rishon LeZiyyon
Nābulus
JERUSALEM
(YERUSHALAYIM)
Bayt Lahm
(Bethlehem)
'AMMĀN
Ghazzah
(Gaza)
Be'ér Sheva
(Beersheba)
Dead Sea
ISRAEL
JORDAN
Negev Desert
Port Said
(Bûr Sa'îd)
Nile Delta
Ismailia
CAIRO
El-Gîza
Suez
(El-Suweis)
Sinai Peninsula
Gulf of Suez
Gulf of Aqaba
Elat
Al-'Aqabah
Beni Suef
El-Minya
Sharm El Sheikh
Eastern Desert

Exiled from the Holy Land

1. Left: Map of the Middle East

Compiled by Horst Blaich

Temple Society Australia Heritage Group
152 Tucker Road Bentleigh 3204
Melbourne Australia

TSA
HERITAGE GROUP

TRANSLATIONS BY

HEINZ ARNDT: 'LOSING HOME AND HEARTH'

PETER G. HORNUNG: 'FROM THE HOLY LAND TO THE HOME OF THE KANGAROO'; 'DESTINY STRIKES'; EULOGY FOR GOTTHILF WAGNER; 'THE CYPRUS GROUP'; KAROLINE KRAFFT LETTERS; ADELHEID GROLL LETTERS; 'THE END OF THE TEMPLER SETTLEMENTS IN PALESTINE'; ARAB AND JEWISH NEWSPAPER REPORTS; *'AUSWÄRTIGES AMT'* LETTERS

MARTHA STRASSER: 'FLIGHT FROM PALESTINE'

GUNHILD HENLEY: 'THE LOSS OF THE AGRICULTURAL SETTLEMENTS'; 'FORCED STAY IN CYPRUS' (FROM PAUL SAUER 'THE HOLY LAND CALLED')

GRAPHIC DESIGN, BOOK LAYOUT AND COMPUTER WORK ON APPLE COMPUTER EQUIPMENT BY HORST BLAICH, MELBOURNE
WITH TECHNICAL ASSISTANCE FROM TREVOR EVANS OF TREE OF LIFE PUBLISHING, RINGWOOD EAST, VICTORIA, AUSTRALIA

Note for Librarians: A cataloguing record for this book is available from Library and Archives Canada at www.collectionscanada.ca/amicus/index-e.html

Printed in Victoria, BC, Canada.

ISBN: 9781-4251-3891-2 (soft cover)
ISBN: 9781-4251-3892-9 (eBook)

Trafford PUBLISHING www.trafford.com

North America & international
toll-free: 1 888 232 4444 (USA & Canada)
phone: 250 383 6864 ♦ fax: 250 383 6804 ♦ email: info@trafford.com

The United Kingdom & Europe
phone: +44 (0)1865 487 395 ♦ local rate: 0845 230 9601
facsimile: +44 (0)1865 481 507 ♦ email: info.uk@trafford.com

10 9 8 7 6 5 4 3 2 1

EXILED FROM THE HOLY LAND

THE LOSS OF THE TEMPLER SETTLEMENTS IN PALESTINE 1941-1950

2. Finally landed in Famagusta

Compiled by Horst Blaich

Foreword

The TSA Heritage Group has made great efforts to preserve Templer history by researching, recording stories, collecting old letters and reports, scanning family photo albums and printing stories known to us from yore. Together with the *Albert Blaich Family Archive - Australia* we have now an extensive collection about the Templer past, widely recognised in Israel and in Germany.

Our aim is to encourage the younger generation to become more interested and get familiar with the unique Templer history.

We hope that this book – like many other activities of the Heritage Group – will help the younger generation understand the trials and tribulations our parents, grandparents and great-grandparents experienced during times of adversity and war.

It was not an easy time for our ancestors, and we pay our sincere thanks and respect to them for their tenacity, their achievements and their faith in the Almighty who brought us safely to this new land of milk and honey – Australia.

We appreciate the Australian Government for their friendly and helpful acceptance. Our special thanks goes to the late Mr H.T. Temby (Government Official in Canberra) for his efforts to help the Templers to settle comfortably in this new country.

The Australian Government encourages New Australians to maintain their inherited culture and language. This is in fact what the TSA Heritage Group is doing; we have received a sizeable grant to purchase modern electronic equipment which was used in our past projects and in the production of this book.

We thank the Victorian Government for their kind support.

We feel privileged to live in this country of freedom and stable political situation and trust that our production is a worthwhile contribution to the history of a people who found safe refuge in Australia.

It was a most interesting project which took us several years to collect, discuss and compile. We owe a lot of thanks to Peter Hornung for his input in thinking and proofreading, without which it would not have been possible to produce this volume.

It was indeed a team effort. First of all I like to thank and express my appreciation to all the contributors: Trevor Evans of *'Tree of Life Publishing'* Ringwood East, Australia, for his invaluable advice and technical assistance. We acknowledge the help and guidance from Peter Lange and Brigitte Kneher, at the TGD Archive for the long-standing cooperation and directions, as well as to the historians Dr Jakob Eisler and Dr Paul Sauer. I thank Dr Danny Goldman for his knowledge and help, as well as his pertinent piece on Waldheim 1948, and Martin Higgins for his ability in finding relevant information in the British archives and depositories. He was the one who discovered the ex-commandant of Waldheim, Alan Tilbury, who was kind enough to report on the Waldheim events of 1948, as he experienced them when he was a young British officer in Palestine. The book presents the Templer history, 1941 to 1950, from different perspectives and point of views, which makes this book unique and we can recomend it to old and young.

May the reader enjoy learning from our pages about the history of the Templers, that is my sincere prayer.

Horst Blaich, TSA Heritage Group
Melbourne, January 2009

TSA
HERITAGE GROUP

Introduction

In 1861, an independent Christian religious community was founded in Germany. Its members believed, and still do, that people, individually and collectively, are components of a living Temple of God; they therefore called themselves the Temple Society. Having evolved from an earlier movement known as the 'Society for bringing together God's People in Jerusalem', the Temple Society separated from the Protestant Church. Its spiritual leader was Christoph Hoffmann.

The Templers – not to be confused with the Knights Templar – moved their centre of gravity to Palestine where, between 1869 and 1948, they established and maintained six Christian communities, which contributed significantly to the development of the country. The consequences of the Second World War led to the loss of their settlements. The Temple Society subsequently formed new communities in Germany and in Australia, albeit not in the 'settlement' style. In Germany, the Society operates as *Tempelgesellschaft in Deutschland* (TGD) and in Australia as Temple Society Australia (TSA).

As a small minority in Palestine, interned behind barbed wire, torn between loyalty to a distant fatherland and love of the Holy Land, forced out by deportation, terror and organised expulsion, the Templers did indeed have a difficult time. Throughout the 1940s, they battled with the spectre of an uncertain future on a rollercoaster ride of fear, hope and despair.

After the publication of *Memories of Palestine* (2005), which is a collection of reminiscences of an earlier era, the question arose: what happened when the Templers had to leave Palestine? An answer to this question is attempted in the book at hand. Although many of today's Templers are still very much aware of this episode, it seems fitting and proper to record it in print for posterity.

Part one contains personal records or diaries written at the time, or shortly afterwards, such as some of the reports about the trip on the *Queen Elizabeth*, Richard O. Eppinger's Cyprus diary or letters of a personal nature, while others were written from memory. In part two, which includes historical contributions by Dr Paul Sauer and Dr Danny Goldman, it is particularly refreshing for many of us to read, for the first time, an in-depth account of the attack on Waldheim from an Israeli perspective, unique not least because it is based on interviews with contemporary observers.

The impact of the assassination of Gotthilf Wagner and its implications – perhaps a neglected aspect of Templer history – is given a measure of information and recognition here. Gotthilf Wagner was a man who steadfastly, not to say stubbornly, adhered to the idea of Templer settlements in Palestine – or elsewhere, if suitably compensated. Like others, he was against selling out, against any kind of break-up, against giving up and against leaving without a firm promise of a viable alternative, because he was for the future and for staying together. His dreams did not come true in the way he envisaged.

We thank all our contributors, be they alive or speaking to us through their families' archives. Who are they? The table of contents provides a long list, too long to reiterate. We, however, do want to express special 'thank-yous' to Dr Paul Sauer and Dr Danny Goldman for permission to print excerpts from their excellent works, as well as to Alan Tilbury for his valuable contribution. In addition – all you translators, indexers, proofreaders, printers, publishers and consultants – none of you shall be forgotten, because your work and your feedback were extremely beneficial and did us proud.

•

Peter G. Hornung, October 2008

Key dates and events

2 November	1917	Balfour Declaration
July/August	1939	Rumours of war
30 August	1939	Eight men leave on an Italian airline
31 August	1939	232 called-up men (including non-Templers) leave on the *Patris*
1 September	1939	German troops invade Poland
2 September	1939	The 'Palestine Police' surround Haifa settlement Local shops close
3 September	1939	Great Britain and France declare war on Germany All men up to 50 and even older are arrested and transferred to Akko prison camp Temple Bank closes down Conversion of the rural settlements of Sarona, Wilhelma, Betlehem and Waldheim to internment camps
19 December	1939	Haifa settlers are sent to internment camps, mainly Betlehem and Waldheim
May	1940	Jaffa and Jerusalem people are transferred to Sarona and Wilhelma internment camps
31 July	1941	665 men, women and children (536 Templers) are deported to Australia on the *Queen Elizabeth*
23 August	1941	The *Queen Elizabeth* arrives in Sydney The German internees are railed to Tatura internment camp in northern Victoria
17 December	1941	First Internee Exchange of 69 women and children
Oct/Nov	1942	Second Internee Exchange of approximately 300 persons
May/June	1944	Third Internee Exchange of 44 persons
July	1944	Some of the exchanged internees die in Stuttgart bombing raid
December	1944	Sarona evacuation to Wilhelma begins
22 March	1946	Gotthilf Wagner murdered
Late	1946	First Tatura internees freed
1946 to	1948	Period of instability in Palestine
17 April	1948	Waldheim raided by the Haganah Two people shot dead, one wounded Inhabitants forced to flee from Waldheim and Betlehem

Key Dates and Events

20 April	1948	Wilhelma residents evacuated on board *Empire Comfort*
21 April	1948	*Empire Comfort* picks up Betlehem and Waldheim refugees
22 April	1948	Refugees arrive in Cyprus to live in tents
13 July	1948	Three people arrive in Cyprus by plane from Germany
10 August	1948	Departure of 27 non-members
21 October	1948	A group of 49 leaves for Germany from Nicosia by plane
5 December	1948	Three families arrive in Cyprus from Haifa
16 December	1948	First *Partizanka* group (37) leaves for Australia from Limassol
17 December	1948	Rumour of stowaway passenger on board the *Partizanka*
26 January	1949	Plane leaves Cyprus for Australia with 45 persons
		Al Misr leaves for Australia with 170 souls on board
31 January	1949	Plane arrives in Sydney
9 March	1949	Second *Partizanka* group (77) leaves Cyprus for Australia
3 April	1949	*Partizanka* arrives in Melbourne, Australia
December	1949	A group led by Samuel Faig leaves Israel for Australia
4 April	1950	Hermann Imberger group leaves from Haifa for Australia
12 April	1950	Nikolai Schmidt flies to Sydney, followed by four others
20 July	1950	Jakob Imberger boards a ship for Australia in Haifa with five others

3. Watchtower in Wilhelma

Table of Contents

Part One
Voices of the Exiled

Erna Tietz nee Tietz (1906-1982)

Losing home and hearth

War

No sooner had Great Britain's declaration of war been announced on the radio, than a British policeman put his hand on my husband's shoulder and declared him arrested

No sooner had Great Britain's declaration of war been announced on the radio, than a British policeman put his hand on my husband's shoulder and declared him arrested. Under guard, he was allowed to go home one more time to say goodbye to us and to take a small suitcase of essentials. He still managed to give me a hundred pounds before he was taken away, together with all German males under fifty.

They were locked up for the night in the city gaol, like criminals, and later taken to a prison camp at Acre together with the men from the other German settlements

They were locked up for the night in the city gaol, like criminals, and later taken to a prison camp at Acre together with the men from the other German settlements. We received no news from them until they were allowed to write to us. However, since all letters were subject to censorship, they always wrote that, under the circumstances, they were well. Not until the German doctor, Dr Wilhelm Hoffmann, was ordered to go to Acre to attend to a seriously ill person, did we learn how awful the food supply was. Consequently, all the German agricultural settlements joined forces to send food parcels to the prisoners.

4. A British policeman (Higgins) of the Palestine Police

The rural settlements of Wilhelma, Sarona, Betlehem and Waldheim were fenced in with barbed wire and had British and Jewish sentries posted at the gates.

A British policeman was stationed in front of our house, which was situated outside the Haifa settlement. We were only allowed to leave the house – with a passport – when it was absolutely necessary for us to go and buy something. Since we were so completely cut off from the other Germans, I preferred moving to the settlement. My mother went to see the community Elder and I called Mayor Pross to inquire about an apartment. When we returned to our house, we found we had been burgled. All the money my husband had left with me and all our jewellery was gone. Even the police were now in favour of us moving to the settlement.

One week before Christmas, we were suddenly ordered to pack our suitcases, because we were to be taken to the fenced-in agricultural settlements. Together with my son and my mother, I opted for Betlehem because this settlement was closest to Haifa and Acre. We were also allowed to take bedding and cooking utensils with us. The three of us were given a room at Mrs Lisbeth Herrmann's. We were to have our meals at Willi Herrmann's. Willi was married to Hilde Dreher, a Tietz relative. The only one happy with this arrangement was my son Jürgen, who found a nice playmate of his own age in Maidi, Willi's daughter.

I suddenly received no more letters from my husband. I learned from other sources that three men had escaped from the camp near Jaffa and that everybody who had assisted them in their escape – apparently including my husband – had been taken to Jerusalem. This created new worries!

EVEN THE POLICE WERE NOW IN FAVOUR OF US MOVING TO THE SETTLEMENT

Bombs

Worse was to come. Planes of the Axis powers had bombed the oil tanks of the IPC (Iraq Petroleum Company) in Haifa several times, always successfully. This happened mostly at full moon. We heard the planes fly in from the Syrian border and were afraid only of the British anti-aircraft fire. However, on one occasion a damaged German aeroplane had to jettison its bombs between Betlehem and Waldheim but was still able to escape across the Syrian border. After this, the British ordered us to seek shelter in the basements as soon as the planes were heard. However, since few houses built by the settlers had deep cellars, this measure was rather pointless. Jürgen had started school in Betlehem and soon sent sketches, drawn with enthusiasm and talent, to his father in camp. All mail was subject to severe censorship; once, when he drew the mushroom cloud which, after a bombardment of the IPC tanks, had extended as far as Betlehem, the entire drawing was cut out. The newspapers had reported that only a few pigeons were hit.

5. Main Street in the German settlement of Haifa

Every now and then, it was rumoured that we were to be deported. Since we did not receive official notification, however, we did not believe this and calmly pursued our daily activities. But all of a sudden we had to register with the police. Our personal details were recorded, and nothing more was allowed to be sent to the men.

6. Haifa after the bombardment of the oil refineries

What was going on? – Jürgen was sick and I had no news from my husband.

WORSE WAS TO COME. PLANES OF THE AXIS POWERS HAD BOMBED THE OIL TANKS OF THE IPC (IRAQ PETROLEUM COMPANY) IN HAIFA SEVERAL TIMES, ALWAYS SUCCESSFULLY. THIS HAPPENED MOSTLY AT FULL MOON

WE ARE ROUNDED UP

Now the time has come. Mayor Krockenberger reads out the names of those who are to be deported. The list is alphabetical. Now it is the turn of Streker Maria, Lieselotte and Lothar; then Tietz Erna, Jürgen, – good heavens, my mother is not included! I ask the Mayor, "Why not?" Answer: "Only those women whose husbands are interned are to be deported along with them and their children." "Where to?" "We do not know."

I now pack a small cabin trunk and a small suitcase with essentials. We are assured that we will have access to our large luggage within two days. Jürgen is still very weak and on a diet. I therefore put cocoa, crackers, glucose and some small kitchen utensils into the hand luggage, together with a warm tracksuit, although we were in a fierce July heatwave. I also pack a small deck chair at the very bottom of the cabin trunk.

GOOD HEAVENS, MY MOTHER IS NOT INCLUDED!

We have to take the luggage to the schoolyard where it is guarded by Jewish policemen. Dr Fürst gives me some painkillers for my frequent gallstone pains. One day prior to departure, Mr Kuhnle manages to kill a calf and gives the meat to the deportees for food on the journey. However, we eat it straight away because our landlady, Aunt Lisbeth, has roasted some chickens for us to take. We did not sleep much during this last night. Where will we be deported to? The uncertain future oppresses us. Will we really meet our interned husbands, or is this another empty promise? Bursch [Jürgen] is looking forward to his father – and so indeed am I!

Straight after breakfast, we have to line up in front of the police in the schoolyard. The buses and the Jewish policewomen are there already. Saying goodbye to our loved ones is hard; will we ever see each other again?

Deportation

One at a time, we enter a room where we have to undergo a thorough body search by a policewoman

One at a time, we enter a room where we have to undergo a thorough body search by a policewoman. Our handbags are also searched painstakingly. All medicines are taken from us, supposedly to prevent us from trying to commit suicide. We look at each other, who would entertain such a stupid thought or – was the future going to be that bad? We now have to board the buses, this is it! As if on command, we all raise our hands and sing the German national anthem. The British have stepped back, and as we were driven out of the village, all we can see is our loved ones waving goodbye.

At Waldheim, the buses with the internees from there are already waiting; we now travel to Haifa together to board the train waiting outside the railway station near the Nesher cement factory. We have to be quick; the train departs at once.

We quickly look out of the window because the German settlement will soon come into view. None of us thought that this would be the last time we would see it. The jacarandas in the *Persergarten* next door are in full bloom.

The train travels fast; we are already rounding Cape Carmel. Bursch enjoys the sight of the mirror-smooth sea, which is not surprising in this oppressive heat. We continue on the well-known route to Ramleh. At the Ramleh railway station, we immediately see the buses with our people from Wilhelma and Sarona. The men from the Jaffa camp are also supposed to be on the still stationary train. I ask everybody about the "black sheep" from the Jerusalem jail. Nobody can give me any information, but I spot a well-known British officer from Haifa and call out to him. He comes over straight away and assures me that the carriage with the Jerusalem prisoners is already hooked up to our train. The men would be allowed to come over afterwards, for sure. He then brings us lemonade and tea. He often used to play tennis with my husband back in Haifa.

Darkness falls. The officer violently pulls and shakes our roller shutter, which showed a small crack. It now refuses to work and does not close at all any more. Secretly, we are glad

We continue the journey as soon as the internees from the southern settlements board the train. The landscape is rather monotonous, everything is parched and the soil is dry, as it always is in summer. Only the sea is wonderfully blue, and a swim now would be heaven.

Darkness falls, and we prepare for the night. A British officer comes and closes the shutters. In spite of this, no lights are allowed, and it becomes unbearably hot in our compartment. After a quarter of an hour, there is another check to ensure that everything is blacked out according to regulations. The officer violently pulls and shakes our roller shutter, which showed a small crack. It now refuses to work and does not close at all any more. Secretly, we are glad. The officer curses softly to himself and then asks us to promise not to switch on any light, and to keep the compartment door closed. We are happy to oblige, and he moves on. At least we now have cool night air and even manage to sleep for a while.

We arrive at Kantara in the morning. Just as we finish combing our hair and are about to give ourselves a lick and a promise with some Eau de Cologne, an officer comes along and says that all of us should get out for breakfast and leave everything in the compartment. I take my handbag anyway, because I keep all our family papers in it. We are now led to a big tent, and to our great joy and comfort, we at last see our husbands standing at the entrance! Meeting again is wonderful, and for the moment, we forget our uncertain future. Hot tea and rolls are available and our spirits become quite jolly.

Hardship on the train

Then comes the shock: we are no longer allowed to return to our train! Our hand luggage, provisions, coats, hats etc. – everything – lies scattered haphazardly on the platform and, just prior to departure, is thrown into another train, which we now have to board. An officer then walks through the train and collects his "black sheep" who are supposed to go to a special carriage. However, I now put my foot down, grab Jürgen's hand and, as the officer is about to send us back, I explain to him that we are the wife and son of the "black sheep" and should therefore also be in his carriage. He grins and lets us pass.

We are now happily united and, in time, our hand luggage, provisions etc. is handed back to us. I even get back my pretty summer hat. Mr Krockenberger had put it on as he walked through all the carriages until, finally, he could give it back to me. Bursch grasps his father firmly by the hand, he is afraid of losing him again.

We now want to eat something. However, I notice that the roasted chickens are no longer perfect and throw them out of the window. This is our good fortune. Several people regret wasting the good snack, eat it and come down with severe food poisoning during the night, in great pain and vomiting a lot. In the absence of any other medicine, Dr Fürst and the British officer administer oil to them from a five-litre canister, as much as they can tolerate. This in due course has a most powerful effect – and it helps! Naturally, a quiet night's rest is out of the question.

The water is terribly dirty, it had just been scooped up from the gutters.

Morning comes, and with it searing heat. We have nothing more to drink. When we stop at a station, we are met by young Arab boys with fresh drinking water, which they sell to us from large clay jars at exorbitant prices. We drink and fill the thermos flask, which I had brought with me, but there is not enough water for everybody; after a short time though, the young lads return with full jars. This time the water is terribly dirty, it had just been scooped up from the gutters. What good luck that we had our typhus inoculations just prior to our departure. We soon resume our journey, the children wail with thirst, and we all suffer from the heat.

We stop at Suez, but the trucks that are to take us to the ship are not yet there. Our train is pulling a long way out of the station. As in the night before, they expect a German air raid. We have to spend another night in the blacked out train. However, we are lucky; the night remains quiet, even though it is very hot.

Some tea and milk is handed out in the morning, and then the waiting continues. At noon, we get mashed potatoes. Fortunately, I had a small cooking container to collect our portion. Those without containers are served their portions into their open hands. Luckily, more tea is available.

The trucks are still not here. We are now supposed to walk the long distance to the jetty and carry our own luggage. We drag ourselves along laboriously under the searing sun. Bursch looks miserable and cries that he cannot walk any further. My husband is about to carry him on his shoulders, when an officer arrives and announces that the men will have to stay back and help unload the bulk luggage from the train. I feel my gall bladder and am so exhausted, that I simply sit down on one of our trunks and declare that I do not want to walk another step without my husband. The officer curses and assures me that we would certainly not be separated; but because I just remain seated, he stops a truck that had collected the older people unable to walk and heaves me, Bursch and our luggage on to it.

The world's largest ship

We get out at the jetty and then have to wait in the tropical midday heat for the men with the big luggage. We are loaded on to a big ferry. Here there is at least some shade and we can buy tea, at a shilling per cup. We are then ferried to the ship, the *Queen Elizabeth,* which had been converted to a troop transport.

Women and children have to board the ship first and are immediately put into cabins. The men go to separate cabins. Three women with one child each and I with Bursch are allotted a cabin intended for two persons, but now containing eight wooden bunks in twos, one on top of the other. To our great joy, we see that there also is a bathroom. The *Queen Elizabeth* had originally been built as a luxury liner. We bathe the children and then ourselves, the bath cleanses, but does not refresh – it is lukewarm sea water.

The children are tired and cry with hunger. I now remember that my sister Erika had sent us a parcel from Wilhelma through a relative. I open it and – oh joy – amongst other items, it contains a few apples and rusks. I hand them out at once amongst the children in our and the next cabins.

The gong sounds at seven o'clock. We are allowed to enter the dining room which, to our surprise, is air-conditioned. The food is terrible, a real hotchpotch, but there is wonderful hot tea, which makes us sweat profusely, but also quenches our thirst. We get only seawater in the cabins.

Unfortunately, we have to return to our hot cabin straight after dinner. To add to our discomfort, a crew member comes and closes the portholes. Light is provided in the passages only. The night is terribly hot, and we are glad to see the cool dining room for breakfast.

Back in the cabins, we have to endure a thorough body search by two nurses. Our luggage is also searched, and money, nail scissors and pocketknives are confiscated. They did not find the money in my corset, and a tiny folding pair of scissors inside a soap container escaped them as well.

7. The "Queen Elizabeth" passing through the "Heads" of Sydney harbour

Now comes the command 'all on deck'. We all look forward to fresh sea air, but to our dismay, only a few windows are open on the entire deck; in fact, these are watched, perhaps to prevent people jumping overboard. It is also terribly hot up here, and when we get tired, we have to sit on the dirty floor. An alarm drill takes place in the afternoon, but nobody knows how to put the lifebelts on or where the lifeboats are. Then we go back to the cabins where the portholes are open, at least during the day.

WE GET OUT AT THE JETTY AND THEN HAVE TO WAIT IN THE TROPICAL MIDDAY HEAT. WE ARE LOADED ON TO A BIG FERRY. HERE THERE IS AT LEAST SOME SHADE

TO AUSTRALIA

The voyage through the Red Sea is sheer hell! We wash our sweaty clothes and put them on while still wet, at least then they don't *smell* sweaty. I have cut off my plait of hair with my saved pair of scissors and throw it out of the porthole. I hope a shark will choke on it! Even the beautiful sea phosphorescence and the flying fish can no longer excite us.

Mr Steller of Sarona passed away; his ailing heart could no longer tolerate the heat. Only his wife and son are allowed to be present when he is buried at sea.

We land at Trincomalee in Ceylon, where the captain takes some fresh lettuce on board. Never have we eaten anything with such appetite!

The poor German prisoners of war who are also on the ship are much worse off than we are. They have made themselves available to help serve our meals. They get to eat only peas and beans, are allowed on deck only once a day and do not have portholes in their quarters. They are allowed to communicate with us only while serving meals.

The time passes – we see only water and sky. When we reach the west coast of Australia – at least we now know our final destination – the weather turns bitterly cold. We are close to icebergs. The transition from the heat into this cold bothers us considerably. We have no warm clothing; we all suffer from coughs and colds. Only the certainty that the voyage will soon be over keeps us going.

MONEY, NAIL SCISSORS AND POCKETKNIVES ARE CONFISCATED. THEY DID NOT FIND THE MONEY IN MY CORSET, AND A TINY FOLDING PAIR OF SCISSORS INSIDE A SOAP CONTAINER ESCAPED THEM AS WELL

Eventually – it is like a fairytale – we enter Sydney harbour. It is said to be the most beautiful harbour in the world, and this was certainly the case for us. The many small islands with green vegetation, the famous harbour bridge and the beautiful city of Sydney are wonderful sights.

Our Bursch has a terrible toothache. However, our doctor has no instruments whatsoever. He tries, unsuccessfully, to extract the tooth by hand. Australian soldiers come on board and take charge. Now everything gets better. We get hot tea, excellent jam, good cheese and fresh bread. Never before have we tasted anything better! After this, we disembark and directly board a train.

In Australia

It feels so good to have firm ground under one's feet at last after such a long sea voyage. The clatter of the wheels is more soothing than the pitching of the ship. Unfortunately, we see very little of the landscape as it gets dark quickly. However, we cannot go to sleep. Jürgen cries continuously. His tooth is aching, and his cheek is very swollen. Day breaks at last. Although the carriages are heated, we feel the cold in our light summer clothing, and are very glad and grateful when soldiers and nurses distribute hot tea with milk and good sandwiches. Everyone gets an apple and an orange. This is a real treat after weeks without fruit!

The landscape is bleak and flat; now and then, there are a few eucalyptus trees, some of which are dead. The train stops at a station built of corrugated iron, and we have lunch: mashed potatoes, sausages and more tea. Metal plates, cutlery and large tin mugs have been handed out before. Then we travel on. We can see farm buildings of corrugated iron, very primitive, built on stumps, with windmills and water tanks nearby. The farms are all sheep and cattle farms.

Towards evening, we stop at a station. Buses are waiting, the women and children must get on, and the men have to look after the luggage. We arrive at the camp after half an hour's drive.

THE TIME PASSES – WE SEE ONLY WATER AND SKY. WHEN WE REACH THE WEST COAST OF AUSTRALIA – AT LEAST WE NOW KNOW OUR FINAL DESTINATION

Horrified, we look at each other. We had not imagined that things would be this bad! All we can see is a large, doubly fenced square, with barbed wire, barricades and watchtowers at the corners. The barbed wire gate is flanked by a small watch-house. The whole thing looks like a gigantic rat trap.

From *Memories of Palestine*

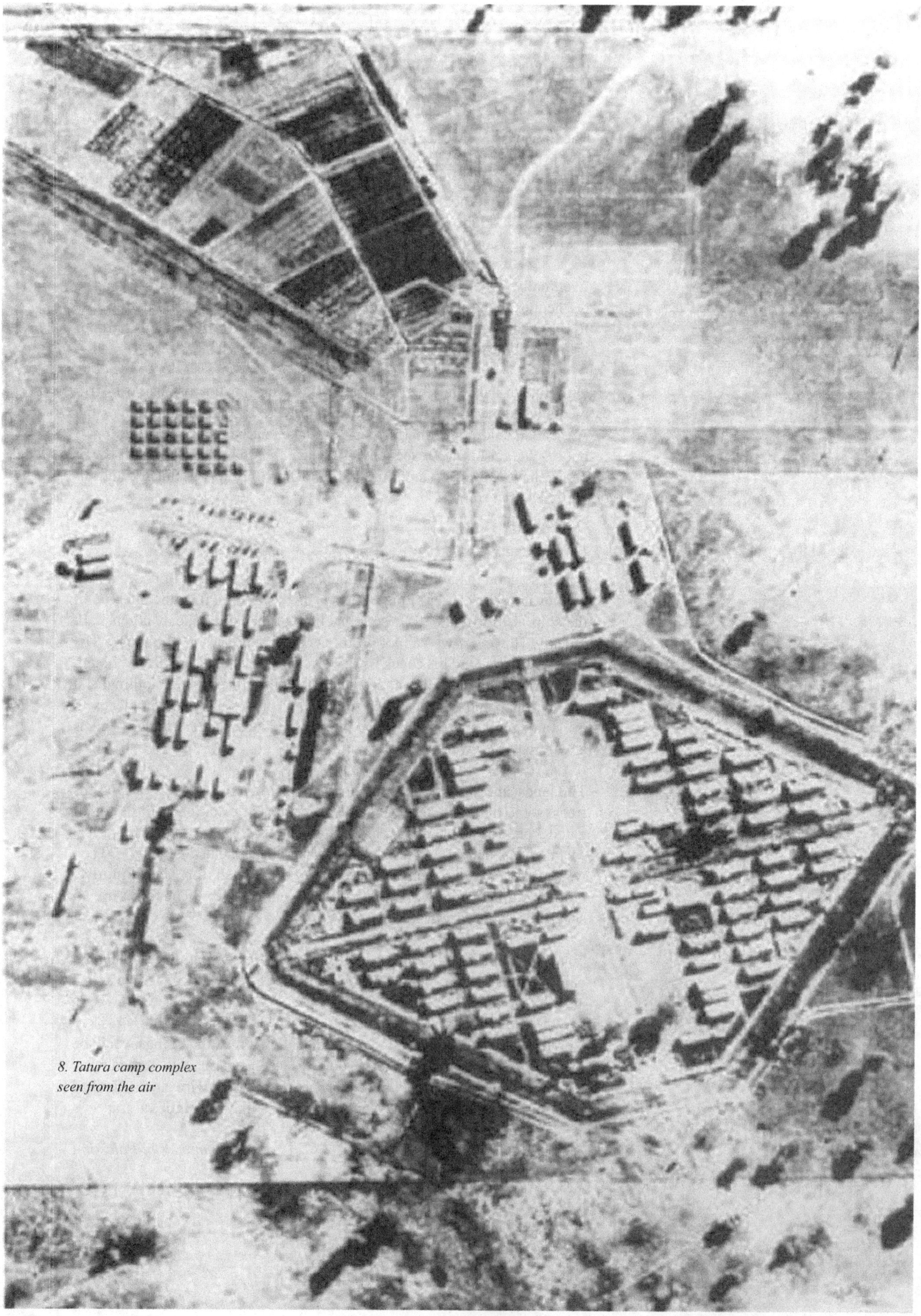

8. Tatura camp complex seen from the air

9. & 10. Drawings of the camp

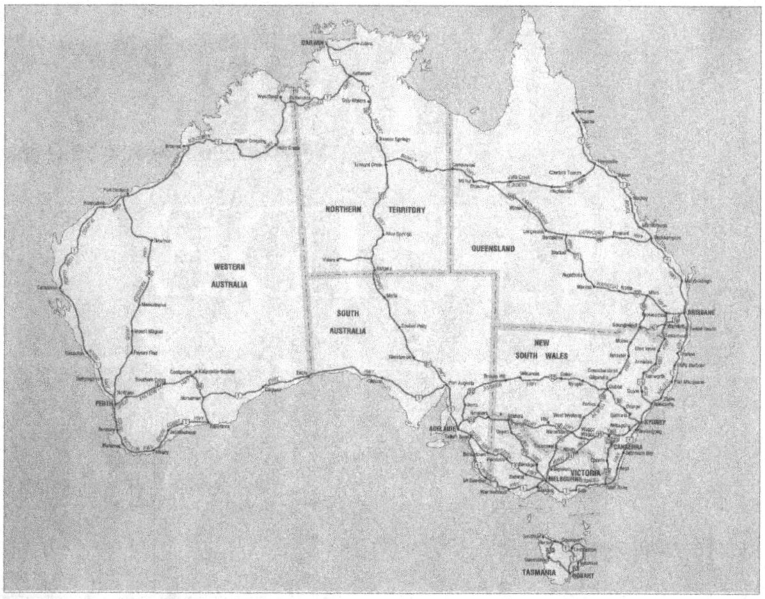

11. Map of Australia

From the Holy Land to the Home of the Kangaroo

German title: *Vom heiligen Lande in die Heimat des Känguruhs*

This article circulated widely in Camp III Tatura. It has been translated with kind permission of C.H. Gohl Publications, holders of ©.

Move

The train with its empty third class carriages and wooden seats was waiting on the open line just north of the Nesher cement factory. Jewish auxiliary members of the Palestine Police kept watch, supervised by a British sergeant. The purpose of the exercise was to deport the majority of the Germans in Palestine to Australia, or so it had been rumoured. This was on the morning of 31 July, 1941.

The first internees arrived by bus at 11:00. Coming from Camp I, Masra'a [Acre] they, with a few exceptions, had already suffered 23 months of internment, cut off from the outside world. By twelve noon, the first families arrived from Camp II (Waldheim) and Camp III (Betlehem), German settlements both, near Haifa. After about thirty minutes the rest of the families had boarded the train as well. Their buses had been accidentally directed to Haifa because of poor organisation.

They were all weighed down with baskets and suitcases, but were of good cheer. A pretty girl handed out bunches of grapes of exceptional quality, grown by diligent German farmers in a foreign land that had been their second homeland since grandfather's day. They had lost their home and faced an uncertain future, yet none showed sadness. They were all convinced that Germany would win the war.

The train started moving around 13:00; nobody knew where the journey was going. When the train traversed the port precinct of Haifa, it seemed a sea voyage would begin right there. Some people were already fiddling with their luggage. At the pier, the *Patria*, a 12,000 ton auxiliary cruiser, was clearly recognisable, sunk with explosives by persons unknown when Jewish illegal immigrants were to be shipped from Palestine to Mauritius.

However, when the train drove right through the port area and left Haifa behind, it became clear to us that we would be on it until Egypt, because embarkation in the shallow waters of Jaffa seemed unlikely.

At 18:30, the train arrived in Lydda to wait for the internees from the other camps. Nine busloads of families had left Sarona (Camp IV) at 17:00, and arrived in Lydda at about 18:30. The internees from Camp V (Wilhelma), Camp VI (Flagellatio, Jerusalem) and Camp XIII (Beit Yam) were already on the train. We could see the joy on the faces of the internees from Camps VI and XIII when they were reunited with their families from whom, with few exceptions, they had been separated by internment since the beginning of the war.

STARED AT BY THE POPULACE, THEY LUGGED THEIR BELONGINGS ACROSS THE PLATFORM IN LONG ROWS LIKE EMIGRANTS, WITH BIG AND SMALL CHILDREN, THE YOUNGEST JUST SIX WEEKS OLD, SOME IN CARRY-COTS AND MANY IN THE ARMS OF THEIR PARENTS

Stared at by the populace, they lugged their belongings across the platform in long rows like emigrants, with big and small children, the youngest just six weeks old, some in carry-cots and many in the arms of their parents. Apart from a modest amount of hand luggage, they had been allowed only 40kg for each adult and 30kg per child. The rest of what they owned, for which they had toiled a lifetime, had been left behind on orders from the C.I.D. [Criminal Investigation Department]. Guards of the Palestine Police made up of Jewish auxiliaries were posted as sentries at the exits of all the rail cars, and inside each carriage sat two or three British sergeants, as well as some women in police uniforms.

Across the desert

After leaving Lydda at 19:00, the journey went to Gaza and then on through the Sinai desert. It was terribly hot in the compartments and became unbearably so when the guards closed the window shutters, presumably for keeping things military along the railway line secret. This triggered strong protests from the internees, upon which they were allowed to open the windows a crack near the top. The drinking water they had taken was used up very soon because of the heat. When the train stopped for a short time under the palms of El Arish at midnight, cries for water were heard from all the compartments, but in vain – the Arab at the small station building did not have any himself. After a bad night, we arrived in Kantara at six thirty in the morning of 1 August 1941.

12. Watchtower in the Wilhelma internment camp

Kantara, on the eastern bank of the Suez Canal, is a well-known supply depot for troops passing through. We were handed some breakfast consisting of tea and sandwiches, and biscuits with milk for the children. Our hand luggage had to be placed on the platform for transfer. The forty-kilo luggage had already been given up at the beginning of the journey for transport in the freight car. While we were having breakfast, all the hand luggage was loaded on to trucks – some of the internees were used as porters – and transferred to the platform for our departure from the western bank of the Suez Canal. The internees were taken across the Canal by ferry. The luggage lay scattered in an awful mess, thrown on to three heaps. With the train about to leave, a desperate search began for food, pillows and blankets which were needed for this journey of unknown duration. The search was without success for most. Many voices were heard asking for some piece of luggage or other on the trip later on.

At 11:00 the journey continued, closely hugging the Canal which could be observed quite clearly with all its craft. The skiffs of the Nile, with their tall, bent masts and sails of remarkable size were in the majority. Pleasure boats and yachts were missing altogether.

It was just twelve noon when the train entered the Lower Egyptian township of Ismailiya, which was not unlike a garden city with its ochre houses, green window shutters and many flowers in small ornamental gardens. In stark contrast, the railway station at the southern exit of the small town made a dismal impression, even though Ismailiya is an important junction of the Port Said–Suez line and the Ismailiya–Benha el Asal line to Cairo and Alexandria.

Again, cries for refreshments were heard from the train. Arabs offered lemonade-like drinks and beer, both of which were refused because of their doubtful composition and because of the exchange rate.

After leaving Ismailiya, we travelled past the old Bitter Lakes and arrived at Suez at 18:00. Just outside town, in the forlorn desert, we suddenly heard shouted greetings. It came from German prisoners-of-war in a tent camp close to the railway line, watched from wooden towers by brown-skinned soldiers with long hair and fixed bayonets. The tents were half buried in the sand because of the heat. The salute was returned from all the compartments on the train. Our military escorts did not like this and the British sergeants threatened to close the windows immediately. In Suez everything was shrouded in darkness because of the danger from aircraft. The train kept shunting back and forth, not a soul knew why. It seemed the engine was too weak to pull the endlessly long train past a level crossing where a number of vehicles and pedestrians had already gathered in front of the closed barrier.

Towards 20:00 it was announced that the night was to be spent in the train once again, and on the open line at that. Everyone was hungry and thirsty; there had been no food since breakfast in Kantara, more than thirteen hours ago. After about an hour we were allowed to leave the carriages to get food from an army truck next to the train. It consisted of tea and English sausages with potatoes, served into our bare hands or wrapped in a piece of toilet paper.

Then came the dreaded night. We had nothing on which to rest our tired heads, for all the things which had been packed for use at night were in the freight car and were not released despite all our pleading. Mothers with infants were given a separate carriage for the night, but pigheaded guards stopped them from taking along the most essential items, like nappies. Commonsense was thus rendered absurd; the intended relief caused additional hardships for both mothers and children. It also has to be said that this Egyptian train was very dirty, unhygienic and uncomfortable and had stopped too close to the Suez oil refinery. It was shunted a little further out later. We could see the outlines of the refinery not far from the port. The beams of huge searchlights were seen sweeping across the sky and at least a dozen barrage balloons were in the air.

It was hard to go to sleep in the poor body positions we had been reduced to in the train; children cried; conversations intruded. According to rumour, our destination could be any of these: India, Ceylon, South Africa or Australia, meaning Tasmania.

Ordeal in the heat

Next morning, 2 August at 7:00, in searing heat and heavily weighed down with luggage, we went on a foot march lasting about one hour from the train to the waterfront. It was a terrible ordeal and will remain etched in the memories of all who took part. Time and again, children, women and ailing men could be seen standing next to their luggage along the way, desperate and unable to go on. Others, themselves heavily burdened, helped them to keep going as best they could. At times, the auxiliary policemen on fast-moving motor trucks overtook this procession of the suffering, not even dreaming of giving women and children a lift or at least transporting the bags.

With great effort, we reached the pier where three freight barges were standing by. The staff of the C.I.D. from Jerusalem were already assembled on the foredeck of one of the barges with their chief, Mr Parkhouse who, together with Superintendent Mansfield and Turner, the interpreter, had supervised the transport.

Before the last and biggest ferry left the pier, the internees were made to carry the entire forty-kilo luggage across a catwalk on to the ferry and were informed in no uncerain terms that whatever was not loaded within the hour would be left behind in Suez. This was hard work in the searing heat, made harder because neither drinks nor food had been distributed since the night before, and our stomachs felt rather stretched by midday.

The trip on the ferry lasted about an hour. A burnt-out giant ocean liner of the latest construction with two stacks was easily recognisable a short distance to starboard. (Our skipper said it was the *Queen Mary* [nonsense, tr]). She was listing badly and her stern was under water. It was said she had been reduced to this state by aerial bombs the day before.

THE TRIP ON THE FERRY LASTED ABOUT AN HOUR. A BURNT-OUT GIANT OCEAN LINER OF THE LATEST CONSTRUCTION WITH TWO STACKS WAS EASILY RECOGNISABLE A SHORT DISTANCE TO STARBOARD. (OUR SKIPPER SAID IT WAS THE *QUEEN MARY* ...

The steamship on which *our* journey was to continue lay far out to the Red Sea because of the danger from aircraft. It was the *Queen Elizabeth*, the largest ship in the world. She had only been completed in England and was then taken to the USA to be refitted as a troop carrier. She has a displacement of 85,000 tons, is 300m long and 36m wide and fitted with turbines and four propellers. She travels at a cruising speed of 29 knots and has 12 decks on top of each other.

The arrival of the ferries was cheerfully greeted from the port holes of the giant ship. After a short verbal exchange it emerged that approximately one thousand German prisoners-of-war were on board already, presumably to be transported to Australia as well. They had come from Libya and had been imprisoned at Latrun.

The Red Sea

The *Queen Elizabeth* sailed at 17:00 on 2 August 1941. The internees were accommodated on B deck. According to displays of the ship's layout, this was the tourist class. The cabins had been fitted with primitive bunks of rough cut boards, fixed on top of each other. The built-in cupboards were partly rendered useless because the bunks were blocking them. Tables and

13. Map of the Middle East and part of Africa

chairs of any description were nonexistent and space within the cabins was insufficient. Fresh air to the cabins was supplied through pipes. This was, however, not enough, particularly when the portholes were bolted down with steel plates even before dark because of the aircraft danger. It was unbearably hot, 35 to 40 degrees Celsius. The *Queen Elizabeth* was not suitable for trips on this run; she was built for voyages in cooler climes between England and New York.

The craving for air was aggravated by insatiable thirst. Often when we did not have a single drop of water, a merciless auxiliary policeman stood at the access to the water pipe and turned away all who asked for a drink. Water was handed out two or three times a day, but only in small quantities. It had been put about that the Captain had not known about women and children coming on his ship and had therefore not been prepared. This turned out to be untrue.

Possibly all of us slept well during the first night on board after the last two almost sleepless nights in the cramped rail compartments. The sea was very calm. The first morning aboard ship was 3 August, a Sunday. Breakfast was taken in the large dining room at tables seating twelve persons each, served by two of our guards per table. After the meals, the internees were to wash the dishes. They had also carried the food from the distant kitchen. This had resulted in a mass migration of food carriers to and from the kitchen, for it *was* a large number of tables with about a thousand internees on board.

The ship's crew was totally helpless in the face of this situation. Someone or other hit upon the idea of leaving the organisation to the German prisoners-of-war. Top management was sceptical, but allowed the sergeant major of the POWs to inspect the mess in the big dining room. The result could be read about in Australian newspapers a few days after the *Queen Elizabeth's* arrival in Sydney where the reporters had asked the crew for their impressions of the Germans during the voyage. The newspapers wrote: "when the sergeant major, pipe in mouth, had surveyed the disorganized conditions in the dining room for a short time, he declared that he and his POWs could handle the service of meals to all the internees, as well as guarantee order in the dining room. The ship's top brass consented, and the dining room henceforth functioned without a hiccup and was a model of order at all meal times."

The beneficial effects of the Germans organising the dining room were evident the next day. Apart from the fact that the service was much quicker now, the scheduled meal times (8:00 breakfast, 13:00 dinner and 18:30 tea), were punctually kept. The prisoners-of-war also played music at meal times.

The internees were, of course, most delighted with this change of personnel, particularly since many families had sons serving in the army. Experiences from the front and from internment were exchanged and plans for the future were discussed. Under these circumstances, the notice on the big blackboard in the middle of the dining room seemed like a joke. It said: "POWs are prohibited to talk to the German families". No one could expect such a prohibition being complied with. The Australian corporal on duty in the dining room also thought it was unfair and, rifle with fixed bayonet slung over his shoulder notwithstanding, only *pretended* to intervene when people talked to the POWs.

The shores of the Red Sea were not sighted and neither was Mecca, even though the ship sailed past close to it. The Red Sea, incidentally, was not red at all, although some travellers insisted they had seen red hues – but it poured out unspeakable heat. At night, even children sweated enough to soak their mattresses; in addition, there was the craving for air and the shortage of water. An eleven-year-old girl (Emma Krafft) turned blue from lack of oxygen.

THE BENEFICIAL EFFECTS OF THE GERMANS ORGANISING THE DINING ROOM WERE EVIDENT THE NEXT DAY. APART FROM THE FACT THAT THE SERVICE WAS MUCH QUICKER NOW

The Indian Ocean

We left the Red Sea behind on 4 August without even having seen a glimpse of Aden. The lowest daily temperature was 33°C, the highest 36°C. The sea was calm and we travelled through the Gulf of Aden at approximately 25 knots. Many small fish were seen in the water with wing-like fins. They jumped out of the water, flew for about fifteen metres and disappeared again in the water.

The guessing game as to what the destination of our journey might be had not stopped. According to new rumours, we were to be taken to Bombay. People tried to calculate the course of the ship by the direction of the few rays of the sun that made it through the small portholes.

Yesterday, there was a life-jacket drill in a longish hall on starboard, one side of which was fitted with nothing but black window panes. These could only be opened by the crew using a special tool. The hall was called a deck and served each morning and afternoon for two hours of "exercise", as the British called it, in which everyone had to take part when ordered "on deck". The room had neither tables nor benches, nor any other furniture and was much too small to provide freedom of movement for that many people. We were herded "on deck" like sheep, there was no turning back. Children screamed for water which, in the beginning, was not available, and when they wanted to go to the toilet it was not allowed. Unbearable as it was below because of the heat, many internees preferred hiding in the cabins just to avoid having to go "on deck".

LIFEBOAT DRILLS WERE NOT CARRIED OUT. THE LIFE-BOATS OF THE *QUEEN ELIZABETH* WERE EQUIPPED WITH TWO-STROKE MOTORS AND DESIGNED TO HOLD ABOUT THIRTY PERSONS

At the second life-jacket drill we were told that, when jumping into the sea, the cork pads on the front of the jacket would need to be held down with our thumbs because they would otherwise be pushed up against our chins on impact, which could entail neck injuries. Lifeboat drills were not carried out. The lifeboats of the *Queen Elizabeth* were equipped with two-stroke motors and were designed to hold about thirty persons.

The lowest temperature on 6 August was 27.5°C, the highest 30.5, and many passengers were seasick. It had become surprisingly stormy the day before and this colossus of a ship rolled quite violently. We were in the Indian Ocean now and, judging by the ship's course, our destination was more likely to be Ceylon than Bombay. The great heat, coupled with high relative humidity, caused many passengers to become afflicted with a skin rash – known to the English as "red dog"– on all parts of the body covered by clothing. Medical care was provided by two German doctors, Dr Fürst and Dr Rubitschung, and two Italian ones, Dr Costero and Dr Tesio, all of whom were fully occupied treating this heat rash which was accompanied by nasty boils in many cases while, for medication, the internees were provided with nothing but aspirin and castor oil.

What luggage in the cabins had not yet been searched in the presence of its owners when knives, scissors, medicines and torches etc were confiscated, this was now thoroughly made up for in people's absence while they were on deck. It was never satisfactorily established what exactly was searched for in the luggage, other than weapons and devices for transmitting light signals. Some items confiscated by some of the officials were not touched by others. The searches were mostly conducted only in women's cabins, by female officials. Our women used to say that the women were the worst.

On 7 August it had become hotter again, from a low of 29.5° to a high of 34°C. Ventilation of cabins and corridors in the men's section was unsatisfactory, while in the women and children's cabins it was non-existent. There were not enough taps for cooled water and none at all in the internee section. The water in the cabins was lukewarm and unpalatable, because it was salty. The only drinking fountain, which was probably intended for the whole of B deck, was situated in the quarters of the auxiliary police who refused to make water available in the required quantities. This led to friction.

On 8 August (low 29°, high 34.5°C), it was warm in the afternoon and a dark outline was seen against the horizon. A bank of fog according to one version, according to another it was the southern tip of India or the southernmost point of Ceylon. A seaplane flew by not long after. Land was obviously not far away.

The dining room, incidentally, was not equipped with chairs, but with benches which were not very comfortable. The prisoners-of-war were happy and of good cheer. They quickly made friends everywhere. Their pants had red or blue patches sown on to them, usually in the shape of diamonds, and often in amusing places. In the meantime, rumours that Australia was to be our destination had percolated down through the grapevine of the Australian guards.

Meeting Australians

Many of these Australians had fought in Libya, Greece, Crete and Syria. They had had a terrible time and were glad to be on their way home. I had a conversation with a New Zealander in the presence of two German flying officers, one of whom, a long range bomber pilot, had been shot down in Libya, while the other had come to grief flying a dive bomber in Crete. The New Zealander said he had fought with a tank division in Greece. He was the only survivor of his tank crew and admitted that it was hell itself; but then he came to Crete where it was far worse. The German planes, he said, had come in such swarms that 'the birds had to walk on foot'.

THE AUSTRALIANS WERE VERY FRIENDLY AND MANY OF THEM HANDED OUT SWEETS AMONGST THE CHILDREN. SOME OF THE AUXILIARIES WERE NOT PLEASED BY THIS AND ASKED WHY THEY WERE GIVING SWEETS TO THE CHILDREN OF THEIR ENEMIES. THIS AND OTHER ISSUES LED TO AN ALTERCATION DURING THE COURSE OF WHICH FIVE OF THE AUXILIARIES HAD TO BE ADMITTED TO HOSPITAL

The Australians were very friendly and many of them handed out sweets amongst the children. Some of the auxiliaries were not pleased by this and asked why they were giving sweets to the children of their enemies. This, and other issues led to an altercation during the course of which five of the auxiliaries had to be admitted to hospital. The Australian soldiers were not inclined to take instructions from auxiliary policemen.

Although everyone knew about the fate of the British vessel *Arandora Star* which was sunk in the Atlantic Ocean on 3 July 1940 with the loss of more than a thousand German and Italian internees being deported to Canada, nobody anticipated a similar thing happening to us. (Later, survivors of the *Arandora Star,* set a memorial plaque in Tatura). An English naval officer told us during a life-belt drill that even a dozen torpedo hits would not sink the *Queen Elizabeth.* We accepted this news with a wry smile.

On 9 August (temperatures from 28 to 32°C) we reached the port of Trincomalee on the northeastern coast of Ceylon. The island is overgrown with strikingly lush greenery, looking as if it was covered with a thick, bright green carpet of moss. We could make out a house of European construction with red roof tiles not far from shore. It was surrounded by a park, similar in colour as the rest of its environment. The harbour consisted of a horse-shoe shaped bay, which seemed to have been created expressly for this purpose by the generosity of nature. The open side of the harbour was protected by U-boat nets which could be opened by two tugboats. The shores of the bay were dominated by the trade marks of fuel supply companies. Thirty oil tanks had been constructed there, perfectly camouflaged with paint against being sighted from the air.

For the first time we actually liked going "on deck" to the long, narrow hall on the starboard side. Everyone jostled towards the windows to see as much as possible of the port environment. Mr Imanuel Steller of Sarona died at 9:00 in the morning. He had been denied admission to hospital although he was seriously ill.

On 10 August (low 28.5, high 34°C) we left Trincomalee around noon. Mr Steller had reached the age of fifty-six; he had not been able to cope with the excitements and exertions imposed by the voyage. All efforts by his family to have him buried in Ceylon failed, because burial in the vicinity of the port was not possible under the religious customs of the local population, and the nearest European cemetery was, we were told, twelve hours away by rail. (In Tatura later on, the Swiss Consul was to deny all of this). Mr Steller was therefore lowered into the ocean, sailor fashion, at 17:30, after a short ceremony and tribute, delivered by Mr Jone Frank. The eulogy was impressive and touching. It was about the suffering of the deported. One hundred internees watching the ceremony raised their hands in salute when the corpse was lowered overboard. The ship was supposed to halt its progress for two minutes, but the organization of the British was not able to achieve this. At the time of the burial, we were out on the high seas, five and a half hours from Ceylon, proceeding in a south-south-easterly direction.

Judging by the lights from the windows of many houses the night before, it had become obvious that Trincomalee was much more densely populated than it had seemed at first when we had seen the thick tree cover in daylight. For the first time our cabins were not blacked out.

LAST NIGHT WE SUCCEEDED IN BORROWING A NEWSPAPER FROM AN AUSTRALIAN SERGEANT. THIS WAS QUITE AN EVENT, CONSIDERING WE HAD BEEN WITHOUT NEWS OF THE OUTSIDE WORLD SINCE OUR DEPARTURE

Last night we succeeded in borrowing a newspaper from an Australian sergeant. This was quite an event, considering we had been without news of the outside world since our departure on 31 July. No sooner had the paper been opened after reading its title, the *Ceylon Times,* than a British police sergeant ordered it returned to its owner. A protest lodged with Superintendent Mansfield regarding the behaviour of the sergeant was of no avail, although it was pointed out to him that internees were entitled to read censored English newspapers. The ship's captain was said to have had newspapers banned.

The sea was perfectly calm. The ship did not roll. A Protestant divine service was held in the morning.

On the Equator

Against expectations, it had become cooler on 11 August (low 29°, high 32.5°C), although we were approaching the equator. The sun was high in the east at 8:00 and we crossed the equator at 15:00 as could be ascertained from the position of the sun. In normal times, this is always an occasion for happy parties on board, with Neptune waving his trident and first-timers receiving the 'Baptism of the Equator'. This time, though, Neptune had remained in the depths of his ocean, five thousand metres below the surface. Only a few jokes were heard here and there. One man insisted having heard a scraping at the moment of crossing, another claimed to know, of all things, that the Brits had removed the equator to a safe location to save it from German U-boats.

As always since the beginning of this voyage, guard duty in the dining room was carried out by Australian soldiers. They had become well acquainted with nearly all internees and were on the best terms with them when the powers that be went out of their way to pour cold water on our friendship with the Australians by banning us from talking to the crew. The British sergeants were in charge and were themselves led by Mr Mansfield and Mr Turner who were their commanding officers. Chief Parkhouse and his staff had left us before the *Queen Elizabeth* had sailed for the Red Sea. – It was bucketing down, the first rain we had seen since April in Palestine. The sea was perfectly calm.

THE FOOD ON THE SHIP WAS ATROCIOUS. THE SHORTAGE OF VEGETABLES AND THE TOTAL ABSENCE OF FRUIT CAUSED DIGESTIVE DISORDERS

The food on the ship was atrocious. The shortage of vegetables and the total absence of fruit caused digestive disorders. The preparation of the food left much to be desired, being unpalatable most of the time because it was too hotly spiced. Anyone sick simply had nothing to eat. It was mostly children and the increasing numbers of the sick who suffered. Diets prescribed by the doctors could only be obtained in the rarest of cases, and in absolutely insufficient quantities at that. Watching the auxiliary policemen eat lettuce, tomatoes and fresh fruit made our mouths water. Being fed lots of rabbit meat all the time made us dub it kangaroo.

The portholes had to be kept closed again after dark because of the dangers posed by aircraft, U-boats and raiders. The entire voyage proceeded with all lights blacked out

The portholes which, to everyone's delight, had been allowed to remain open throughout the night during our stay in Trincomalee, had now to be kept closed again after dark because of the dangers posed by aircraft, U-boats and raiders. The entire voyage proceeded with all lights blacked out.

On 12 August 1941, the low was 29.5°C, the high 32°C. The young people met almost every night in one of the cross corridors. Some of the girls had brought along their accordions and all sang German folksongs together and songs of the idealistic youth movement of 1899, which emphasised return to truth and nature, but eventually was dissolved by the National Socialists in 1933. One of their songs typically was *Wildgänse rauschen durch die Nacht* [Wild geese are swooshing through the night, by Walter Flex]. Space was tight in the narrow corridor and it was hideously hot but everyone enjoyed the songs. Both ends of the corridor were tightly packed with listeners, including the Australian soldiers. Many a listener forgot he was in the middle of the Indian Ocean on board the *Queen Elizabeth*, when his thoughts wandered back to his home in the Spessart Mountains, in the Black Forest, or in Palestine.

14. Rabbits in plague proportions

The songs rang out loudly from the confines of the corridor, which displeased one of the auxiliary police. He complained to an Australian soldier at the door about one particular song, urging him to forbid singing it, because he thought it said that Germany wanted to conquer the whole world. The Australian sergeant replied, "I do not speak German and have no idea what they are singing, but they sing very beautifully and they may continue to their hearts' content."

On 13 August the temperature fell to its lowest range yet, 25° to 27°C. A violent storm had blown up during the night and it was pouring with rain, but the ship majestically held its southerly course at a speed of thirty knots. Judging by the howling rage outside, the storm should have flattened everything, but the ship hardly rolled.

On the previous day, we were on the same latitude as the southern tip of Sumatra, but could see no land. Everybody welcomed the warmth of the sun when it reappeared at 15:00, for all the travellers, still in their summer clothes, had keenly felt the drop in temperature.

On 14 August, the temperature had fallen to 22° and 26.5°C respectively. It was exactly two weeks after our departure from Palestine. The sea was calm and the voyage proceeded with undiminished speed. The crossing of the Tropic of Capricorn put an end to the hot weather. Everyone searched their hand luggage for warm underclothes, in vain. The heating was out of order and the rest of our belongings was inaccessibly stowed away in the belly of the ship with the so called 'forty-kilo' luggage. We had been told at departure that we would get access to all of our suitcases on board ship. No one knew what to do. We froze like wet rats. All our pleas to get our bags were flatly refused. We were unable to get warm even in our beds.

15. Jumping kangaroos

Australia in sight

The sea looked like black ink during these days and was as smooth as oil. There were whales to be seen, but often no more than their spouts.

On 15 August, the temperature ranged from 16 to 20.5°C. We had arrived on the roadstead of Fremantle at six o'clock in the morning. Fremantle is one of Australia's earliest mail ports, important today as a commercial transit centre for the city of Perth, twenty kilometres inland. We had dropped anchor about one thousand metres offshore. The ship took on provisions and fuel during the day.

On 16 August, the thermometer showed from 14 to 19°C. Fortunately we had been allowed, as in Trincomalee, to keep the portholes open at night, although the craving for fresh air had abated somewhat compared to the hotter legs of the voyage.

On 17 August (16-19.5°C) an Australian Government physician, who had come aboard accompanied by an intelligence officer, examined people's lower arms and hands for scabies to prevent its introduction to the country, we were told.

On 18 August the high and low temperatures were both 17°C. The intelligence officers who had come aboard the day before took thumbprints of all men, women and children over the age of sixteen.

On 19 August (13-16.5°C) the Australian Army had relieved the British Police. We sailed from Fremantle at 6:00 and continued full steam ahead on a southerly course. The onset of a storm in the afternoon actually caused the ship to roll.

On 20 August (13-20°C) a number of seats at meal times had remained empty. People were seasick. On 21 August the weather was a little better, but still they were seasick.

Fortunately, it had become 3.5°C warmer on Friday 22 August when some rocky land came into view. Some said it was Tasmania, while others assumed it was the southernmost tip of the Australian mainland.

Sydney

We dropped anchor one thousand metres offshore in the harbour of Sydney

We dropped anchor one thousand metres offshore in the harbour of Sydney on 23 August at 9:30. Some thought they had worked out that we had reached Sydney by circumnavigating Tasmania, rather than via Bass Strait.

Sydney, rising up from the harbour, presented a wonderful view, particularly at night, with colourful displays of neon lights reminiscent of the New York harbour entrance.

The entire panorama was dominated by the great harbour bridge, which had been opened to traffic in 1932. It is the longest single span bridge in the world. Many of the travellers saw the Southern Cross for the first time, high up in the sky. Everyone pushed towards the portholes to catch a

16. Jumping kangaroos

We were filmed for the newsreels on the way from the ferry to the train, probably by *Cinesound*. The quality of the contact with the Australians was the best possible as, indeed, it had been on the ship

glimpse of the view. For most, though, the longing for freedom may well have been twice as strong as wanting to see the view.

We disembarked on 24 August 1941 and were taken to the railway station by ferry where everyone was given an ex-army coat dyed red. Numbers for allocation to the rail cars were handed out to avoid crushes when boarding the train. This was organized by the internees themselves and proved very effective. An Australian sergeant, who was in charge on the ferry, tried a few times to upset this arrangement by his loud bullying, but did not succeed in doing so.

We were filmed for the newsreels on the way from the ferry to the train, probably by *Cinesound.* The quality of the contact with the Australians was the best possible as, indeed, it had been on the ship. What pleased us most of all was that none of the auxiliary police were allowed to leave the ship and we were rid of the spoilers of nocturnal peace with their yelling and screaming. The Australians tolerated no nonsense from these persons, who then became quite subdued.

Towards Tatura

Enough rail cars on the two trains had been provided for us. There was a comfortable seat for everyone in upholstered first and second class compartments. The rail trip went through Sydney, starting at 11:00. Being a Sunday, people wore their Sunday best and happily waved to us. The many small single-family houses were conspicuous by their fenced gardens and backyards. Many were gaudily painted and presented an altogether colourful picture. People waved to us from their houses. We passed Campbelltown at 12:50 and Bargo at 13:30; an hour later, we were at Bowral and arrived in Moss Vale at 15:00; Goulburn at 16:45; again, people were friendly at all the stations and waved to us. The police officer who happened to be on duty at Yass Junction had been to Sarona during the previous war. He delighted in reminiscing and wished us a safe trip.

We arrived in Berrigan in the morning of 25 August, after having received woollen blankets for the night and having been well looked after with food. Everything had been served cleanly wrapped in enticing packages. Well-dressed Australian ladies from the best circles [probably CWA, tr] took care of our wellbeing. We had been travelling all night and had actually slept a little, thanks to the upholstered seats which were much more comfortable than the third class wooden benches in Palestine and Egypt. We reached Tocumwal on the Victorian border at 8:30. Up to now, the track had a gauge of four feet eight and a half inches, corresponding to the European standard gauge [1435mm]. Even though they are united in a federation, the Australian states do not enjoy a uniformly gauged rail system countrywide. This meant we had to change trains at Tocumwal in order to continue on the Victorian train which runs on a gauge of five feet three inches [1600mm].

17. Australian Merino sheep

We had been well supplied with food on the first day of our trip, and when we arrived in Shepparton at 11:00, an ample, warm lunch, consisting of fresh sausages, mashed potatoes and stewed carrots, was waiting for us. We also had a chance to walk up and down the platform. This sounds as if it

EVERY COMPOUND MEASURES 16,600 SQUARE METRES. WORKING OUT THE DENSITY OF POPULATION FROM THIS PRODUCES A FIGURE OF CLOSE TO 17,000 PERSONS PER SQUARE KILOMETRE, WHICH COMPARES TO AN AUSTRALIAN AVERAGE OF 0.9 PERSONS PER KM^2. WE ARE FORTUNATE IN THAT THIS IS A FAMILY CAMP AND THAT THE FOOD IS REALLY GOOD

isn't worth mentioning but gains in significance when considering we had spent twenty-four hours in railway compartments.

After lunch, the first train arrived at Rushworth [Hammond siding] at 13:15, which was the end of the line for us. The second train arrived a few hours later. At the station, buses stood ready for women and children and trucks for men and youths. After a trip of about twelve kilometres we found ourselves in internment camp No 3, Tatura, behind barbed wire once again.

18. Drawing of "Tatura Camp" by Wilhelm Kübler

Helmut Ruff (1928-)

Transported to the End of the World

Written 1997

A forced farewell

The German Templers have been confined to their settlements since the day Britain and France declared war on Germany

July 1941! The war has been raging for almost two years. In Palestine, administered by Britain under mandate from the League of Nations since 1923, the German Templers have been confined to their settlements since the day Britain and France declared war on Germany. The agricultural settlements Betlehem, Waldheim, Sarona and Wilhelma have been turned into internment camps by the authorities. The Germans from the cities of Haifa, Jaffa, Jerusalem and Nazareth were transferred to those camps. A number of men, apparently considered a higher security risk, were separated from their families within hours of the outbreak of war and held under primitive conditions first in a camp at Acre (Akko), later near Jaffa. Amongst them was my father. My mother, sister, brother and I were transferred from Haifa to Betlehem in December 1939.

In July 1941, we are informed that a large group of us is to be transported to another country. Each adult is allowed 40kg of luggage, children less. The destination is not disclosed but we are told it is to a warm country, no heavy winter clothing would be needed!

Thursday, 31 July 1941: we have to say goodbye to Grandfather and the aunts and to all the other friends and relatives who stay behind. We assemble in the school grounds and our hand luggage and the contents of our pockets are inspected. Then the Jewish guards order us on to buses. My brother Ernst and I get separated from our mother and sister, who are still in the school building being searched. When our bus reaches Haifa central railway station, we wait in vain for the others from Betlehem and Waldheim. Now I am really getting worried; I am, after all, only thirteen and Ernst not yet ten. Eventually, a police motor cyclist turns up and we return the way we had come. At the Nesher railway siding, east of Haifa, we are reunited with Mother, Sister and the others and board a train.

The train leaves, we pass through Haifa and get a last glimpse of our *Koloniestraße* [Main Road] and, shortly after, of the German cemetery and then the *Muschelesberg* [Mound of Shells], where we had spent many a Sunday with our father, swimming and collecting shells. Then we round Cape Carmel and travel south along the coast. We pass Neuhardthof, the small Templer settlement where we used to enjoy many hot summer days on the beautiful surf beach.

Lydda: Our train is joined by internees from Sarona and Wilhelma and the men from Jaffa. Mother and children are excited to see our father again. But no, the guards in our carriage will not let anyone enter! The men are allowed to join their families in the other carriages, but not in ours. Eva, my sister, gathers up all her courage and asks the British police sergeant in her school English to let our father through to us. She gets the curt reply "I haven't seen my mother either for a long time." I hate our guards! – A group of Italian internees is also on our train.

We cross the Sinai desert during the night. The hard seats are uncomfortable; we are tired, dusty and hot. The air is stifling; all windows have to stay closed. We are disturbed frequently by the sergeants coming through to count us. Finally, one of them relents and lets us open the windows a little. Fresh air, but also smoke and cinders from the engine come in as we are in the first carriage behind the tender.

EGYPT

Early in the morning we stop at Kantara on the eastern bank of the Suez Canal. This is Egypt. We are given something to eat and drink in a large shed or tent, then cross the famous canal on a ferry. African soil, another continent!

Our hand luggage had to be left behind when we got off the train. We find it lumped together with the 40kg luggage in several huge heaps on the other side alongside another train. Utter chaos reigned as we try to find our belongings whilst the men stow the big luggage into the baggage vans and the guards urge us on to the train. Finally, people just grab anything still lying around, hoping to sort things out on the train. Wishful thinking!

Our guards prevent any movement from carriage to carriage, even when it turns out that in the rush to get on, some cars were overcrowded, while others had seats left vacant. Is it pure chicanery and harassment? Or are they so frightened of us and worried that we might escape? British police sergeants continuously come through, counting us whilst Jewish policemen with fixed bayonets guard both ends of the carriage.

We lost the bag with our food during the luggage scramble, so we have nothing to eat all day. Someone else has taken care of the bag but cannot get it to us on the train. When we receive it late next day the food has spoilt in the heat – mid-thirties every day – and has to be thrown away.

One good thing comes out of all this; our father is with us at last, mother and children feel much safer now.

The train takes us south along the western bank of the Canal. We see the upper structures of ships and boats, occasionally the distinctive large lateen sail of a Nile felucca.

At Ismailiya, our elders wonder whether the train will branch off towards Cairo, where Templers had been interned during the First World War after the British forces occupied Palestine. No, the train continues south. The Bitter Lakes appear. Here the ships travelling the Canal in opposite directions wait to pass each other. The desert, baking in the heat, stretches away to the right.

We pass huge depots of war material, vehicles and aeroplanes parked by the hundreds. Then troop trains travelling north pass us. The soldiers, stripped to the waist in the heat, yell and wave: they are Australians on their way to war. (We learned later that they had arrived on the very ship that was to take us away).

Then a large camp appears, the tents partly buried in the sand, surrounded by barbed wire and guarded by armed sentries on towers: German prisoners-of-war. Our guards object when we call across.

Darkness comes and with it Suez. Our train shunts back and forth, and then backs up the way we came, and stops. Another night on the train! An Australian Army officer comes up and talks to my father, who mentions that we had nothing to eat or drink all day. The officer returns with a field kitchen and other vehicles and speaks to the guards. We are allowed off. Having no plates or dishes, we hold out our open hands: mashed potatoes into one hand, a piece of meat in the other. It tastes beautiful.

I shall never forget that night: trying to sleep on the hard, dirty floor, babies crying, men cursing the guards, sergeants coming through with torches shining into our faces, counting and recounting. Father demands to be taken to the police superintendent in charge of the train in order to complain, the guard threatens him with his bayonet. A woman calls for help, her husband is ill. A sergeant comes through with the Italian doctor who gives the man an injection.

In the direction of Suez, searchlights reach up into the sky. Occasionally a faint rumbling can be heard; is it an air raid?

Eventually the night ends. Our train starts again, reaches Suez and finally stops in the port area. All off again!

We struggle towards a long pier with our hand luggage. The sun is high and burns down relentlessly. Elderly people and women with little children sit exhausted at the roadside. Men carry additional loads. Trucks carrying our heavy luggage and the guards pass but do not stop to help. Finally, we reach the end of the pier and are directed on to large ferries.

An Arab seaman tells Father that we are to be taken to a ship anchored well out in the Gulf, safe from air attacks on Suez. We see the results of such a raid, a burnt-out steamer, stern down in the water. After about half an hour, we reach a huge grey ship. It is the *Queen Elizabeth*, 85,000 tons, the largest passenger ship in the world.

Before we board, our heavy luggage has to be transferred, hard work in the hot sun for our men who had nothing to eat or drink all day. I see some of the big luggage slings dip into the sea as they swing across from our ferry. Accident or design? Will the contents of the wet boxes and cases be all right?

Men look down to us from a row of portholes, call out in German. They are prisoners-of-war, destined to share our voyage.

On board, the men are separated from their families again. We four are allocated an 'inside' cabin without portholes to let in light or air. All light globes have been removed, all we have is the dim light from the passage. But there are four comfortable beds and, what luxury after the past three days, a bathroom. It does not matter that only seawater seems to come out of the taps.
Our ship weighs anchor in late afternoon and heads south, into the Red Sea. It is Saturday, 2 August 1941. We have survived the first leg of our journey into the unknown. What does the future hold in store for us?

On the high seas

We are on board the *Queen Elizabeth*, somewhere in the Indian Ocean, on a southeasterly course. I am in Uncle's cabin with my head out of the porthole, breathing fresh air, watching the waves and looking out for flying fish. Two portholes further along, a boy my age is doing the same thing and we conduct a sporadic conversation at the top of our voices above the noise of wind and sea. It seems a long way down to the water. Somewhere closer to the waterline are the German prisoners-of-war. Would the waves reach their portholes when it is stormy?

After leaving Suez on 2 August 1941, everyone speculated where we would be taken. Kenya? South Africa? These were ruled out when the ship turned east after leaving the Red Sea. Was it to be India? Then the 'Queen' steered a southerly course and put on speed. After stopping at Trincomalee in the North of Ceylon, our ship turned southeast again and we were still on board. So it must be Australia. The Australian soldiers guarding the German POWs confirm this. Our own 'minders' never informed us of our destination. Perhaps they do not know themselves.

The *Queen Elizabeth* was brand new when the war broke out. She was immediately converted to a troop transport. Additional double-decker bunks were built into the cabins. Four or six-berth cabins now hold eight to ten persons. In most cases, the original furniture had not been removed but was made inaccessible because of the additions. Space to move about is therefore very restricted. In some cabins, people have to climb over a bunk to get to the bathroom.

Mother and we three children are more fortunate in that respect, with only the four original bunks in our small 'inside' cabin. But we have no porthole and, therefore, never any natural light or fresh air.

The heat and humidity are really bad. It is terrible in the Red Sea and later in the tropics. The Q.E. was obviously built for the colder North Atlantic run. We make frequent use of our bath. Even if it is only lukewarm seawater, it is refreshing while you lie in it. In the dark of the room, the microscopic phosphorescent marine organisms in the seawater provide a fascinating spectacle in the bathtub, like glow worms swimming in the water. This phenomenon is very noticeable in the Red Sea, but it disappears gradually as we reach deeper, colder waters.

All portholes are closed at night by ship's personnel; this is to prevent us from giving light signals. To whom? To German submarines, or raiders? As another precaution, all light globes have been removed from the cabins and all mirrors have been confiscated. Some women even have the small mirrors cut out of their handbags!

Our cabin has only the dim light coming in from the passage; therefore, the door has to be open all the time. When mother drops a hairpin, we crawl around the floor on all fours, feeling for it.

After a few days, Father manages to get hold of a light globe with the help of Tommy, a young German seaman, who is good at 'organising' things. (Tommy had been taken off an Italian ship by the British in Suez, before Italy entered the war, and had been interned with our men at Jaffa). Unfortunately, our light globe is discovered and confiscated one morning when our cabin is searched whilst we are 'on deck'. Tommy 'finds' another globe for us. This now goes with us in Mother's handbag when we leave the cabin.

Jewish Palestine Police guards are stationed with fixed bayonets at strategic points along the passage, such as the stairways leading up and down and the only drinking water fountain in our part of the deck. We need permission to fill our containers.

We are sent up to the Promenade Deck for exercise every morning and afternoon. This deck is enclosed by windows, which are usually shut; it is almost as hot and humid as below. There are no seats anywhere. All you can do is walk up and down or sit on the dirty floor. During these exercise periods, our cabins are periodically searched. What are they looking for? One day I feel ill – is it seasickness? – and stay in bed when the call 'All on deck' echoes along the passages. Suddenly one of the guards and a ship's nurse enter the cabin, shine their torches into my face and order me up to the promenade deck. My feeble protestations are to no avail. I feel very wonky and spend the time sitting in a corner.

The dining room where we have our meals is on a lower deck. It must be the only place that is air-conditioned. Coming from our humid cabins it always feels very cold at first. The food is monotonous and not what we are used to: kidneys for breakfast and old frozen rabbit meat almost every day, with potatoes for lunch or dinner. I prefer the corned beef. No fresh vegetables or fruit for us! (For many years to come, any mention of rabbit evokes in me unpleasant memories of the peculiar taste of thawed rabbit meat).

The first meal resulted in chaos when we were expected to return dishes, plates, cutlery and leftover food to the kitchen and to wash up. It was therefore suggested to those in charge that perhaps the German POWs could take over in the dining room. This they did with great efficiency and everything runs smoothly now at mealtimes. What is more, our POWs entertain us with music and songs while we eat, accompanied by guitar and violin. We hear many of the old, well-known folksongs and learn new ones. The *Edelweißlied* and its *Afrika Korps* version and *Jung an Jahren* with its haunting nostalgic refrain *Grüß mir die Mutter* will always remind me of our POW friends. The Australian guards of the POWs are very relaxed and friendly about all this. In between music and songs, an elderly little Aussie corporal, his rifle with fixed bayonet taller than he is, strolls amongst our tables, whistling Australian birdcalls.

19. Ewe and lamb

Eva's lute finally comes into its own. She has lugged the precious instrument in its large, cumbersome case with her since we left home. On the long trek in the burning sun along the pier of Suez, Father threatened a few times to throw the damned thing into the water as it was so awkward to carry and prevented Eva from helping with the other luggage. Now she lends it to one of the POWs who plays it beautifully.

Music and singing is about the only entertainment we have on the Q.E. Every evening, the young people gather in one of the connecting passages and sing, with most of us sitting on the floor. Some of the older girls take turns playing the accordion. We sing all sorts of songs and I learn many that are new to me. The Jewish guards are not too happy about this singing but the Australian soldiers often stop to listen. The Australians, on the whole, are very friendly. They frequently pass on their apples to the children, our first taste of Tasmanian 'Jonnies'.

After the stop at Fremantle, the Australian guards seem to take over. Speculation arises on where we are going to land. The weather turns cold and stormy. Now we are glad of our warm cabin. Many people come down with colds. We learn that it is winter in Australia. The sighting of whales is reported. I am annoyed that I missed this spectacle.

Modern day 'Convicts'?

On the morning of 23 August 1941, three weeks after leaving Suez, the Q.E. enters Sydney Harbour. We admire the beautiful scenery, the lush vegetation coming right down to the water's edge, the many bays and above it all, the mighty harbour bridge. Our POW friends leave the ship the same day. We watch and wave from the portholes as they file down the gangway on to waiting ferries. Years later, we are to renew the friendships made in the dining room of the Q.E.

20. An Australian soldier helping the Decker family to disembark in Sydney

We disembark the next day. Our contingent of about 665 German and about 170 Italian internees has been divided into two groups for the next leg of our journey. Our family is in the second group. Father tells us that three internees are too ill to travel with us; they are to be transferred to a hospital. I feel sorry for them. It is late morning when we leave the ship, not sorry to see the last of the Palestine Police. A ferry takes us under the famous bridge to a railway station. Another train journey lies ahead of us, but what a difference from the dirty, uncomfortable Egyptian train. Everybody gets a comfortable seat in a clean carriage and our Australian guards are friendly and helpful.

We travel through Sydney, see many small, single storey houses set in their own gardens. Then we are in the countryside. It is all so different to what we are used to. Everything is green, but a different green. The countryside varies. We pass through little towns; see farmhouses and native bush. The journey goes on and on. Night falls and we get tired. Ernst and I climb into the overhead luggage racks to stretch out and to make more room for the others.

21. The Johann Decker family disembarking in Sydney, 24 August 1941

An Australian sergeant comes through the carriage calling out for a Mr 'Rough'. When he returns, still searching and now calling "Mr Are-you-double-eff", Eva sits up suddenly: "This must be our name!" It is the first time we hear it in English. The sergeant sits up with Father most of the night, talking non-stop about Australia, the war, the camp we are being taken to, his family etc. Father just nods and says "yes" now and then. Our friendly sergeant never realises that most of what he says is not understood. I get the impression that Eva understands more than any of the others. Listening to him, I am fascinated and intrigued by the way he moves his false teeth around with his tongue.

Next morning we are in flat, open country with fields stretching to the horizon. Many of the large eucalypts we see are dead. The men in our carriage discuss the possible reason for this. Is it a terrible disease that is killing off these trees? Our friendly sergeant from the night before explains that the trees have been ringbarked by the farmers so that they die and make cultivating easier and to provide more grazing for the sheep. The men shake their heads in disbelief.

At Tocumwal, we have to change trains in order to continue across the River Murray and into Victoria. Why change trains? Aren't we still in the same country? We know so little about Australia. Our train stops at Shepparton. We are allowed off to have a meal. The first meal in weeks that tastes absolutely wonderful. Soldiers guard the station. The journey continues on to Murchison East, where we have to get off and board buses. Heavily armed soldiers are everywhere. They really must consider us dangerous and desperate!

WHAT ARE THEY DOING TO US? HAVE WE DESERVED THIS? DID THEY BRING US ALMOST ONE THIRD AROUND THE GLOBE TO FINISH UP IN A PLACE LIKE THIS? WE FEEL LIKE CONVICTS 'TRANSPORTED AT THE KING'S PLEASURE TO THE END OF THE WORLD'. ARE WE THE LAST CONVICTS TO BE DEPORTED TO AUSTRALIA?

It is late afternoon on 25 August 1941, when the buses drive through a large wire cage into the camp, which is to be our home for the next few years. We are surrounded by barbed wire, guard towers and searchlights.

What are they doing to us? Have we deserved this? Did they bring us almost one third around the globe to finish up in a place like this? We feel like convicts 'transported at the King's pleasure to the end of the world'. Are we the last convicts to be deported to Australia?

22. Basic shelter in "Tatura Camp"

23. Improved entrance of a corrugated iron hut in "Tatura Camp"

Bringfriede Steller nee Weberruss (1917-)

Destiny strikes

After years of unsettled times, the Second World War broke out on 3 September 1939. Willy [Weberruss] had gone to Germany for work service in the spring and Paul [Weberruss] was on his way to Germany on a Greek steamer.

The parting

Our houses were encircled by British army tanks. We were ordered to the schoolyard. The British soldiers now searched all our houses

There was a commotion outside the village. We assumed it had to do with guerillas in the forest and were not much concerned about it. We learnt very soon, however, that the raid was aimed at us. Our houses were encircled by British army tanks. We were ordered to the schoolyard. The British soldiers now searched all our houses. Cameras and radios were confiscated. This was the beginning of our internment.

We were allowed to go back to our houses for the night and, within a week, we heard what our fate was to be. The rural settlements of Betlehem, Waldheim, Wilhelma and Sarona were to remain, but the urban settlements of Haifa, Jerusalem and Jaffa had to be abandoned. We were fenced in with barbed wire. Each household in Betlehem was allocated a certain number of displaced people.

Every day brought news of new events, but my mother grabbed her seed box, undeterred, and began to sow the seeds in the garden. In our igno-

24. Wilhelm and Päule Weberruss

rance, we young ones thought this was nonsense, but it soon became obvious how right she was when we had to make do with the allotted rations. A table of fifteen persons was a large family, for whom lettuce and vegetables were welcome supplements.

My parents were granted only forty-two years in the small colony built up with so much hard work. In 1948, long after the war had ended, they had to flee with all the others. Not until they reached the island of Cyprus were they able to catch their breath.

Of all the things that had to be left behind, what saddened my mother most was the loss of her handwritten family history and her photo collection. All her free time had been dedicated to this chronicle. She wrote, collected, composed poetry and pasted her 'finds' into the book for the next generation and their descendants to read. God only knows what has become of it.

The Weberruss Tree of Destiny

25. The Arab family helping on the farm for many years were regarded as part of the Weberruss family

A violent storm split it in half and it had to be felled. My parents often talked about this hour of destiny, an omen of the end of the Weberruss family in Betlehem

As a newlywed, Mother 'Päule' had planted a small peppercorn tree next to the garden gate. Under this tree, all her babies had been parked in their prams for their pre-lunch naps and all her children played their games. The bench under the tree was good for a chat at any time. It was cool and shady there in summer, yet sheltered in winter. The garden gate was within easy reach to look up and down the main street. Here was the 'hair salon' for men and boys, and the 'arrack spot' where the men discussed the village news and world events. It was lovely to sit out there, even late at night, for up to eight months of the year. People on their evening stroll loved to drop in when they heard someone talk inside.

During the wartime curfews, we made music under the tree every night. We never tired of playing and singing by heart all our beautiful German songs. We needed no lights and no invitation; the tunes just came to us as if flying through the air. Many times, we had an 'audience' of guards out in the street.

All our family celebrations, such as confirmations and our parents' silver wedding, had been held under the tree, with all relatives attending. Shrubs and trees enclosed the area and a myrtle hedge lined the garden path. The big grapevine covering the yard was a sight to behold. Even the peppercorn tree was adorned with small red and green berries. It was a treasured spot.

In the spring of 1948, the fateful hour of the tree had struck. A violent storm split it in half and it had to be felled. My parents often talked about this hour of destiny, an omen of the end of the Weberruss family in Betlehem.

The expulsion and tragic flight of the settlers was not long in coming. The cattle in the stables had to be released from their chains; home and hearth were abandoned. Loyal Arabs helped arrange the sale of some cows in Nazareth. This was the end of the Betlehem settlement.

From *Memories of Palestine (2005)*

Ewald Wagner (1926-2008)

My last days in Betlehem

As told to Werner Blaich 2006

Editor's note: *Betlehem, not to be confused with Bethlehem in Judea, was a Templer settlement in the Galilee of about one hundred inhabitants. Apart from community buildings, a schoolhouse and a water tower, there were nineteen houses, with stables, sheds and other outbuildings.*

During the Second World War, the settlement was turned into an internment camp with guards, watchtowers and a strict control regime which, although eased after the war, was never completely removed. The settlement continued to function as a rural village, with benefits for the residents as well as the British Mandate Administration. On 17 April 1948, nearby Waldheim – another German settlement – was raided by the Haganah. This event directly affected the inhabitants of Betlehem and caused the displacement of all the Germans in Palestine. Ewald Wagner, who was there as a 21-year-old, continues:

26. Ewald Wagner with his horse

29. The Wagner house in Betlehem in 1947

27. Cows coming home to their stables

28.Cyclamen, native to the area around Betlehem

When the war had ended, we were allowed to obtain passes to get out of our barbed wire enclosure. The fields had been somewhat neglected without proper supervision. We were now able to inspect our fields and check on the work of our Arab employees. There were still full-time guards in Betlehem for about two years. Before that, the only person allowed out for servicing the pumping station of the water supply two kilometres outside the camp was Mr Weber or his deputy.

Betlehem was once surrounded by extensive oak forests, which we loved. They were our forests, where our shepherds grazed herds of dairy cows and where we went for picnics, festivals and all-day school hikes before the war, in a sea of wildflowers during springtime. We were outraged to see that the British had cut down all the trees to make charcoal to fuel their steam trains. When the extent of the devastation was realised, we sued the British Mandate Government for damages by engaging the services of Mr Levi, a Jewish lawyer. The case was decided in favour of Betlehem, and compensation was paid.

After the war, the longstanding tensions between the Jews and the Arabs escalated. We felt quite unsafe and packed some things in case we had to leave in a hurry. When the shooting started in Waldheim, five kilometres away, we knew it was time to leave. Our people were in panic; some left right away and others waited a bit longer. Eventually, they all left by horse-drawn wagon for the Arab village of Saffuriyeh, about ten kilometres away. The first to leave were the British officers and their guards when they took off through the upper gate in their motor vehicles. I was on horseback and followed my father's wagon to Saffuriyeh.

My father said it was silly not to have released the cattle, would I mind going back to do this. I quickly rode back on my horse. Our Arab ranger agreed to come along. When we got there, we saw a young Arab who was quite upset. Hassan, his father, was sitting on the roof of the Weberruss house with a gun, ready to defend the settlement. We said, come and give

30. Refugees (Heinrich Wagner, Marie Beck and Frau Brofeld) leaving their home

WE LIFTED SOPHIE ON TO THE TRUCK SITTING IN A CHAIR, BECAUSE SHE WAS DISABLED

us a hand with the cows. Some of the cattle were trotting around in the yards; others were still chained in the stables. Two of us got them out, working from the lower gate up towards the upper gate, while the third kept the growing herd together on the main street.

Back in Saffuriyeh, we discussed the plight of six older people who had stayed behind in Betlehem. Old Mr Andreas Beck and his wife were there, the elderly sisters Caroline Sus and Sophie Rothacker and an old uncle of mine, Fritz Pfeiffer and his adult disabled daughter. Uncle Fritz had insisted he would not leave. My father ran into a friend of Mr Beck's, an Arab, who had a truck. He was willing to get them out with his truck, as long as I would come with him. Again, I rode back on my horse and told the people to get ready to be picked up. We first helped Mr Beck and his wife into the cabin and loaded their belongings on the back of the truck. We then went to pick up Caroline Sus and Sophie Rothacker. We lifted Sophie on to the truck sitting in a chair, because she was disabled. Fritz Pfeiffer with his sick daughter declined to come; he said he would stay and take his chances.

As I rode back through the settlement on my horse – the truck had already left – I heard a kind of rustling in the trees and when I saw bits of leaves

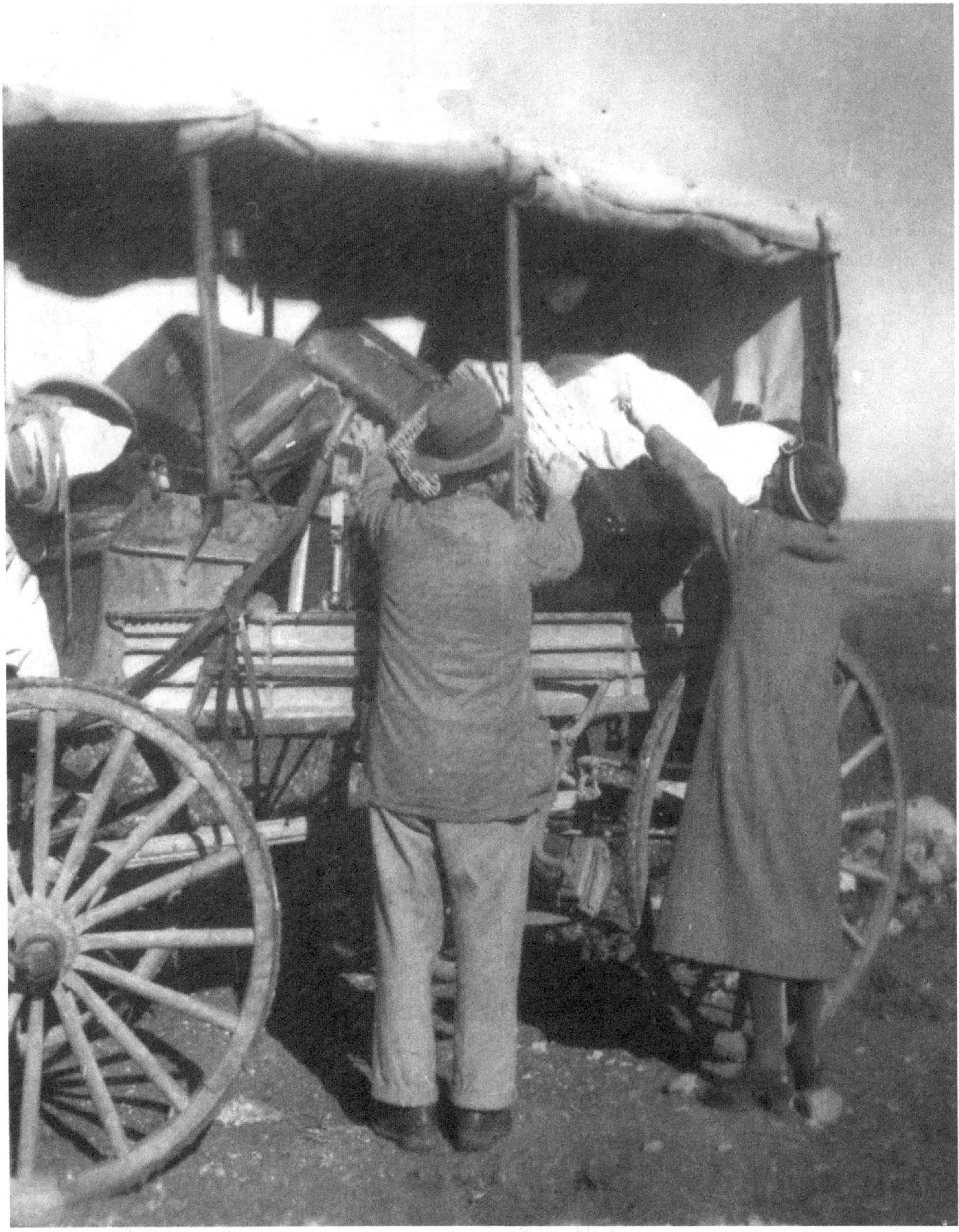

31. Loading the wagon before fleeing from Betlehem

I HEARD A KIND OF RUSTLING IN THE TREES AND WHEN I SAW BITS OF LEAVES FALLING OFF THE TREES, I REALISED IT WAS FROM BULLETS, NOT FROM BIRDS. I SAID, "I BETTER GET THE HELL OUT OF HERE"

THE SHOOTING HAD COME FROM A TRACTOR WITH A BUCKET SCOOP DRIVING ALONG THE OUTSIDE PERIMETER FENCE. TWO MEN WITH GUNS SITTING IN THE BUCKET TRIED TO HEAD US OFF. THEY WERE STOPPED BY A HEAP OF ROCKS

32. Last farewells to the Arab helpers

33. Karl Wagner minding the cattle

falling off the trees, I realised it was from bullets, not from birds. I said, "I better get the hell out of here."

I have since heard that the shooting had come from a tractor with a bucket scoop driving along the outside perimeter fence. Two men with guns sitting in the bucket tried to head us off. They were stopped by a heap of rocks blocking a five-foot gap between the perimeter fence and a fence running at right angles to it near the Blaich and Beilharz orchards. The only reason they did not get us was the fact that they had to clear away the rocks.

34 The Convent in Nazareth where the refugees took shelter

36. The small group found refuge with the nuns in Nazareth. From left to right. seated: Frau Beck, Karoline Sus, Sophie Rothacker. Back row: standing, second Anna Wagner nee Beck, Heinrich Wagner and Sisters of the Convent

A lucky escape indeed for a young man, four elderly settlers and a brave Arab truck driver.

35. The grave of Ewald Wagner's grandmother who died during the flight and was buried in Nazareth

As it turned out, Hassan, the lone gunman on the roof had indeed put up quite a fight later on and was wounded, shot in the stomach, but made a full recovery. We have no further news of him or his son, who helped us with the cows, nor of the truck driver and the ranger. It is tragic that so many good and decent Arabs have to go through such tough times.

The four old people, as well as my father, mother, grandmother and myself, found refuge with the Borromeo Sisters in Nazareth. The rest of the people were taken to Haifa by the British. Before they left, the farmers authorised my father to sell the cattle at twenty-five pounds per cow, not a great price, but the best that could be obtained under the circumstances. My greatest regret was having to leave my horse behind. It had been brought up starting with milk from a bottle. To me, the horse that had performed so magnificently on that eventful final day in Betlehem was like family. The Sheikh who bought the livestock promised he would see to it that the horse would be looked after; but in wartime nothing is certain.

Shortly after our people arrived in Haifa, they were transferred by ship to Cyprus, an overnight trip. They lived there for the best part of a year in tents provided by the British Army until they could find transport to Germany or Australia. Even Uncle Fritz and his daughter had ended up in Cyprus, but I do not know how. While we were with the Borromeo Sisters, my grandmother died the night before the Haganah took Nazareth; she was quietly buried in the German cemetery by a Catholic priest and an Arab, who dug the grave. We could not attend the funeral, because it was deemed too dangerous. After a few months, the priest said it was time we notified the Israeli authorities of our presence. Some time after that, we were transferred to the camp in Cyprus. Within days of our arrival in December, a number of Templers left by ship for Australia. We followed soon after with the next group.

Eleonore Braun (nee Ruff 1913-1998)

Flight from Palestine

We lived in the rural settlement of Betlehem before the war. At the outbreak of war in 1939, the British turned it into an internment camp called a perimeter settlement by surrounding the entire village with a high barbed wire fence. There was a gate with guards at either end of the Main Street. Most of the inhabitants of the Haifa settlement were moved to the camps of Betlehem and Waldheim. During the war, groups of internees were repatriated to Germany via exchange programs. My family and many of the older people stayed behind. In 1941, most able-bodied men and their families were deported to internment camps in Australia.

37. Betlehem with water tower

In April 1948, all Germans were ordered to pack their bags. It was rumoured that we were going to be taken to a safer environment, because the political turmoil in Palestine was rapidly getting worse. My mother wanted to stay put, but I said: "We are going to pack; we are not going to stay behind by ourselves!"

Attack by the Haganah

On Saturday [17 April] at about five in the morning, we heard shots from nearby Waldheim. We hastily loaded some of our packed bags on to our horse-drawn cart. Our neighbour, Mr Imanuel Katz, came across and asked us if we also intended to leave. We said "Yes." "Then my Walter shall drive you." When the shooting had started, our Arab stable boy who had arrived earlier to do the milking, untied the cows, opened the gate and drove all the cattle out into the street. Cows and calves came trotting out of all the other farmyards as well, and Ewald Wagner, helped by some Arab herdsmen, drove the entire herd out the upper gate to Saffuriyeh, the nearest Arab village.

Walter Katz took the reins of our wagon with my mother, my sister and me. All the Arab farm hands also fled to Saffuriyeh

We, together with the Katz and Weber families, set off in four wagons. Walter Katz took the reins of our wagon with my mother, my sister and me. All the Arab farm hands also fled to Saffuriyeh. Our Arab horse groom suddenly met up with us on the way. He asked, "Where are you off to?" We said, "To Saffuriyeh." He: "Then I can drive you there." Walter was therefore able to rejoin his father.

When we arrived at Saffuriyeh, some of the men continued to the nearest British police station in Nazareth to report what had happened. Our own Commandant at Camp III [Betlehem] and his driver had been the first to flee in an armoured car out the upper gate and on to Nazareth.

We were now told to drive to the German hotel [Heselschwerdt] in Nazareth. When we arrived there, we found a large table in the kitchen loaded with provisions so we could start cooking meals for all the people. Afterwards everyone selected one of the rooms, but we only stayed there for two or three days and were then taken to Acre to join the people from Waldheim.

One married couple had been shot dead in front of their three small children, and Mrs Deininger, when emerging from her cowshed, was shot in the head

They had gone through a terrible and frightening experience. One married couple had been shot dead in front of their three small children, and Mrs Deininger, when emerging from her cowshed, was shot in the head. All the others were herded together and forced into one room where all their money and their jewellery were taken from them. Later in the day, they were allowed to go home under heavy guard to pack a few things. Whatever they packed was immediately pulled out of their suitcases again so that they ended up with only the barest of necessities. This, of course, was not a pleasant experience.

38. Haifa, view from Mount Carmel

From Acre we were taken to Haifa and loaded on to a freighter, which had collected all the internees from the southern settlements. There was not much room. Several people had brought their dogs along, but all the dogs were shot dead on the wharf. We had left our dog at home. It probably suffered the same fate, but at least we did not have to watch. Waiting for our papers being sorted out, we were shot at from across the water and had to take refuge on the far side of the ship to avoid being hit.

39. Arriving in Cyprus

Cyprus

It was evening by the time we steamed out of Haifa. We were given some food to eat, like rice, carrots and peas; it was not too bad. This was going to be a terrible night! I was lucky to find a deck chair for my mother, whereas I slept on the floor next to her, wrapped in a rug. We did not see my sister; she must have been below deck. We did not see her again until we disembarked in Cyprus.

Army vehicles took us to a tent camp pitched on bare sand near Famagusta. We had to pick a tent, take bed frames and trestles and make them into beds by stuffing straw into bags for mattresses for us to sleep on from now on. The German prisoners-of-war who lived in tents across the road made life much more bearable for us. They made half of their large kitchen available for our group to do our own cooking. The prisoners-of-war also provided us with solid floor bases for our tents. The sand was not so bad now and things had become more comfortable.

Our camp was very close to a beautiful beach called Golden Sands. We could go for long walks along the beach, but it was very hot during the day. We lived there for half a year, all summer long.

We now had to decide whether we wanted to go to Germany or to Australia. We opted for Germany because our sister and her family lived there. All our other relatives had been deported to Australia in 1941. We left by plane in October 1948.

Most of the other refugees at the Famagusta camp had yet to endure the whole winter in their tents before they were finally on their way to Australia.

From *Memories of Palestine (2005)*

MOST OF THE OTHER REFUGEES AT THE FAMAGUSTA CAMP HAD YET TO ENDURE THE WHOLE WINTER IN THEIR TENTS BEFORE THEY WERE FINALLY ON THEIR WAY TO AUSTRALIA

40. Cyprus refugee camp

Imanuel Katz (1896-1969)

Gotthilf Wagner
MEMORIAL SERVICE

Text: Job 5:17-19; Job 35:2-15; and Romans 14:8.
Hymn no 299, 1-5, 6-7.

Llike a bolt out of the blue, we were hit by the horrifying news that our leader and old friend Gotthilf Wagner was murdered

On Friday 22 March 1946, like a bolt out of the blue, we were hit by the horrifying news that our leader and old friend Gotthilf Wagner was heinously murdered at the insidious hands of common thugs. His foes, who were no match for him and could not touch him in the open, have resorted to the vilest depravity to remove by cowardly murder the irreplaceable man who, to us, was a blessing, but for them, a person to be feared because he stood in their way.

The severity of loss

There had been repeated attempts to destroy him by bomb attacks, but God, through His Providence, had graciously saved him and preserved his life, but now a horribly tragic fate has caught up with him. There rages

41. Gotthilf Wagner was an accomplished public speaker

within us a holy tempest of repugnance against the damnable deed, but we are reduced to impotence in the face of this dastardly act. If the authorities cannot find the ways and the means to deliver the culprits to lawful punishment instead of letting them off scot-free, we are left facing the fact that any one of us could be struck down with impunity.

The severity of the loss the Jaffa-Sarona community and indeed each one of us, as well as our Society as a whole, have suffered through the death of Gotthilf Wagner does not bear thinking about. His service, which included representing the Society to the authorities, was dedicated to community life: the entire management of the Society had rested in the hands of our esteemed departed friend and we cannot imagine how we can go on from here. Why did we have to suffer this blow, why has God allowed it to happen? Are we abandoned by all men and forsaken by God? Our pain is justified and so, too, is our gloomy and desperate question, why, Why?! – Let us, however, be mindful that if we go down the path of brooding, of letting ourselves go, of doubt and despair, or even of rebelling against God, we will be led astray and lose our way.

Gotthilf Wagner

Mr Wagner had intended to visit and stay with us in Betlehem for a while to recuperate from working tirelessly for the common good when, just before his visit, he had taken a trip to Jaffa on business. He was accompanied by his sister Frida, who observed motor cyclists pursuing them. Alarmed, she pleaded with her brother to turn back or at least take another route, to which he replied: We are in God's hands and He will protect us. The steadfast trust in God that inspired him and his upright and fearless attitude do empower me, I believe, to say it would not be in keeping with the philosophy and character of the departed if we were to go down the path of doubt and despair.

Blessed is the man whom God corrects, therefore do not despise the chastening by the Almighty.

These are words that our natural human mind cannot accept, for not only does punishment cause pain, but also injures our self-esteem. What is more, we mostly are so convinced of our innocence that, surprised, we resist trying to justify ourselves even when we begin to see the reasons for our punishment. How many questions are crowding our minds, how many 'whys' has the death of our departed triggered within us! God must know we have nobody left, He knows that we have always fulfilled our duties, even under the most difficult conditions! The time seems to have come from which it is said:

It is true that even superstition is not as dangerous as lack of faith

That God has darkened the minds of men that with open eyes they do not see, and with open ears they do not hear; the hearts of men are harder than stone, and they do not want to change; it seems that knowingly and with diabolical intention, they no longer want to respond to what God demands of us. It is true – as one out of our midst has once said – that even superstition is not as dangerous as lack of faith. Spiritually and religiously, superstition is still active, whereas unbelief is too indifferent and superficial, and too

42. Gotthilf Wagner (1887-1946)

lazy to think about facts, to ponder realities or to establish useful ideals. Through brainwashing and incitement, superstition affects only individuals and has ruined relatively few (such as in witchcraft trials), whereas unbelief seizes entire nations and sweeps them to their doom. Its aim is decay and the dissolution of order, human or divine, and the destruction of social, religious and ethical morality which, in the last analysis, spells chaos and the doom of humanity. As we can observe in the world today, humankind is doing its best to be on the path to self-destruction. The use of atom bombs for the destruction of our fellow human beings without limitation serves as a foreboding of the catastrophe it will entail.

That God has darkened the minds of men

Since humanity, us included, has drifted on to paths so slippery and far from God, God intervenes time and again, for He does not want death and destruction for man, but wishes that we mend our ways, which means that we come to our senses, stop and examine ourselves, recognise and rectify our mistakes and proceed to walk on God-pleasing roads and live, really live, even if we die. Therefore: *Blessed is the man whom God corrects; do not despise the chastening by the Almighty, for He makes sore but also binds up; He wounds, and His hands make whole; He will deliver you in six troubles, and in the seventh no harm will befall you.*

To give this sorrow the right expression and perspective lest we are not only crushed and beaten, but will find the strength to walk upright once more, we want to listen to a time-honoured passage from Romans 14:8: *For whether we live, we live unto the Lord; and whether we die, we die unto the Lord: whether we live or die, therefore, we are the Lord's.*

Prayer

Almighty God, dear Heavenly Father! In this hallowed hour of remembrance, we humbly bow to you, conscious, as always, of our indebtedness to you, for we live and exist only through you and in you. We praise you also when in pain and deepest mourning because we know that what you have ordained for us is right and comes from a good and wise Father, who knows all things better than we do. We thank you that you had given us him, whom you have now recalled; we thank you for everything he, with your assistance, was able to do for us. Take us all into your care and do not deny us your fatherly help and shelter, protect us from coming to grief in body and soul; make us recognise that happiness is only found in the obedience to your commandments, and give us your spirit who guides us on to your path. Give that our life's work will consist of serving your cause so we may be yours, even in death, and forever!

Amen

As a last salute to you, Gotthilf Wagner, and as a visible sign of our heartfelt condolences to the bereaved family, I place this wreath on your grave on behalf of the Betlehem Community.

Rest in Peace

Richard Hornung (1933-)

Reminiscences of the Middle East

Written 2002

The turmoil

Millions are reeling under the impact of the news and the images of violence and terror

The turmoil in that area is a daily spectacle on TV screens throughout the world. Millions are reeling under the impact of the news and the images of violence and terror. There are some older folk for whom it has an all too familiar ring, to the point of the somewhat cynical reaction: what's new?

Take the Swabian Templers. This little known group of former Palestine residents originating from southern Germany had its brush with terror that was rife in pre-Israel Palestine.

The Templers had emigrated from their native Swabia – the area now called Baden-Württemberg – during the last four decades of the nineteenth century. Their motivation was religious. The Holy Land was their choice for practising what they believed to be genuine Christianity in contrast to the repression they had experienced under the perceived fossilised Protestantism of their homeland at the time.

Two and a half generations and many hardships later, they had built excellent lives for themselves in seven settlements in various parts of Palestine. The Templers, tough and resourceful Swabians with the characteristic work ethic of that stock, had introduced progressive practical methods in many fields, such as irrigation bores – water was often found thirty metres below the surface – and water pumps driven by Deutz kerosene and Diesel motors. This made possible large plantations from which the famous 'Jaffa' oranges were exported to many parts of the world. Irrigation also revolutionised agriculture for many other products of this dry land. Old Palestinian Arabs have not forgotten this and their ongoing gratitude to the Templers is quite touching.

Twice, the Templers' status was reduced to that of prisoners of HM the King of England

.

Twice

Twice, the Templers' status was reduced to that of prisoners of HM the King of England and, after 1945, they became personae non gratae: enemy status German nationals in the midst of the fierce Arab-Israeli conflict erupting into war after the fighting had stopped in Europe. This was the period leading up to the expiry of the British mandate in 1948. It was a time of daily shootings, bombings, killings, savagery and terror that also did not spare the British.

The secretary of the Templers was Gotthilf Wagner, a man in his late fifties, their de facto leader, very energetic, stubborn and unafraid of the none too clearly defined 'authorities', making negotiation particularly difficult. He was also one of the few fluent English-speakers of the group. In his view, the Templers had earned the right to a future, if not in Palestine, then elsewhere in the British Empire, with just and fair compensation for assets lost. His negotiations involved discussions with the British, the Zionists, the Arabs – with all of whom he stuck to his guns, convinced that the line he had adopted was justified.

This was the time when he began to receive anonymous phone calls, messages to the effect that 'we will make certain that you will never see your grandchildren in Australia again'. In 1941, large numbers of younger Templers and their wives and children had been deported to Australia on the *Queen Elizabeth*, tearing apart many families. This set the stage for the eventual migration of the bulk of the Templers to Australia.

The warning

The warning Gotthilf Wagner had received materialised as a bomb explosion in the Sarona settlement, one of the Templer communities near Tel Aviv, where he was to preside over a meeting of Elders. A major mess with many dead bodies was averted because the meeting was twenty minutes late, a mere non-routine coincidence. I never found out why the meeting had been postponed.

Then, on 22 March 1946, Wagner drove with three others, one of them his sister Frida, from the settlement of Wilhelma near Lydda, now Bnei Atarot near Lod, to nearby Jaffa and Sarona.

At the time of this business trip, unrest was all around: tensions, daily killings, mutual atrocities between Jews and Arabs, occasionally involving the British as well, who found all this increasingly beyond their control. Once more: what's new? Gotthilf's wife Lina had pleaded with him not to go this once because she had been frightened by dreams about his safety – all very much like Calpurnia of 'Ides of March' fame.

In his somewhat gruff manner, Wagner had brushed it all aside saying *"Allah ma na"* – God is with us – in Arabic, although he was not a Muslim. Many Templers, normally not given to too many words, were less reticent and less inhibited when using the Arab tongue in which some were as fluent as native speakers. After they had driven off in the car, Frida observed two motor cyclists following the car at some distance. They overtook the car, taking a good look at the occupants and disappeared up ahead. The ambush was set up close to the outskirts of Jaffa, in front of a narrow cast iron bridge which, incidentally, had been built by Gotthilf's foster father Georg Wagner before the First World War. The road was blocked by a truck.

FRIDA, IN UNSPEAKABLE PANIC, TRIED TO MOP UP THE BLOOD POURING OUT OF THE FATAL WOUNDS

TWO KILLERS

Two killers jumped forward at the slowing car, pumped bullets into Gotthilf's head and took off on their motorbikes. The deed took less than a minute. Gotthilf was almost instantly dead, trying to frame a word resembling '*Ende*' – the end – as he switched off the ignition in an already automatic reflex action. Frida, in unspeakable panic, tried to mop up the blood pouring out of his fatal wounds.

In the afternoon, Wagner's body was returned to Wilhelma. The entire community, and later all Templers, were stunned and speechless. Feeling time had stood still, they wondered who and what would come next. They certainly felt that their days in Palestine were numbered one way or another. There was no one remotely capable of guiding them through this chaotic time with the same conviction as Wagner had done, toughing it out with those in power.

THIS WAS THE BEGINNING OF THE END FOR THESE SWABIANS IN THEIR HOLY LAND

THE BEGINNING OF THE END

This was the beginning of the end for these Swabians in their Holy Land. After yet another atrocity committed by the Haganah, most of them became displaced persons, as they were called then, refugees in a tent camp in Cyprus, hoping to find a boat to Australia. This roughly coincided with the end of the British mandate in the spring of 1948.

How do I come to know this story of terror in the Middle East?

I was a thirteen-year-old in the Templer community and I was Gotthilf's nephew and he was my mother's cousin. Gotthilf had been raised by Georg Wagner, my mother's father, the man who had built that bridge and had introduced and masterminded the irrigation systems mentioned above. Gotthilf had lost his own parents in a typhus epidemic when he was a boy. My brother Hans and I both knew Uncle Gotthilf particularly well, were extremely fond and admiring of him, appreciated his generosity, his sense of humour and his ability to have fun. He taught me to swim in the midst of going through hell in his own daily struggles, while the terror encroached upon him in the manner related above. None of this ever showed in the man. He goaded me on in the water, finding it difficult not to laugh outright at my grimacing face. Through his hilarity and confidence in himself and in life, I very quickly lost all water shyness. Gotthilf was a positive personality and a role model.

Like me, many people puzzled over the need to kill this man. It had nothing to do with the strife in Europe. It had a lot to do with the all too familiar use of terror as a political weapon. No one felt safe after this killing, all stared at an abyss from that date onwards until, in April 1948, the British ex-troop ship *Empire Comfort*, crammed full with Templers beyond passenger capacity, left full steam for Cyprus. It departed Haifa harbour, a city in which the former Templer settlement was conquered by Jewish forces on the very day the ship berthed to collect the refugees from the two Templer settlements east of Haifa. I remember it as a day of ceaseless gun and mortar fire, of bullets flying and feelings of unrelieved tension, older folk despairing of the future and an almost zombie-like stare on many faces.

The impression persists that the intention was to terrorise and to create situations where those so terrorised simply leave while they can 'of their own volition', situations well known to hundreds of thousands of hapless Arab Palestinians.

THE MURDER OF GOTTHILF WAGNER IS RELATIVELY UNKNOWN

The murder of Gotthilf Wagner is relatively unknown. It, however, is well known to most Templers and is recorded in the Templer chronicle entitled *The Holy Land called* by Paul Sauer 1991.

I believe we simply cannot strike out in fresh and positive directions if we dwell on 'knowing' dreadful things. One of the great findings of modern psychology is, what we fill our mind with at one end comes out at the other in the form of action: achievement or non-achievement, fulfilment or frustration, dreams-come-true or nightmares-come-true. There is much more to this approach than meets the eye. The positive side is seized by those who are productively involved in the present with a sense of and a longing for a worthwhile future.

THE POSITIVE SIDE IS SEIZED BY THOSE WHO ARE PRODUCTIVELY INVOLVED IN THE PRESENT WITH A SENSE OF AND A LONGING FOR A WORTHWHILE FUTURE

And what of the negative side? Continued mourning, permanent black armbands? Nourishing hatreds in the spirit of revenge? No – it is inconceivable to all who knew him that Gotthilf Wagner, had he lived, would have travelled down that road to nowhere.

43. British guards on watch

Richard Otto Eppinger (1902-1976)

The Cyprus Group 1948–1949

On 3 April 1949, the last section of the Cyprus group arrived in Melbourne on board the Yugoslav passenger liner *Partizanka*. Anxiety about the future was mixed with the gratitude of being reunited with friends

On 3 April 1949, the remainder of the Cyprus group safely arrived in Melbourne on board the Yugoslav passenger liner *Partizanka.* Anxiety about the future was mixed with the gratitude of being reunited with friends and members of the Temple Society and standing on terra firma once again, looking forward to creating new homes and reviving community life in true Templer spirit.

Above all, I want to thank the members who, in selfless effort, after their discharge from internment in Australia, have cordially welcomed and provided accommodation for the Cyprus group despite the very limited means at their disposal. The future oppressed us like a nightmare. With deep trust in God, we embraced the old saying, 'where there is a will, there is a way'. In recognition of the efforts made by the Commonwealth Department of Immigration, I want to mention our truly caring Mr H.T. TEMBY, whose name had become known to us all, down to the youngest child.

44. Leaving the settlement of Wilhelma, April 1948

45. Arrival in Cyprus

46. *H.T. (Harry) Temby, Australian Government official*

Turbulent Times

Yes, they were disturbing days before the corvette *Empire Comfort* (1600 tons) of the Royal Navy finally docked at Famagusta on 22 April 1948, and British Army trucks transported 300 Palestine-Germans to a tent camp in the sand dunes three miles away, under the auspices of Sir GODFREY Collins KCIE, CSI, OBE, Commissioner for Refugees.

On 22 March 1946, our highly respected Mr Gotthilf WAGNER was brutally murdered in his car on a business trip from Wilhelma to Sarona. This exacerbated the already existing insecurity and increased the anxiety of the people enormously. Additional murders of camp residents (at the time of our departure the losses amounted to 2%) further aggravated the tension and the distress, as did the growing number of shooting incidents. In broad daylight, shots were fired at the houses of Wilhelma from a newly built road through German-owned land close to the settlement. A young girl employed as a nanny by the British District Commissioner was just feeding the Commissioner's child, when a cup she was holding was shot from her hand, missing the baby by sheer luck. The management urged the father to have the child evacuated. In another incident, a bullet crashed through a kitchen window, narrowly missing the owner of the house. Then, also in broad daylight, two city louts kidnapped an elderly widow, who was on a shopping trip in Tel Aviv. Exhausted and angry, she returned after two days and told how she was pushed into a house where she was gagged and blindfolded. This was not the only case.

These events caused the camp management to look for protection as far as this was possible in captivity, and to try to prevent knee-jerk reactions in the three still existing camps of Wilhelma, Betlehem and Waldheim. The Sarona residents had been evacuated to Wilhelma one year before. It is to be noted that the populations of all these camps consisted predominantly of women, children and men over sixty, except for seven younger men.

Our appeals for help were first heard by the Archbishop of Canterbury, then by the International Red Cross. Unitarian friends in the USA did not reply. The Secretary [of the Mandate Government] for German affairs appeared in person, on the instructions of the High Commissioner, for private talks to which, contrary to usual practice, the British commandant had not been invited.

47. *The last volunteers leaving Palestine*

Business activity throughout the country slowed down considerably as the situation became more dangerous. Acts of terror, shootings and political murders happened on an almost daily basis. For a year or so, only seven or eight Arab auxiliary police armed with primitive shotguns guarded our camps. From time to time, one guard or other went missing, gun and all. Suddenly, there was the great shock. Waldheim and Betlehem had been attacked and occupied by armed Jewish forces. On the next day, 18 April, a representative of the Mandate Government unexpectedly appeared in Wilhelma, confirmed what had happened and informed us that the Royal Navy was standing by to evacuate Wilhelma residents. The destination was not revealed. We had to be ready within 48 hours, with 40kg hand luggage each (children 25kg); the RN would not wait. The bulk luggage would be sent later.

48. *Nikolai Schmidt (1876-1953)*

49. *Imanuel Katz (1896-1969)*

The race against time was on. A conference with the director of the International Refugee Organisation (IRO) was planned for twelve noon. At 1pm his plane finally arrived at Lydda airport – without the noble gentleman from Cairo.

After that, the District Commissioner ordered a conference in Jaffa concerning storage and insurance of our bulk luggage, to be delivered there in two days. A heated discussion ended with the Commissioner's request that the luggage be left with Levant Bonded Warehouses Ltd in Jaffa. It was the right thing to do. We heard later that all the warehouses of the customs office had been looted.

Meanwhile in Wilhelma, all hands were busy packing. Night was turned into day, lists had to be made, goods were sold at throwaway prices, and willing buyers amongst the Arabs were few and far between. Boxes had to be made, measured and marked, and trucks ordered for their transport at inflated prices. There was no end to the rushing and fixing – forty-eight hours were not enough!

Some stay behind

A small band of fifty-two, mostly older persons and three children stayed behind and were given shelter at the Hospice [hostel] of the Borromeo Sisters in Jerusalem. Six of our younger men (Siegfried HAHN, Walter IMBERGER, Wilhelm GROLL, Hans STEPHAN, Heinz VOLLMER and Adolf BAMBERG) under the direction of Mr Gottlob LÖBERT remained as volunteers to sell the remainder of the cattle (about 300), but were at first busy with the dispatch of the bulk luggage. The District Commissioner helped them to get on to a plane to join us in Cyprus.

On the morning of 20 April 1948, a long column of eight buses, five trucks, three tanks and two armoured cars appeared on the long street of Wilhelma. The adults were in a sombre mood, but composed, and counted their children, who looked forward to the 'outing', the like of which they had not experienced in their nine years of internment.

50. *Boarding "Empire Comfort" off Jaffa*

51. On board "Empire Comfort" April 1948

52. Hilda and Richard Eppinger with their son Otto on board "Empire Comfort" April 1948

53. Sailing into port

54 Leaving the ship in Famagusta, April 1948

55. Young people on a boat

56. Karl Richter, Elfriede Doh, Herbert Petrick, Rosemarie Imberger and Elisabeth (Mausi) Frank on "Empire Comfort"

57. Trucks waiting for the new arrivals

58. In the port of Famagusta

59. The Golden Sands camp with the small tents where the refugees stayed first

60. Camp with the large tents where the German POWs stayed until September 1948

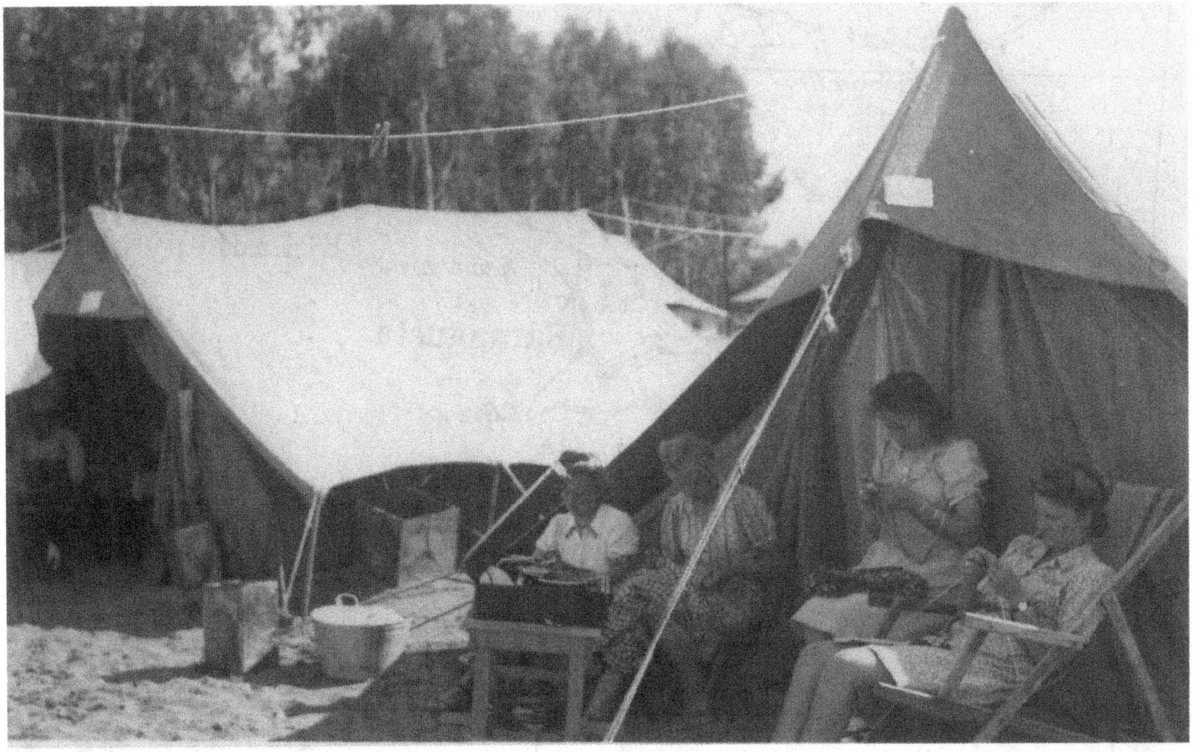

61. Relaxing in front of the small tents

62. Theodor Doh, Walter Imberger, Rose Imberger and Siegfried Hahn preparing the catch of the day

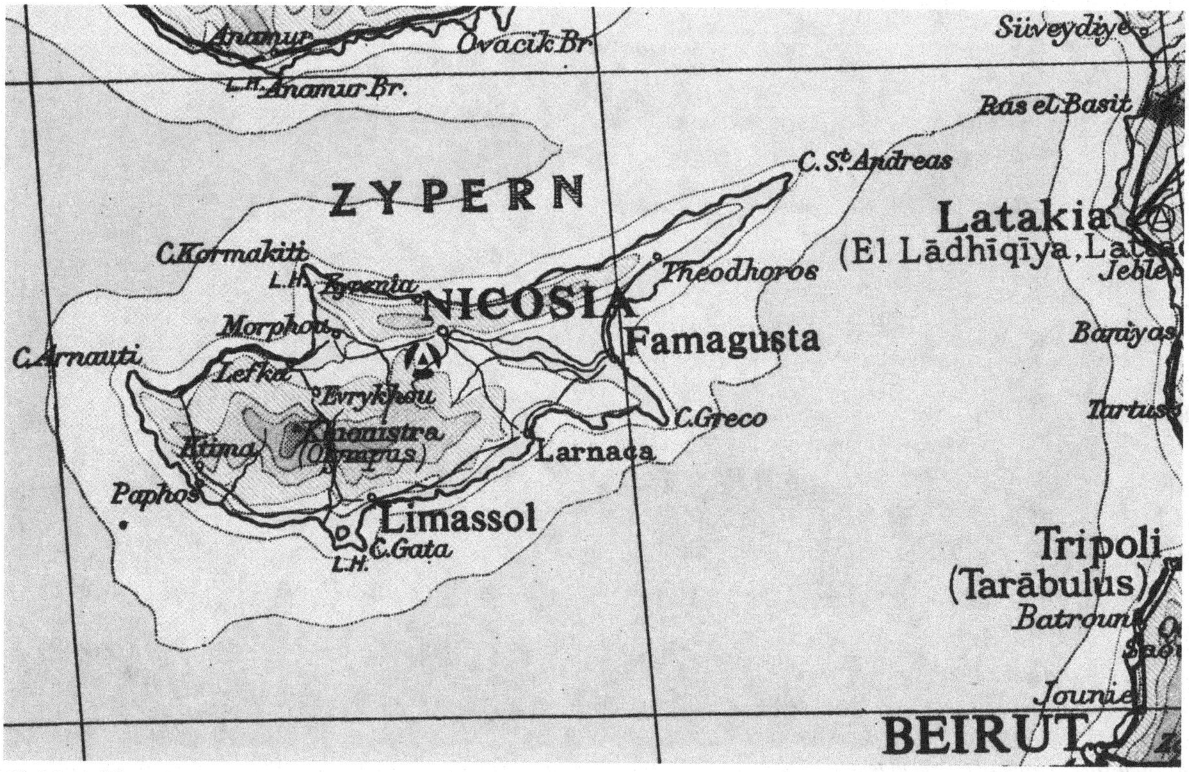

63. Map of Cyprus

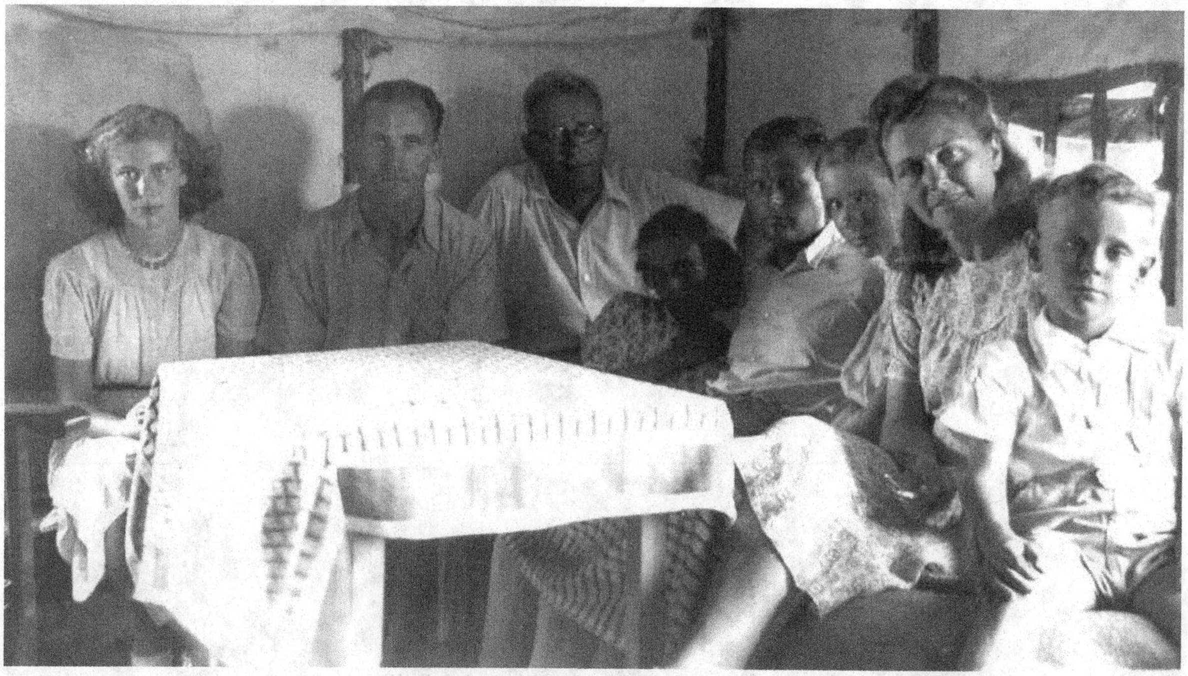

64. The Eppinger family in the "living room" corner in their tent in Golden Sands

65. The Eppinger family with some German POWs

66. The Eppinger family and friends inspecting an old cannon in Famagusta

67. In the port of Famagusta

At a slow pace, the convoy left our beautiful, much loved Wilhelma with its red roofs and green eucalypts. As we waved good-bye, we knew it was for ever.

Before we left, the president of the Temple Society, Mr Nikolai SCHMIDT, had silently grabbed my right hand and then said: "Who knows if we meet again. As president, I place this group in your charge. I appoint Mr Imanuel KATZ from Betlehem as your Elder. With trust in God, you will be able to perform your duty. My thoughts will be with you always. Farewell!" Our eyes were moist when we parted.

68. Golden Sands tent camp

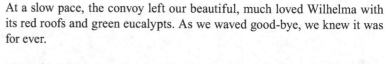

SOON AFTER ARRIVAL, YOUNG AND OLD WERE BUSY FILLING THE MATTRESSES WITH STRAW AND A HAPPIER MOOD BEGAN TO PREVAIL

I wish to express my deep gratitude for Mr Schmidt's tireless work and his care for us and for the Temple Society, even though his eyes have now long closed forever. We honour his memory.

Two smallish ships lay at anchor in the blue sea off Jaffa. One, a destroyer of the Royal Navy, and the other, the *Empire Comfort*, normally used to collect illegal Jewish immigrants on the coast of Palestine and to transport them into temporary banishment to a camp in Cyprus, two miles north of Famagusta. It was fitted with large wire cages to keep warring factions separate from each other. We boarded the *Empire Comfort*, which sailed at noon, heading north in a calm sea, accompanied by the destroyer for protection. In the late afternoon, two km off Haifa, the *Comfort* dropped anchor. We could see our picturesque Haifa settlement spread out at the foot of Mt Carmel. Few lights were visible after dark, but one could see a

69. Sgt. Walker and the captain of the "Al Misr"

flash here and there, followed by a crash as if the Jewish-Arab war already had begun.

On the following day, 21 April, the *Comfort* docked in the harbour. Mr Charles V. BOUTAGY [hotel owner and agent] paid us a short visit to see if he could help. We thanked him sincerely for his offer, which he had made in spite of the danger, even though we made no use of it. We had been advised not to arouse attention and to stay away from the railing.

Our loved ones from Betlehem and Waldheim joined us on board ship at noon, exhausted and depressed. The army had taken them directly from Waldheim and Nazareth to a camp called 'Sydney Smith Barracks' at Acre. The people from Betlehem had fled by horse and cart via Saffuriyeh at the last minute. They all breathed easier when they were reunited with and welcomed by their fellow sufferers from Wilhelma.

When leaving Palestinian waters at around five pm, the destroyer vanished over the horizon. We watched wistfully as Mt Carmel disappeared into the sea, until only the monotonous noise of the engines could be heard.

In Cyprus

We sighted Cyprus early in the morning on 22 April and soon reached the harbour of Famagusta, adjoining the old Byzantine fortress with its backdrop of ancient churches and chapels from the time of the crusades.

In a camp called 'Golden Sands' we found many small tents erected on sheer sand to the left of the access road, and heaps of fresh straw. Every tent contained two to four iron army bedsteads with blankets and an empty mattress cover each. To the right of the paved road stood large Indian tents (so-called tepee tents). This was the camp of the German prisoners-of-war [POW], who were wearing yellow diamonds on their jackets.

70. The luggage of the refugees being unloaded in Famagusta

In general, the exhausted refugees were cheered up by the presence of German compatriots, and their morale improved noticeably. They began to forget the unrest and the worries of the recent past and were glad not to have to endure hateful glances any more as in Old Palestine. In spite of this, the Cyprus secret service thought it necessary to warn us of strangers who might approach the camp.

71. At the kitchen barrack entrance

Soon after arrival, young and old were busy filling the mattresses with straw and a happier mood began to prevail. The exhaustion was almost forgotten. A huge marquee was our 'dining room' where the military had prepared our food on the first day. A large shower block made of cement blocks was made available, half of it for women, the other half for men. It even had hot water at times, but we still could see only a real nomads' life ahead of us and we were worried about how the old and frail would cope, even though the more serious cases had already been taken from the ship

72. German POWs watch as the refugees arrive in Golden Sands

by army ambulances and kindly accommodated in a home at Kantara in the mountains. We actually had two sick women on stretchers among us.

WE SENT A TELEGRAM TO THE REGIONAL COUNCIL IN AUSTRALIA, 'ALL COLONISTS ARRIVED SAFELY CYPRUS'. THE FORMER COMMANDANT OF WILHELMA, B/SGT. WALKER INTRODUCED HIMSELF TWO DAYS LATER AS LIAISON OFFICER (LO), APPOINTED BY THE COMMISSIONER FOR THE PALESTINE MANDATE GOVERNMENT IN NICOSIA. WE LIKED THAT BECAUSE WE KNEW HIM.

On the next day, we sent a telegram to the Regional Council in Australia, 'All colonists arrived safely Cyprus'. The former commandant of Wilhelma, B/Sgt. WALKER introduced himself two days later as Liaison Officer (LO), appointed by the Commissioner for the Palestine Mandate Government in Nicosia. We liked that because we knew him and appreciated his friendly attitude. He disclosed that we would be only temporary guests in Cyprus. We were expected not to seek work and steal jobs from the islanders. The campsite selected – Golden Sands – was one of the healthiest of the whole island. Our group of German Templers would be under the auspices of the Commissioner for Jewish refugees ['Comjews'], Sir GODFREY [Collins]. He would be responsible for and in charge of our funds that had been set aside for this purpose by the Public Custodian of Enemy Property in Palestine for our stay in Cyprus and for our eventual transportation from here. We were to sort out later who had originally owned the money. On entering Cyprus, we were no longer internees but 'free' civilians and, as such, we no longer had a claim to 'free board'. The facilities and tents were provided by the British Army for our use, but we would still be liable for all losses, damage and expenses. All submissions, applications or requests were to be directed, via the LO, to Sir GODFREY himself. We were not to get involved with the Cypriot authorities.

73. Right: The volunteer kitchen gang in the kitchen barrack. From left to right: Mischka Persztik, Paul Reichert, Karl Scheerle, Margarete Vollmer, In front: Irmgard Aberle, Erna Scheerle, Else Sus, Anneliese Lippmann, Lotte Frank, Elly Wennagel, Margarete Blaich

74. Walter Imberger and Karl Richter running over hot sand in the camp

75. Right: Elly Wennagel (Grant) and Martha Hoffmann (Gentner) at lunch in their tent

At first we wondered about Sir GODFREY's official title, but it was explained that the soon to expire Palestine Mandate Government would not want to create a special office just for our small group, since we would be guests of Cyprus only for a short time anyway. It is well known how long and how expensive this 'short time' turned out to be, but on the other hand, our suspicions regarding the official title of the commissioner proved groundless.

Organising camp life

Because of this information from Mr WALKER, we expected to be moved very soon and therefore would not need to build an organisation other than for a food and kitchen roster; we made a deal with a food company and hoped for the best. However, we did get organised anyway. Mr Werner STRUVE helped by taking on the hard job of treasurer and community accountant.

76. Inside a typical tent in Cyprus

Mr Walter ALBRECHT became an active deputy camp chief. Mr Eugen KAZENWADEL and Mr Theodor DOH took on the difficult task of purchase officers in the pre-dawn markets. Thanks to their circumspection and experience, they managed to buy food and vegetables at almost half the price and of far better quality and wider range than the contractor did. Mr Walter IMBERGER became our postmaster, who walked the long way to the post office every day to collect the mail and to post letters.

77. Sister Maria Wagner

Sister Maria WAGNER, her qualifications having been recognised by the government physician, looked after the sick, and the women in general organised the kitchen service and associated work in a very commendable way and kept clean the twenty-four showers in the shower block. The highest standards of hygiene and cleanliness were observed from the beginning.

In short, everyone had their little jobs or was otherwise engaged in the administrative processes of the camp. The best result was that, as everyone was doing their duty, a cheerful harmony was emerging that also very much impressed our compatriots, the German POWs.

It was a blessing for our children that school was started again under the proven direction of Miss Luise DREHER, actively supported by Mrs Hulda STRUVE as well as by Mr Adolf BAMBERG and Mr Walter IMBERGER for more advanced students of English.

Last, but not least, our revered elder, Mr Imanuel Katz, who was in charge of our spiritual guidance is to be commendably mentioned. He also won over our esteemed friend Mr HEINRICI, the missionary, for services as representative of the small Lutheran section and to help where he could, which greatly enhanced our harmonious cooperation. A grateful mention goes to our auxiliary speakers such as our seniors Mr Heinrich SAWATZKY and Mr Eugen JOHN. I refer to the report by Mr Imanuel KATZ in the Templer Circular of May 1959.

Our period of internment of close to nine years had found its official conclusion in Cyprus. We were now considered to be, at least in name, free civilians or better perhaps, free 'children', for as such we were treated and patronised. In 1946 a high official of the CID (Criminal Investigation Department) had explained to me that we were no longer interned for security reasons, but only for our own safety.

Financing the camp was a big and difficult problem. In the beginning, three shillings [sterling] per head per day (=37.4¢ Australian) were released via the LO to pay for the cost of living in the camp. This rate of 3/- was soon increased to 4/- (50¢ Australian) and reached 6/- a little later. Ordinarily, this would have fully met our needs, but we, the camp management, were forced to provide an advance of £2 ($A5) per head per month out of the 6/- rate. Except for a certain amount for 'rehabilitation' (see remark on 6.7.1948 in the diary below), this money predominantly supported the Betlehem and Waldheim people who had been robbed and had had to flee at short notice. The number of hardship cases soon climbed from 77 to 97 recipients. No one from the camp management was a beneficiary of these payments.

This was followed by special pleas for clothing, linen, glasses, medication and dental requirements etc. The camp management, who always derived satisfaction from approving applications, separately and conscientiously examined every request. Whether one owned assets held by the Custodian or in Palestine was of no consequence in these cases. It must be mentioned here that these circumstances would have been aggravated a great deal if the German POW dentist in the other camp at Larnaca (he held the rank of a Major) had not treated all patients free of charge and if the government physician in Famagusta had not granted us free consultations and free medication.

In addition, there were requests for sizeable amounts from our Regional Council in bombed-out Germany, who wanted to help its own members in their predicaments. Similar calls came from Jerusalem and there were even certain hints from Australia. Perhaps they were afraid we would needlessly squander the money in our ignorance. The camp management was fully conscious of the fact that transfers would be made to our official Regional Councils only if there was a need – and *if* there was a surplus. In my opinion, the money released to us was sacrosanct and would only be spent – and most sparingly at that – for our immediate needs, because one day we would have to pay it back. In our circumstances, we considered an iron reserve as being absolutely necessary, because we had not that much trust in our guardians to take everything on blind faith. This gave us cause to draw as much of the reserves as possible, being conscientious custodians, without anybody enjoying personal benefits. That is how we succeeded to draw a daily rate of 7/- per head which enabled us to transfer the surplus. This was possible thanks to the camp residents subjecting themselves to a regimen of the utmost frugality.

This also enabled the camp management, after due consideration, to increase the [monthly] rate for cases of hardship from £2 to £3 ($A7.50), because apart for food, funds for other articles were not released.

In questions of finance, the director of the Famagusta branch of the Barclays Bank, Mr J. WINDSOR, a personal friend, was always helpful with active advice

In questions of finance, the director of the Famagusta branch of the Barclays Bank, Mr John WINDSOR, a personal friend, was always helpful with active advice. Our relationship, going back to Palestine, was much enhanced by our encounters in Cyprus. He and his family also had plans to settle in Australia, eventually. Unfortunately, he died suddenly in 1966, only weeks before his retirement.

Even after the death of my dear wife in 1964, we maintained a lively correspondence, and to this day, I gratefully remember how he served us in Cyprus in many ways.

78. Fetching food in the kitchen barrack

80. Impromptu meeting in Golden Sands:
Back: Richard Eppinger, Friedrich Hornung, Brig. White, Sgt. Walker
Front: Martha Katz, Lina Wagner and Siegfried Hahn

Below is a chronological summary of important events in Golden Sands, Cyprus:

22 April 1948

Johannes WAGNER (Nazareth)............................... Fritz KATZ (Waldheim)
Imanuel KATZ (Betlehem).....................................Georg EHMANN (Haifa)
Gottlob LÖBERT (Wilhelma)..............Eugen KAZENWADEL (Wilhelma)
Friedrich HORNUNG (Wilhelma).................... Wilhelm GROLL (Sarona)
Walter JUNG (Sarona) .... Werner STRUVE (Haifa)*
Walter ALBRECHT (Haifa)*............Richard O. EPPINGER (Wilhelma)*

*these three formed the executive committee with R.O.Eppinger as head. We adopt the name of 'Temple Society, Refugee Branch'.

79. Fritz Katz (1880-1955)
Mayor of Waldheim

23 April	Took over camp kitchen (wooden hut, corrugated roof) from British army, oil-fired, situated next to POW kitchen; established kitchen roster.
24 April	Internal camp regrouping: 51 non-members given own section. Caused protest, but compromise of LO unanmously rejected.
25 April	Many go to explore Cyprus and its people. Delegation visits old people in the Kantara home (all are homesick).
30 April	Telephone connected to office tent.
7 May	Return of the sick from Kantara, cordial welcome.
8 May	First visit by Mr TEMBY in Golden Sands.
12 May	First interrogation by Mr TEMBY.
14 May	Mrs Katharine WEINMANN dies (Anglican cemetery, (HEINRICI).
15 May	Begin to fill in Australian immigration documents.
16 May	1) First divine service, Pentecost (I. KATZ). 2) First news from Jerusalem (J. IMBERGER).

17 May	1) Golden wedding of C. & T. KRÜGLER, Haifa. 2) Begin medical examination for 'Australian' immigrants.
25 May	1) Palestine currency changed to Cyprus money (via Barclays Bank). 2) School opened, director Miss Luise DREHER.
2 June	Gottlob and Elise LÖBERT celebrate Silver Wedding.
21 June	Erika KATZ born (parents F. & I. KATZ, Betlehem).
1 July	1) Talks to give cash advances to cases of hardship. 2) Tentatively work out powers of attorney, but only in agreement with Australia. 3) Suggestion that Jerusalem gentlemen Nikolai SCHMIDT, Jakob IMBERGER and Hermann IMBERGER temporarily come to Cyprus because concrete cash offers for sale of colonies are being made.
6 July	1) Decided: One off cash advance for hardship cases is granted: Waldheim people £C500 ($A1250); Betlehem people, £C230 ($A575); other colonies £C55 ($A137). 2) Daily rate 7/- (shillings) per head approved by Commissioner. 3) Statistics show we spend 2½ Cyp.shillings ($A0.32) per day/head.
13 July	Trudel ORTH, Peter HORNUNG & Hedwig STICHT (Mrs W. Groll to be) arrive from Germany by plane.
16 July	Mr TEMBY flies in from London without positive news re departure.
17 July	August HAAR to Famagusta hospital, then Nicosia.
23 July	Karl WAGNER to Famagusta hospital.
27 July	1) Mrs Maria HARDEGG dies (Anglican cemetery, Imanuel KATZ). 2) Conference in Platres (Troodos mountains 1952m or 6420ft): R.O. EPPINGER & wife, W. ALBRECHT, Brigadier WHITE, Mr TEMBY and IRO delegates (car rolls along the way on embankment, Mrs E.'s left hand crushed, freed, drove on). Also talks with Mr CANTAROCH.
30 July	Money transfer to Jerusalem.
2 August	Mrs Barbara SAWATZKY breaks down (loss of strength). August HAAR operated on in Nicosia.
4 August	1) Brig. WHITE and Mr TEMBY take leave and say there were prospects for Dutch ship; they would also look around in Egypt. 2) Decided to pay £C2 per month for hardship cases.
5 August	Greetings and receipt arrive from hospice in Jerusalem.
10 August	Departure of 27 non-members.
18 August	W. ALBRECHT starts lists for plane to Germany.
24 August	Talks with Lloyd Triestino; Commissioner refuses again.
27 August	Saw Palestine Government Commission re copy of Divesting Order of April 1948 concerning Enemy Subjects.
3 September	Departure of German POWs to Germany.
4 September	POW ship passes camp; much waving, loud cheering.
14 September	1) Power of attorney for Central Fund Jerusalem refused. 2) Jerusalem head asks to have deposit of Ottoman Bank Amman, transferred to Barclays Bank. Was made possible thanks to friendly relations network. 3) Jerusalem head asks R.O. EPPINGER to stay behind in

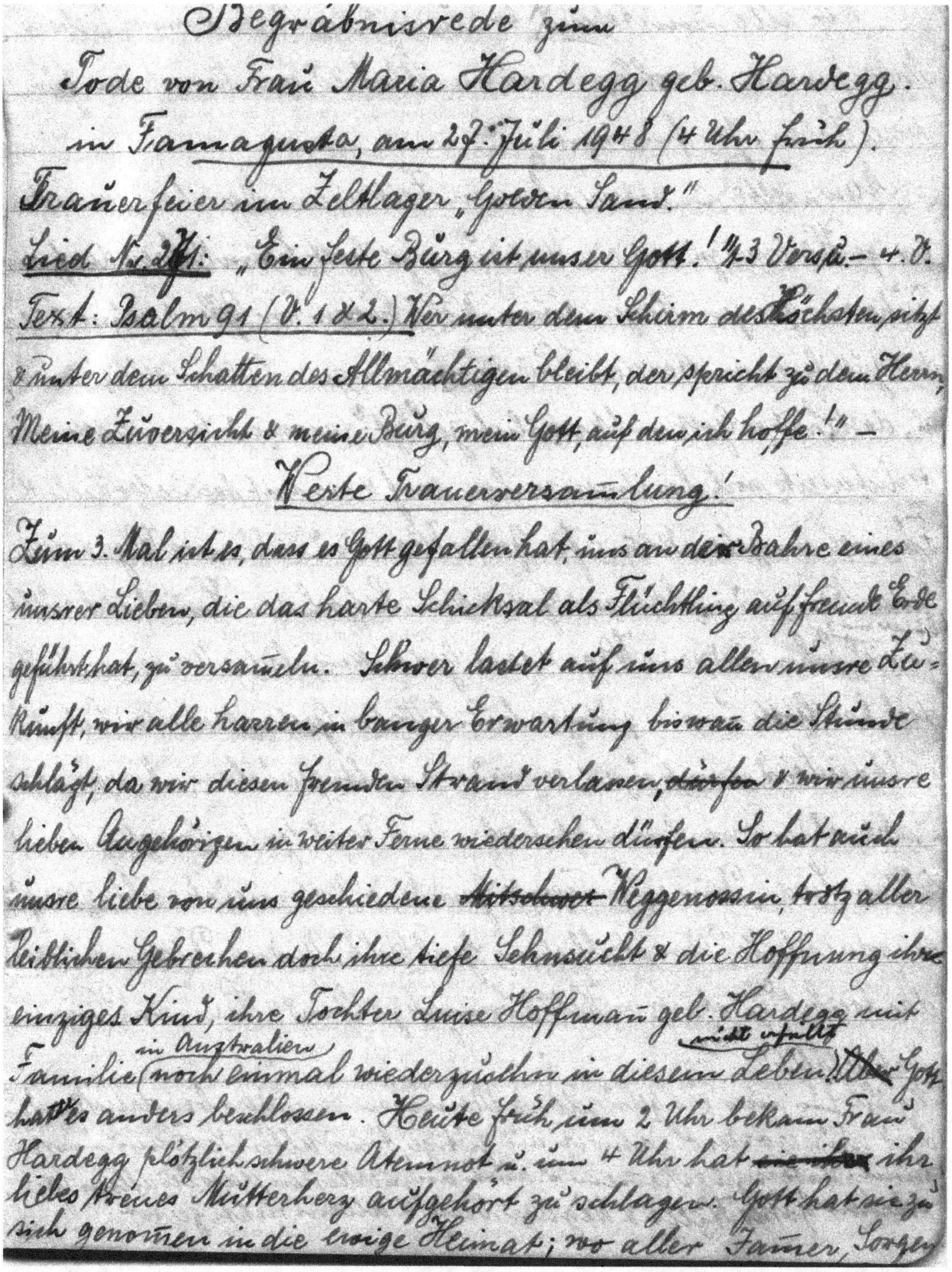

Begräbnisrede zum
Tode von Frau Maria Hardegg geb. Hardegg.
in Famagusta, am 27. Juli 1948 (4 Uhr früh).
Trauerfeier im Zeltlager „Golden Sand."
Lied Nr. 271: „Ein feste Burg ist unser Gott!" 1-3 Vers u. 4. V.
Text: Psalm 91 (V. 1 & 2.) Wer unter dem Schirm des Höchsten sitzt
& unter dem Schatten des Allmächtigen bleibt, der spricht zu dem Herrn,
Meine Zuversicht & meine Burg, mein Gott, auf den ich hoffe!" –
Werte Trauerversammlung!
Zum 3. Mal ist es, dass es Gott gefallen hat, uns an der Bahre eines
unsrer Lieben, die das harte Schicksal als Flüchtling auf fremde Erde
geführt hat, zu versammeln. Schwer lastet auf uns allen unsre Zu-
kunft, wir alle harren in banger Erwartung bis wann die Stunde
schlägt, da wir diesen fremden Strand verlassen, ~~dürfen~~ & wir unsre
lieben Angehörigen in weiter Ferne wiedersehen dürfen. So hat auch
unsre liebe von uns geschiedene ~~Mitschwester~~ Weggenossin, trotz aller
leiblichen Gebrechen doch ihre tiefe Sehnsucht & die Hoffnung ihr
einziges Kind, ihre Tochter Luise Hoffmann geb. Hardegg mit
Familie (in Australien) noch einmal wiederzusehen in diesem Leben (nicht erfüllt) ~~Aber~~ Gott
hat es anders beschlossen. Heute früh, um 2 Uhr bekam Frau
Hardegg plötzlich schwere Atemnot u. um 4 Uhr hat ~~[illegible]~~ ihr
liebes treues Mutterherz aufgehört zu schlagen. Gott hat sie zu
sich genommen in die ewige Heimat; wo aller Jammer, Sorgen

81.Eulogy for Maria Hardegg nee Hardegg, by Elder Imanuel Katz

82. Camp conference: Richard Eppinger, Brig. White and Sgt. Walker in front of the office tent

	Cyprus to cooperate with Jerusalem. The idea is rejected. 4) Monthly cash advance is increased to £C3. 5) Bulk luggage from Jaffa supposed to be on its way, but is registered at Levant under name of Palestine Government.
17 September	Managed to get hold of copy of Divesting Order of April 1948 in Platres.
20 September	Bulk luggage arrives on Turkish sail ship, extensively damaged.
21 September	Bulk luggage collected and stored in large stone barrack.
22 September	Everyone starts to repair or renew containers (boxes).
24 September	Commissioner is confident we leave in October.
26 September	Engagement Gerda SCHEERLE and Werner STRUVE.
29 September	1) Georg EHMANN exits camp council. 2) S/S *Ernesto* is out of the question. 3) Mr TEMBY announces other ship in prospect. 4) Learn according to telegram that 13 persons would join us: 5 Germany, 6 Palestine, 2 Lebanon. 5) Seriously consider flying to Australia.
3 October	1) Presentation of three girls: Helga REICHERT, Irene WAGNER, Erika KATZ. 2) Thanksgiving celebrated as in Palestine. Announcement that a ship had been found. Arouses loud amusement (p.s. was again only air bubble). 3) Discussed how further family members could be attracted from Germany.
5 October	Registration for flight to Germany.
12 October	Heavy storm during night, some tents blow over.
19 October	First group to fly to Germany gets ready.
20 October	First group, 49 head, leaves camp in evening.

21 October	First group leaves on Danish plane at 2 am from Nicosia.
23 October	Permission from OC to move old and sick to large stone barrack.
24 October	Miss Emma BÄTZNER dies in government hospital (Anglican cemetery, Imanuel KATZ).
8 November	M/S *Partizanka* has 28 berths. Commissioner is not interested, prefers *Al Misr.*
9 November	Telegraphed Australian Regional Council: we must have free hand to get away at last (was in vain).
12 November	LO comes at 10pm, announces new ship.
15 November	Big storm with rain: thank God, the Aged are in the large stone barrack.
17 November	1) London rejects ship of 12.11. 2) New prospect from Paris for ship.
19 November	First group for ship to Australia inoculated (plus 3 reserves), 28 persons envisaged for *Partizanka.*
23 November	Lawyer SALOMON visits us with letter from Nikolai SCHMIDT re power of attorney for Central Fund Jerusalem. Rejected, because signature might have been obtained under duress.
27 November	1) Received letters from lawyer LEVI re safeguard of our interests (sale or compromise). – Rejected, because this could be done only in agreement with Australia [Regional Council]. 2) Decision to prepare power of attorney for Wilhelm EPPINGER, Fritz C. ABERLE and Fritz LIPPMANN. 3) New ships are announced again.
1 December	First *Partizanka* group prepares for departure.
4 December	1) Mrs Martha STELLER telegraphs from Beirut that Karl STELLER died of a heart attack in Chamlan, Lebanon. 2) Ship *Volendam* rejected by Commissioner. 3) *Al Misr* still available for Dec – Jan departure.
5 December	Families Heinrich WAGNER, Janczy GENTNER and Miss Mina FRÖSCHLE arrived from Haifa.
7 December	1) Commissioner urges to grab *Al Misr.* 2) S/S *Continental* said to offer opportunity for mid December out of Port Said. 3) Further applications for monthly advance granted.
9 December	LO reports that Commissioner is advised by Mr TEMBY to recommend *Al Misr* (I can hardly believe it).
11 December	Preliminary lists prepared for 170 persons.
12 December	Celebrated Founder's day.
13 December	Inoculation for *Partizanka* group. London is silent re *Al Misr.*
14 December	Signed general powers of attorney for Australia (about 200 persons).
15 December	1) Decision under pressure to accept *Misr.* 2) Reported in evening: Embarkation *Partizanka* tomorrow morning in Limassol. 3) Motor cars to be arranged, shops are closed, camp head gets back at 1am, all done. Raging storm increases.
16 December	Camp is up at 4am; buses and trucks arrive from 6am but

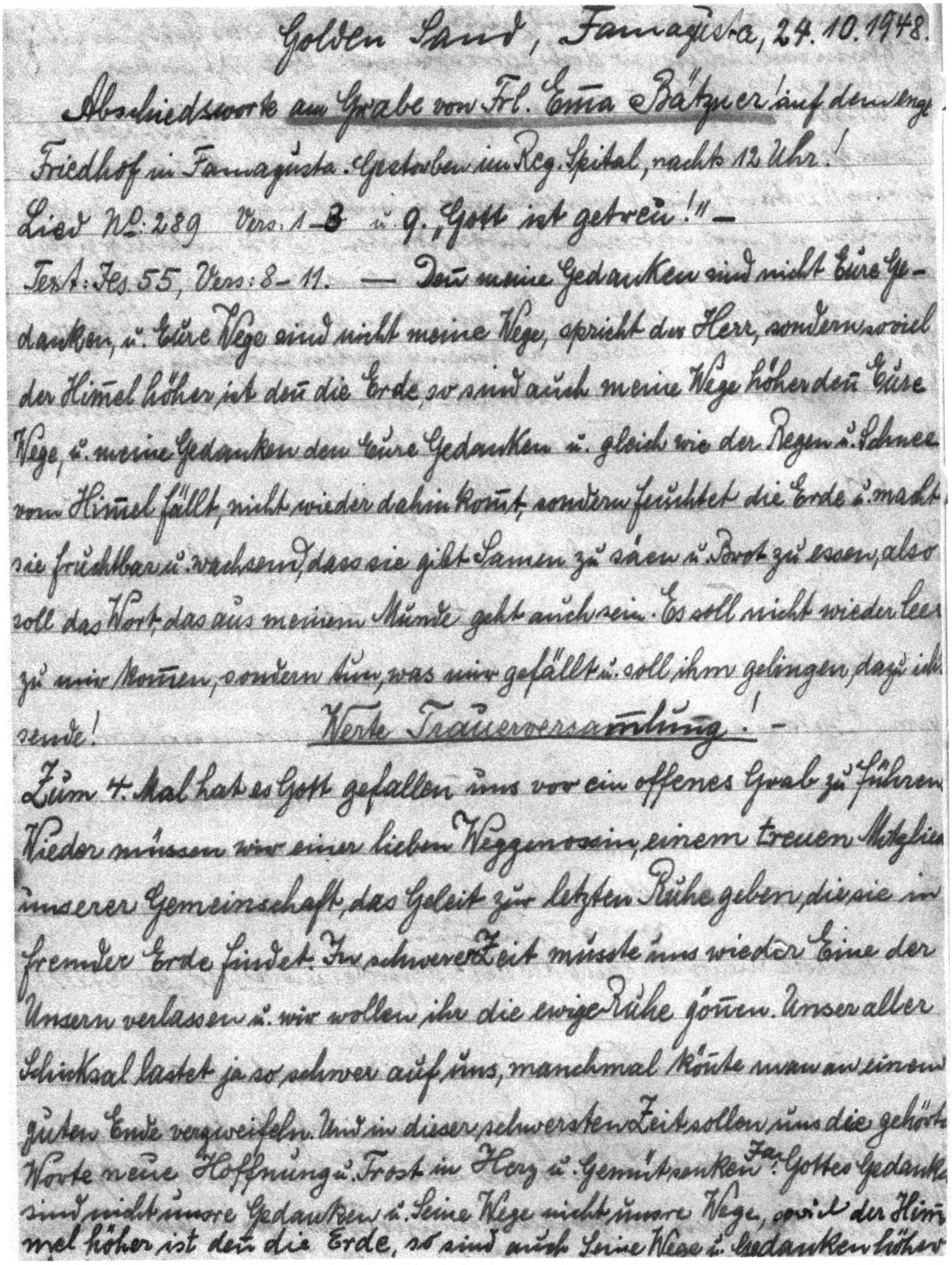

Golden Sand, Famagusta, 24.10.1948.

Abschiedsworte am Grabe von Frl. Emma Bätzner auf dem engl. Friedhof in Famagusta. Gestorben im Reg. Spital, nachts 12 Uhr!

Lied No: 289 Vers. 1-3 u. 9. „Gott ist getreu!"–

Text: Jes. 55, Vers: 8-11. — Denn meine Gedanken sind nicht Eure Gedanken, u. Eure Wege sind nicht meine Wege, spricht der Herr, sondern soviel der Himmel höher ist denn die Erde, so sind auch meine Wege höher denn Eure Wege, u. meine Gedanken denn Eure Gedanken u. gleich wie der Regen u. Schnee vom Himmel fällt, nicht wieder dahin kommt, sondern feuchtet die Erde u. macht sie fruchtbar u. wachsend, dass sie gibt Samen zu säen u. Brot zu essen, also soll das Wort, das aus meinem Munde geht auch sein. Es soll nicht wieder leer zu mir kommen, sondern tun, was mir gefällt u. soll ihm gelingen, dazu ich's sende!

Werte Trauerversammlung!–

Zum 4. Mal hat es Gott gefallen uns vor ein offenes Grab zu führen. Wieder müssen wir einer lieben Weggenossin, einem treuen Mitglied unserer Gemeinschaft, das Geleit zur letzten Ruhe geben, die sie in fremder Erde findet. In schwerer Zeit musste uns wieder Eine der Unsern verlassen u. wir wollen ihr die ewige Ruhe gönnen. Unser aller Schicksal lastet ja so schwer auf uns, manchmal könnte man an einem guten Ende verzweifeln. Und in dieser schwersten Zeit sollen uns die gehörten Worte neue Hoffnung u. Trost in Herz u. Gemüt senken! Ja Gottes Gedanken sind nicht unsere Gedanken u. Seine Wege nicht unsere Wege, soviel der Himmel höher ist denn die Erde, so sind auch Seine Wege u. Gedanken höher

83. Eulogy for Emma Bätzner, by Elder Imanuel Katz

	leave Famagusta only after noon because of storm. Embark in Limassol only after 5pm in rough sea. Luggage not inspected.
17 December	Rumour of stowaway passenger on *Partizanka*.
20 December	LO reports that Secretary of State, London, rejects *Misr*; but we have free hand. Re-established connection to agencies immediately, flying reconsidered.
21 December	1) Commissioner reports that sub agency tried again to gain approval for ship (*Misr*). 2) Full camp council decides unanimously to reject *Misr*, even though one senior observed it was incomprehensible and he would be inclined to accept. The meeting was thanked for their unanimous trust.
22 December	In spite of all goings on, preparations are made for Christmas.
23 December	1) *Misr* sub agent personally pleads for acceptance of *Misr* in the camp: 'golden opportunity'. 2) Decided to pay a visit to the High Brass concerning Christmas & New Year.
24 December	German Christmas traditionally celebrated in the large stone barrack with burning candles on Christmas tree, modest presents, songs and nativity plays.
25 December	Christmas Service: Peace on Earth! How paradoxical!
28 December	Young people busy with New Year's Eve preparations.
31 December	1) New Year's Eve service by Eugen JOHN. 2) New Year's Eve congenial get together with amusing plays etc. Hot tea and sandwiches were very welcome in the unheated large stone barrack. At an advanced hour, *Glühwein* was served. To the credit of our young people, they succeeded in drawing us into their spell, so we could forget our nagging worries for a few hours. We faced the New Year with more courage, even though hopes were not justified.
1949	
1 January	The year begins with quiet seriousness, '*Mit dem Herrn fang alles an'*.
4 January	Newspaper ads: *Misr* sails to Australia mid January. (The search, the bargaining, the chase, and the talks about ships or planes go on endlessly, without achieving anything positive, neither here nor there; and criticism disrupts at best; is never encouraging.)
7 January	Fly party to Australia prepares.
10 January	Sent SOS telegram to Australia Regional Council (we ask for free hand in self determination for departure): fruitless.
13 January	1) Excited committee meeting: should berths on ships be booked at own risk or should we grab *Misr*? 2) Received telegram from F.C. ABERLE of 12.1. 'Yours 10th TEMBY in Sydney have cabled him without success hoping refusal Comjews means other ship'. This is certainly not encouraging for us.
14 January	Australia fly party may well leave on 25.1.
15 January	Bad news about the passengers en route on the *Partizanka*: Mr Fritz KATZ (Waldheim), stroke Mr Heinrich SAWATZKY, pneumonia

	Mrs Barbara SAWATZKY, broken arm Mrs Karoline WURSTER, pneumonia Mr Jakob WEISS & daughter, angina.
16 January	Telegram from Mr TEMBY, group should not fly if possible, Commissioner said to have replied: flight finalised.
24 January	1) *Misr* lies off Limassol. LO demands to inspect the ship. 2) Looked up agency 'Manaro' in Limassol. 3) Go with *Misr* is accepted – reluctantly.
25 January	1) *Al Misr* arrives in Famagusta. 2) Bulk luggage moved to harbour. 3) Advised: Fly party to go to Nicosia tomorrow morning.
26 January	1) Fly party, 45 head, leaves camp at 6am under direction of Werner STRUVE. Plane flies over camp around 9am. Much waving! 2) The remainder of bulk luggage to the dock. 3) After 1pm, nearly all of the camp are on their way to embarkation, 145 souls, leader Siegfried HAHN. 4) After 5pm *Misr* pushes off the quay.
27 January	Dismantle empty tents for removal by army.
30 January	Confirmation: Irene EPPINGER, Walter GROLL, Richard & Hans HORNUNG, Walter KAZENWADEL, Hilda KATZ (Elder Imanuel Katz). Heavy rain. Report at night, *Partizanka* to sail again to Australia on about 4.3.1949.
31 January	1) Commissioner orders 45 to fly, remainder by ship. 2) Morale in camp very low, [they] insist on *Partizanka*.
1 February	1) LO reports, after our renewed pleas, that Commissioner Order is irrefutable, i.e. split between plane and ship. London was advised by wire. 2) Wire: All well on *Misr*. 3) Wire from Werner STRUVE: Arrived safely Sydney.
2 February	Delegation (without camp head) rejected by Commissioner, denied audience morning and afternoon.
3 February	1) Same delegation, third time refused: Commissioner does not want to see anybody. 2) Delegation of women in the afternoon (on instigation of the above) tries in vain to gain admission to Commissioner. Delegation reports 'Com. feels insulted'.
4 February	The same women make another trip, cap in hand, to Commissioner (without knowledge of camp head) and report, Commissioner had no time, he had to see officials in Nicosia re our departure. Big protest in the camp, because this is seen as excuse. Our gentlemen are determined to book berths on *Partizanka* without Commissioner (What the camp head did at this time you will read later in this report).
5 February	1) LO telephones, application granted, all can go on *Partizanka*. Cook's in Cairo are already informed by wire so as not to lose time. 2) Mrs Karl STELLER arrived from Beirut.
7 February	Today LO officially confirms firm booking on *Partizanka*.

All are happy with this success.

10 February It turns out *Partizanka* will not sail until 12.3.

12 February 1) Removal of empty tents, beds, etc.
2) Hull Blyth & Co agency in Famagusta informs: *Partizanka* to depart Limassol on 9.3. afternoon.
3) Nine persons from Germany will be on board.

17 February *Partizanka* will not come to Famagusta, only Limassol.

19 February It seems the whole group of 'Illegals' (non-members) were financed from our funds by Commissioner. We are outraged, cannot find out details, LO is as silent as the grave.

21 February Decision: Women and children to leave camp Tuesday morning, to be accommodated in hotels, to be ready next day to go on ship. Men and boys to stay behind to dismantle camp, counting, help with removal (army trucks) and supervision.

22 February Group of non-members leave camp for repatriation.

25 February Allocation of cabin berths on *Partizanka.*

27 February No 'Saal' service today, no tent available for it.

28 February Great excitement behind the scenes, because camp head had booked hotels 'high-handedly' (Note: not true; had only ascertained exact details about number of beds and prices.)

3 March 1) Amman transfer arrives at Barclays Bank.
2) The deposit at the Jerusalem Central Fund belonging to the group that followed us, as well as the cow money from Betlehem and Waldheim, is acknowledged by Barclays Bank.
3) OC (Military camp commandant) advises to dismantle camp on the 8th and hand over on trucks.

4 March 1) Official information: depart Limassol 5pm.
2) Booked hotels in Limassol and Famagusta.

6 March LO informs us nothing doing, hotels have to be booked to free camp for handing it back to the [British] army.

7 March Camp head announces 'Tomorrow morning trucks will take bulk luggage to Limassol'.

8 March Early in the morning the last cup of tea. Camp residents go by bus to hotels in Famagusta and Limassol. Very few men and boys begin the huge job of dismantling and removal of the camp by army trucks. It was, of course, made more difficult because some of the available men went ahead with their families to Limassol and had a nice day while their mates toiled all the harder. Not until late at night could they go to their hotels, completely exhausted, while the camp leader did not reach his hotel until after 10pm, quite run down, because not until then could he finish his business with the OC and with Barclays Bank for everything to be in order. He did not have time to see the Commissioner, but he could express his thanks on behalf of the Camp over the phone at 10.30pm.

9 March After breakfast, the larger group leaves Famagusta by bus to join the others at Limassol. Embarkation goes ahead 4pm, after a thorough luggage check. The LO is thanked for his effort and, since the Commissioner had excused himself through the LO, the latter was asked to express our deep respect for him. By 9pm on a choppy sea, the great journey began. The lights of Limassol faded into a quiet night.

11 March Arrived in Port Said. A delegate of the IRC (International Red Cross) from Cairo saw us on board ship, to help us, among other things, to organise a trip to the pyramids near Cairo for a group of 25. This fell through, however, because the fanatical captain of the *Partizanka* thwarted us with every difficulty imaginable.
Pity! This could be considered the final stroke of the epistle about the long and bitter epoch of the Cyprus group, which also practically sealed the fate of our communities in the Holy Land, begun in 1868.

However, I would like to add a few short words to provide further insights into the developments arising out of the conditions of camp life, to tell of these hard times as I remember them, to the best of my knowledge and ability.

Review

If I have so far restricted myself to describe the life and activities of the Cyprus Group, I would now complement this report by a few remarks as seen from the perspective of the camp leader.

The leader's task was, first, to establish and maintain an organisation necessary for the group's existence, second, he had to represent the group to the outside world, especially to the authorities. The first task was solved relatively satisfactorily, I think. We adopted the name 'TEMPLE SOCIETY, REFUGEE BRANCH', but were usually addressed as 'German Templers'. In any case, we have tried, as best we could, to look after the interests of all long-established Palestine Germans, regardless of denomination. In general, this was readily acknowledged, although one cannot always please everyone. Living in close proximity to each other inevitably creates tensions, but I dare say we have tried to be impartial.

Living in close proximity to each other inevitably creates tensions, but I dare say we have tried to be impartial

To represent the group and its interests to the outside world was much more problematic. We were supposed to be free civilians in Cyprus, but in reality, we were homeless refugees without money, who depended on the authorities for living expenses and for transport to Australia. The members were less keenly aware of this than the leadership, sandwiched as it was between the group and the authorities, whose goodwill it needed if anything was to be achieved. We knew that our progress depended to a large degree on the goodwill of the Liaison Officer (LO) and of the Commissioner for Jewish Refugees (Comjews), Sir Godfrey. This was most apparent in the question of a departure from Cyprus, which weighed heavily on our minds.

After the departure of the first *Partizanka* group which, as a first successful effort to get away, seemed like a ray of light to the ones staying behind, it became known that a stowaway passenger had been among that group. The otherwise good-natured and kindly disposed LO came back irate and excited. Without exception, he accused everyone of 'infamous intrigues and machinations', above all the camp leader. He could not be convinced that no one had known, or even suspected, anything. All protestations were in vain. However, it emerged that there was, in fact, an accessory among us, which was the basis of the LO's accusations.

Crossed wires

On the following day, the LO unexpectedly paid me a visit in my family tent. Having obviously regained his composure, he wanted to talk things over. An inner nervousness was distinctly noticeable. Unfortunately, this developed an intensity of hitherto unseen proportions, as if a fury had been released. He gave the impression of enjoying 'sweet revenge!' Taken by surprise, and practically paralysed, we endured this avalanche of a speech. Talking back was useless. This unforgettable scene caused us much chagrin. On the other hand, his anger was understandable, considering the consequences arising out of this affair for him: loss of prestige, facing the music from his highest superiors, suspicion of aiding and abetting etc., for it was he who, on his own initiative, out of an honest desire to help, had persuaded the Customs Office not to have our bulk luggage checked. The whole affair was extremely embarrassing to the camp leader. As a consequence, the LO from then onwards dealt with all matters pertaining to us without zest and full of suspicion. Our task was in no way made easier by this.

The days and weeks went by without any prospects to get away, making a shambles of our hopes and creating a morose mood. Spurred on by this tendency, the camp leader tried even harder, not sparing himself and leaving no stone unturned. He was in Larnaca or Platres one day, in Limassol, or Nicosia, or even in Kyrenia the next, apart from the city of Famagusta. (Kyrenia also had a crusader sea fortress and there had been an internment camp there during the war). I was hoping to relieve the feeling of discontent by some kind of success, any success.

At first, we were strictly forbidden to do our own research for travel possibilities (which caused rebellion and outrage) because that was solely 'the domain of the Comjews', in cooperation with London and Canberra. Our searching would only produce 'unnecessary and time-consuming confusion'. Unfortunately, and against expectations, the first Australian Commission (TEMBY and WHITE) agreed with this. Thus, our hands were tied for a long time until, finally, we were graciously allowed to look around for ourselves, but not to make any firm arrangements! No less than fourteen ships were investigated, of which the LO notified the Comjews, who in turn had to obtain London's approval by telegram before arrangements could assume concrete forms. The wired replies were always a big NO, 'not up to British standards' except for one case that the Comjews rejected on his own, ex officio, without batting an eyelid, and without wiring London.

Setbacks

In July 1948, the head office of the agency acting for Lloyd Triestino in Cyprus informed us (the camp management) that they had reserved 300 berths, tourist class, at £125 per full ticket ($A313) and would take us aboard at Famagusta in the first half of October, provided we would give a firm commitment within 48 hours. Full of jubilation and grateful joy, this was immediately announced in 'High Places', by meeting them in person together with the LO. Without even having considered this liberating chance, we were tersely given a curt reply to the effect of: "How dare you? Mid October? Out of the question! By that time you will long be in Australia, and forgotten in Cyprus!" Reproachful, as if we had committed the greatest wrong in the world! Further pleas and requests were useless.

We went 'home' quite dopey and tried to console ourselves with the idea, without real faith, that this Caring Master must have firm possibilities at his disposal and only had to push a button at the given time. On the other hand, some individuals began to quietly ask the question for the first time: are we really at the mercy of the capriciousness of this dignitary? – Yes, it almost seems our nine-year internment had turned us into blindly obedient little children who listen to big 'Mummy's' every word. Today, after 21 years, I say it was the biggest mistake the camp leader unwittingly made at the time, namely, not having appealed immediately to the highest authorities.

At another time, it was suggested to us to charter a refitted freighter with 900 (or 1000?) berths in conjunction with the IRO (International Refugee Organisation) in the name of the TS Refugee Branch. The IRO would then assume 600 berths to ease the financial burden. This sounded very nice, but when one considers the details: full ticket at £220 with the IRO only paying £110 at most, one understands that our reply could only be a spontaneous and indignant "no!" – With a little humour, like, "you are not serious, you are fooling us", the 'generous' offer could be dismissed as a joke. The price for us would have been £440, or $A1100, per person!

As an alternative, we were surprised with another offer. A smallish coastal luxury steamer of about 1600 tons, which plied the Adriatic and the waters of Greece, was available and could take on our group of 300. It was about the same size as the *Empire Comfort*, which had brought us to Cyprus. The top price, the offer said, was *only* £400 ($A1000) and available immediately, which would save us costly delays and frustration. Hm, madness! It is rejected without hesitation: 'impossible'. This enraged the promoter who irritably let slip: "What do you want? Do you expect a *Queen Elizabeth*? In the end *we* are making the decisions, there is plenty of money at the Comjews'!"

The traditional 'no' from London arrived three days later, but in this case, we breathe easier. Not long after this, we read in the Cyprus Mail that the said little ship was sold for scrap in Piraeus.

Hope

Among such confusion, *Al Misr* is coming into contention. London had already refused. A general assembly in the camp had also unanimously supported the leader to that effect. He thanked them for their confidence, but alas, time went by, and a festering mood caused a heaviness not known before. 'We want to leave! Just leave! Nothing but leave!'

The news of our first *Partizanka* mariners was not encouraging, but still, people wanted to leave! The emerging rumours, that this or that ought to have or not have happened, only created confusion. The management was powerless, and sometimes divided in itself. This is how the idea took hold in the minds of the people that the Egyptian ship had to be better than we had imagined previously. Under such pressure we began to prepare lists so we would be ready for any eventuality. '*Misr* lies at anchor on the roadstead off Limassol – grab this golden opportunity!' Supported by official approval, the sub-agent took this opportunity to appear in the camp to promote *Misr*. He was literally thrown out of the camp, which did not deter eight men (not to say laymen) of the camp committee from driving to Limassol with the LO to 'inspect' this *Misr*. It would have been funny if it hadn't been so bitterly serious. It was known that *Al Misr* was of welded construction, without rivets, a so called 'Liberty Supply Ship' of which many dozens had been produced in the USA because of the U-boat war. It was rumoured that vessels of this kind had broken in half at sea. Nota bene! Today we know that loss of life caused by material failure of these ships exceeded that of the navy during action engaging the enemy!

The result of the inspection can be summarised thus: (1) the ship was nice and clean, (2) smelt strongly of fresh paint, obviously thickly applied, (3) was registered in Panama, (4) was not insured with Lloyds, and (5) the captain was a 'free' Austrian, a strapping seaman in advanced middle age.

The responsibility of having to send our people away on the *Misr* weighed on me like a load of lead. I decided to see the harbourmaster, an Englishman personally known to me, on my own, because trust among my colleagues had been somewhat impaired. No one in the camp had any idea what seaworthiness meant. I wanted to have absolute certainty as far as this was possible. The LO joined me on the way, against my wishes. When the harbourmaster heard what we wanted, he, after a short reflection, excitedly said he considered sending these decent Templers away on a liberty ship a criminal offence and he was quite frank and open about that in my presence. The LO was visibly embarrassed and tried to talk me out of it. – However, the majority wanted to go, no matter how, just GO!

The International Red Cross in Cairo replied to our letter diplomatically – after two reminder telegrams.

84. "Partizanka"

The great day dawned with a cheerfulness I did not dare to dash. Without having heard any more from London, the bulk luggage went to the Famagusta dock to be loaded on to *Misr*, which had arrived there in the meantime.

This was 26 January 1949. First, at 6am, the party for the flight to Australia, 45 head, left the camp led by Mr Werner STRUVE to catch their plane in Nicosia. After 8am, the plane flew over the busy camp. People cheered loudly and waved 'bon voyage'. Shortly after noon the group for the ship, 170 strong, started to move on their way to board *Al Misr* in the company of many friends. Mr Siegfried HAHN was the group leader. Everything went according to plan.

Shock, Horror

The Comjews and the LO watched the happy throng from a respectful distance. The LO sent someone to call me and my wife over to them. A formal handshake, then: "Is everyone on board? Can the signal for departure be given?" I acknowledged; he thanked me; and then, yes, then – came the unexpected, the entirely unbelievable!

A telegram from London is condescendingly handed to me for my attention. Astonished and perplexed, I take it. Is it a death notice? But now I read, feeling as if a rug was pulled from under my feet, that if *Misr* was used against advice, "You and Mr Eppinger" would be totally responsible for all consequences.

Stunned, I hand the note to my wife while I hear a calm voice like distant thunder, "this does not affect me. You and you alone, as leader of the German Templers, who were pushing for this, carry the full responsibility!" Stepping forward, I stand directly in front of this Lord and Master, looking him straight in the eye, as my reply came desperately and seriously, "I beseech you in the name of God the Almighty and humanity! Full responsibility rests solely on your conscience, on your soul! You could have told us this long before now!" Long silence – then we part!

Al Misr departed. I did not notice; I do not know how I returned to the camp, the shock still held me in its spell. I was at the end of my tether, but – I remained silent. Thank God, all of them reached Melbourne safely, eventually!

The camp of Golden Sands seemed so empty now, with the remainder of the group reduced to 77 people. The general mood is one of temporary relief. Everyone is pleased with the successful departure of 215 camp residents, everyone that is, except two, my wife and I. After a while, the future looked rosier again, we did what had to be done, cleaning up and removing the tents. But soon another black cloud descended on to our small flock.

We heard, that *Partizanka* was going to sail to Australia again via Cyprus in early March, and we imagine it to be the most natural thing in the world that all of us would travel on this ship together. – Then the bomb went off:

Comjews advises 45 are to fly, and the rest to go by ship with all the bulk luggage!" Outraged, we take a stand; our pleas are in vain; the 'King's' heart of stone cannot be moved to change his mind. London is informed, he says, and that's that.

Under pressure from the camp inhabitants, the gentlemen of the committee are having a meeting without the camp leader and send a special delegation of their own to gain an audience at the Comjews', but are rejected. In the afternoon, they repeat the hopeless undertaking – in vain; undaunted, they tried once more on the next morning – again without success. Then, in the afternoon, without knowledge of the camp leader, follows a delegation of ladies, who are finally promised a hearing for the next day. Courageous and self-confident, they now go cap in hand on their way to 'Canossa'. They are told to go home under the pretext that the Comjews had urgent talks in Nicosia about our departure. This was seen as an excuse or even a lie. This happened in the afternoon of 4 February 1949.

I consciously allow these secret things to take their own course. I hear that the LO had secretly and confidentially whispered to the delegation that the camp leader had 'insulted' the Comjews without telling them how. It must have been the scene of the *Misr* telegram.

Withdrawn into myself, I let the past unfold before my inner eye. I search for a solution to the Gordian knot. In my considerations and reflections, I recall the secret reproaches made against our beloved TS president, Christian ROHRER [1860-1934] in 1919, in relation to the deportation of half of the German internees from 'Al Hayat' in Helouan near Cairo. I remember the earnest words of Mr Nikolai SCHMIDT [1876-1953], our president, when he farewelled me in Wilhelma. I further have memories of a piece of advice that our revered president, Mr Philipp WURST [1882-1941] had for me at a discussion in Wilhelma in 1940, when he said: "Remember you must never pound the table unless you know deep in your heart that things cannot get worse!"

Courage

I am sure that this moment has arrived and I see clearly in my mind: (1) We are no longer captives, but free civilians, (2) *We* are paying for our voyage, not the state, (3) the Comjews has orders from London to treat us as British migrants. So, in my dilemma, I take the decision to compose a telegram, aware not only that I am bypassing our own camp council but also that every single word would count. I seek the advice of a trusted friend to make sure that protocol is observed in all respects.

At noon on 5 February 1949 a wire is sent from the Famagusta telegraph office to the government of Cyprus in these words:

Templer community presents greeting Colonial Secretary and respectfully requests authority 77 berths sufficient remainder our community offered Cooks Cairo sailing s/s Partizanka March 4 Cyprus Australia direct instead part only air separating from remainder to which all members object stop may Commissioner for Jewish Camps be notified accordingly – Eppinger.

In the morning, the camp telephone rattled "all OK".

If, after twenty long years, I now reveal all and look back on to the harrowing times in Cyprus, some, if not all 'Cyprus people' will admit that we enjoyed good times as well, in good health, generally. We remember the unique sights of the many interesting historical monuments predominantly from the days of the crusaders, such as castles, churches, chapels and maritime fortresses. And who could forget the wonderful beach! I, for one, enjoy a certain satisfaction when I hear young people say they had the time of their lives in the tent camp of Golden Sands which, after all, was only to be expected, given they had never tasted true freedom during their long internment.

Everyone would have to gratefully concede, however, that the high price fate exacted from us in the shape of trouble, danger, as well as money, had brought about worthwhile results as well: we were now free citizens of a country rather than tolerated guests, as in Palestine, albeit respected, and even favoured, thanks to the reputation of our forefathers. We want to give thanks to the grace of God in Heaven, from the bottom of our hearts.

Here we also want to thank the Australian authorities, who have not only opened their doors and welcomed us here, but also helped us in word and deed concerning our properties abroad. Everyone has a job and a livelihood.

Something would be very amiss if in this space we would not, on behalf of the community, belatedly, but no less sincerely, remember with the greatest and most grateful respect the Palestine Mandate Government for its substantial efforts and help concerning our well-being, especially in the weeks before and during our hurried departure in 1948. In this context, it is absolutely essential to mention the Government in London as well.

Even at the risk of perhaps inadvertently overlooking one entity or another, we want to mention the following in recognition of their merit:

(1) The government and military authorities of Cyprus
(2) The Archbishop of Canterbury, Dr FISHER
(3) Lord ASQUITH, House of Lords
(4) The International Red Cross, Cairo
(5) Barclays Bank, Famagusta branch
(6) Mr H.T. TEMBY
(7) Our own Regional Council in Victoria
(8) Our Liaison Officer in Cyprus, Mr G.R. WALKER.

WE ALSO WANT TO THANK THE AUSTRALIAN AUTHORITIES, WHO HAVE OPENED THEIR DOORS AND WELCOMED US HERE

On behalf of the Temple Society, Refugee Branch, I express with deep respect a sincere 'God bless you' to all the above.

In conclusion, I take this opportunity to warmly thank all those involved in fulfilling all the tasks in the camp (men and women), for without their support even less would have been achieved.

So be it, Amen.

Richard Otto Eppinger

85. Richard Eppinger's wooden travel trunk

86. The tent camp in Golden Sands viewed from the sea

87. View from the camp towards Famagusta

Peter G. Hornung (1932-)

From Palestine to Cyprus

Written 2003

Three years after the Second World War

the Templer settlements were still behind barbed wire. What had begun as numbered concentration camps (in British parlance) in 1939, when the villages of Sarona, Wilhelma, Betlehem and Waldheim were fenced in, had now become oases that provided some shelter for their inhabitants from the world outside.

The Jews were fighting to get the new state of Israel established, the Arabs were fighting to retain their ancestral homes and lands, and both were fighting to oust the British who had been running the country since 1918

The Jews were fighting to get the new state of Israel established, the Arabs were fighting to retain their ancestral homes and lands, and both were fighting to oust the British, who had been running the country since 1918. The last Templer settlements were like islands in a turbulent sea and their days were numbered. There was no place for them in the new scheme of things. In April 1948, Waldheim was attacked one morning by the Jewish Haganah. Two people, Karl (63) and Regina Aimann (42) were shot dead in front of their children, Traugott, Helmut and Gisela, aged nine, four and three, and another person, Katharina Deininger (65), was wounded.

There had been other murders preceding the above, notably Wagner, Mitscherlich, Müller and Schumacher, as recorded in 'The Holy Land called' by Paul Sauer.

PANIC ENSUED IN WALDHEIM AND NEARBY BETLEHEM WHERE THE SHOTS HAD BEEN HEARD. PEOPLE FLED WITH NOT MUCH MORE THAN THEIR SHIRTS ON THEIR BACKS.

Panic ensued in Waldheim and nearby Betlehem where the shots had been heard. People, not having had time to pack the bare essentials, fled with not much more than their shirts on their backs, on foot and in horse-drawn vehicles to Saffuriyeh, and from there by bus to Nazareth, from where they were taken to a camp in Akko (Acre) to await further developments.

THE BRITISH AUTHORITIES ADVISED they could no longer guarantee the safety of the Templers. It has to be understood that the Templers were still prisoners or at least internees of Great Britain and therefore her responsibility. The British said they could evacuate them by bus and ship to Cyprus, if they could be ready in two days. The people of Wilhelma had exactly that much time available to get their things together as best they could, a luxury not afforded to the Germans of Betlehem and Waldheim. The people took this chance, packed what they could, sold what they could, and were ready in three days. Their flight from home and hearth thus proceeded with a semblance of order, but a flight it was all the same, no, it was in fact an expulsion.

In Jaffa, after a bus trip of sixteen kilometres, they were transferred by rowboat on to a British corvette, a small vessel by the name of *Empire Comfort* that had not been designed with passengers in mind. There was the open deck and there was the hold, that was all. The ship soon weighed anchor and sailed north, hugging the coast until it reached Haifa, where the others, brought from the camp at Akko, were to be picked up. The refugees (which they now well and truly had become) were ordered to move to the side of the ship facing away from the wharf because of the gun battles in progress around the harbour area and in the city, and the bullets could be heard hissing past the ship. When all were aboard, it sailed in a westerly direction on 21 April 1948. It was a terrible night on a rough sea. On deck it was bitterly cold, but the stinking hold made people more seasick than they were before, and not a shred of the comfort suggested by its name was to be found anywhere on the ship.

88. The camp with the small tents

THEY ARRIVED OFF FAMAGUSTA in the morning, and eventually disembarked at that port. Another short trip by truck and they were at 'Golden Sands', a stretch of beach where a sloppily pitched tent camp had been provided for them. Most of the transition was supervised by Sergeant Walker, who, as an officer of the Palestine Police in the service of the British Empire, had long been commandant of Wilhelma. He, in a way, had undergone a metamorphosis, from camp boss to supervisor to friend, who even spoke German when he felt like it. The escape of the Templers from Palestine was financed by the Templers' own money, frozen and held in trust by the Public Custodian appointed by the British Mandate government for such purposes. The Public Custodian also released money from these funds on an ongoing basis to pay for the group's living expenses in Cyprus.

Next to the slack tents was an already established, much neater tent city, occupied by German prisoners-of-war, who had been taken there from Egypt. What a surprise on both sides: here German families in exile, there young German ex-soldiers who had not seen women and children since before they had fought under Rommel in North Africa, where they had eventually been taken prisoner. There was much relief and rejoicing in each group for having found such good neighbours in the other. They quickly came in droves to straighten out the defects in the tent camp for the new arrivals and to take the slackness out of it. Social contact was instant, friendships were established everywhere, each family 'adopted' their own POW, and romances blossomed, some of which led to lifelong unions.

89. Walter Albrecht and Werner Struve in Golden Sands

Our family's POW was a toothless twenty-six-year old, happy go-lucky kind of a fellow with the nickname of Bimbo (which bears no relation to this term's present day meaning). He didn't say how he lost his teeth, so my father asked him, 'had he perhaps been born without them?' "Oh no", he said, "Heaven forbid."

Approximately three hundred persons were accommodated in the tents. A kitchen roster was organised, the cooking was done in a Nissen hut, which had been fitted out with huge oil-fired stoves by the British army who was trying to develop this beach area, four kilometres south of Famagusta, into a rest and recreation complex for its soldiers. A large tent next to the kitchen served as a dining room; alternatively, meals could be taken home to one's tent. For supplies of fresh fruit and vegetables, Eugen Kazenwadel and Theo Doh walked all the way to Famagusta markets, carrying large baskets, hiring taxis only on the way home, to save money for the community. Days became weeks, weeks turned into months and this slightly different camp life became routine, for once without barbed wire, yet a far cry from freedom: Cyprus was an island and there were no jobs for anybody. Besides, one had not expected to stay there for very long.

Problems arose

Problems arose and had to be dealt with. There were quite a few old people who were not considered fit enough to live in tents. They were taken to a home in Kantara with beautiful views of the sea. This, however, proved to be too expensive and they felt homesick while separated from the community, so they were brought back when bigger and better tents had been erected for them. To the relief of the management, they took it all in their stride. The three deaths that occurred were not attributable to living conditions. (They were Katharine Weinmann on 14.5.1948; Maria Hardegg on 27.7.1948; and Emma Bätzner on 24.10.1948).

THE THREE DEATHS THAT OCCURRED WERE NOT ATTRIBUTABLE TO LIVING CONDITIONS

Toilets were the portable type, set up in the open, surrounded only by sheets of hessian stretched from post to post. It was almost impossible to use them when the sun was high. They were emptied at night by men employed for the purpose, called honey extractors by my father.

The people from Betlehem and Waldheim were short of even the most essential utensils because they had had no time to pack anything when they had to flee. They lined up at meal times with tin plates and condensed milk tins for cups.

90. Theo Doh cleaning a fish

91. A POW boarding the ship in Famagusta, 3 September 1948

The prisoners-of-war were very good at making things with their hands. One plentiful material at their disposal was corrugated iron which, when beaten flat, could be shaped into anything. They made suitcases for instance, to take home their gear and their souvenirs on that uncertain day of their release sometime in the future, or to sell them to the refugees for their journey to Australia. They were proper suitcases, mind you, with tightly fitting lids and lockable hasps. Quite a few of them ended up in Australia.

On 3 September 1948, nine years to the day after the British declaration of war in 1939, the day of freedom finally arrived for the prisoners and it was a sad farewell for the families. The POWs were allowed to take with them whatever they could carry and one of them suffered greatly along the hundred metres from his tent to the lorry. He had made his cases much too big or filled them up a little too much, or both: he practically dragged them on the ground and, after many stops, he was the last to make it to the trucks under the cheers of his comrades. Another had to leave behind his beloved 'armoured cruiser' so dubbed by his mischievous friends. He had said he would build a yacht that he would sail to Turkey or Greece in an effort to escape. He built it all right, but it was made from corrugated roofing iron beaten flat and wasn't very seaworthy and, because it lacked balance, it badly needed an outrigger, which was promptly added, again made of iron. The mast was only for decoration and to hide the true purpose of the craft. When it was finished, the only way it could be moved was by pushing it along by hand, wading in the knee-deep water close to the beach. Everybody laughed about this lame duck of an 'armoured cruiser'.

As it happened, however, a concrete wall was being built along the beachfront of this holiday resort to be, and it was built by the POWs who, to satisfy the Geneva Convention, were paid one shilling per day. This was about one twentieth of a respectable wage. Now this enterprising skipper made sure during the day that some unused bags of cement remained on the job, and at night he came back with his 'armoured cruiser' to pick them up, stacked them on to what served as a deck between the hull and the outrigger and pushed them through the knee-deep water for half a mile or so to a secluded spot well beyond the tents, where he sold the cement to the local Greeks. When asked during daytime when he would finally make his escape, he just smiled and said, "Good things take time!"

Yet another POW was a cellist who had once played in the Nuremberg Symphony Orchestra. He helped my fifteen-year-old brother with his violin lessons. God knows how he came by a violoncello. Perhaps the British supplied it because they wanted him to perform at functions in their officers' mess. He pressed his Sunday pants by placing them under the bag of straw serving as a mattress on the planks of his bunk.

When the POWs had departed in September, the refugees from Palestine moved into the tents vacated by them. The slack ones would not have withstood the winter. Time hung heavily on everybody's hands. It was very frustrating not to have something definite to look forward to and the odd geometry lesson and boot-mending session were not enough to prevent unrest in the younger ranks. They formed the so-called 'young committee', designed to protest against the establishment, the 'silly old fools, who sat on their backsides doing nothing, while they, the Young Turks, were condemned to rot in tents'. There was more brawn than brains to it and it was soon recognised for what it was – the Templer equivalent of a teenage rebellion.

In spite of the continuous and strenuous efforts by our committee, expertly guided by Mr Richard O. Eppinger, the leader of the Cyprus Group, to procure berths on ships headed for Australia, none were forthcoming until December 1948 when a small group of mainly elderly and frail people, as well as a family or two with small children could leave on the *Partizanka*, a formerly German ship now flying the Yugoslav flag. It was a stormy old day when they embarked at Limassol, a hundred kilometres away on the south coast of Cyprus. This was also the beginning of the 'saga of the stowaway sweetheart' which, I am sure, is adequately recorded elsewhere, if not in print, then in the memories of the people to whom it matters most.

THIS WAS ALSO THE BEGINNING OF THE 'SAGA OF THE STOWAWAY SWEETHEART'

THE MAJORITY DECIDED TO GO TO AUSTRALIA

Although the majority had decided to go to Australia, a small number had opted to return to Germany, which they did in October 1948, by air. The next group left for Australia by chartered plane in January 1949. There were many people from Betlehem and Waldheim on that plane, travelling light, with no luggage to speak of. The flight was most uncomfortable in the ex-troop transport and took five days to reach Sydney. One dear old soul was asked on arrival, whether she had seen the equator. "No" she said, "I looked, but it was too cloudy."

The group after that found accommodation on the Egyptian ship *Al Misr* (Arabic for 'Egypt'), reputedly an ex-liberty ship. Liberty ships were ships mass-produced in the United States to replace losses caused by submarines during the war. This filled its prospective passengers with misgivings, but the ship 'sported a fresh coat of paint and had a German captain'. It turned out to be more luxurious than anything anybody had been used to for years and everything turned out O.K., at least to cause my brother Hans, fourteen years old, to quip: "Isn't it strange, having travelled miserably on *Empire Comfort*, but comfortably on *Al Misr.*"

The last occupants of the tent city of Golden Sands had to wait until the *Partizanka* had completed her round trip. They boarded her, again at Limassol, to arrive in Australia on 3 April 1949, almost a year after they had left Palestine. When the ship berthed at Victoria Dock in Melbourne, my father called out to friends on the wharf to hear what this new country was all about. He got the reply: "Make your last will and testament!" – He stepped on to Australian soil with somewhat diminished expectations.

HE STEPPED ON TO AUSTRALIAN SOIL WITH SOMEWHAT DIMINISHED EXPECTATIONS

92. The Richter family and their POW friends in front of their tent

93. The heavy trunks and baggage have arrived in Famagusta at last

Manfred Löbert (1938-)

Templers in Cyprus 1948

Written 1998

In April 1948

most of the Templers still in Palestine were forced to pack up and leave on the insistence of the departing British, whose Mandate was about to expire. A convoy of buses came to transport us to Jaffa harbour, where barges waited to ferry us out to a small ship called *Empire Comfort.* This little piece of 'Empire' turned out to be anything but comfortable for its overcrowded passengers.

We boys slept on deck to get away from the smell of vomit pervading the decks below, only to awake next morning covered in soot from the ship's coal-fired boiler. Breakfast consisted of porridge and tea, cooked in large laundry coppers on deck. All these tastes and smells were new and strange to us country boys and remain indelibly etched in my mind to this day.

Breakfast consisted of porridge and tea, cooked in large laundry coppers on deck. All these tastes and smells were new and strange to us country boys and remain indelibly etched in my mind to this day.

The ship called at Haifa to pick up more Templers, including three recently orphaned children from Waldheim. Their father and mother had been killed

94. The large tents in the Golden Sands camp

in their home just days before by the Jewish Haganah waging a war of intimidation and murder against non-Jews to force them to leave Palestine. Two years earlier, Templer leader Gotthilf Wagner had been assassinated; he had been advocating that the Templers remain in Palestine. There also had been other killings of Germans in Palestine. Thus, it was made abundantly clear that our welcome had expired and that, when the last British ship left Palestine, we would have to be on it!

95. Arrival in Cyprus

We landed at Famagusta

We landed at Famagusta in Cyprus and were transported on British army trucks to a crowded tent camp a few kilometres from Famagusta. Our camp, part of a British Army base, had been hurriedly pitched by German prisoners-of-war, POW for short, who were interned there.

We quickly organised everything as best we could. A roster for cooking and kitchen duties was drawn up. Gottlob Löbert (my father), Eugen Kazenwadel and Theo Doh were detailed to buy fresh meat and vegetables at the Famagusta market for the 300 men, women and children. Others were rostered to buy groceries etc.

We lived off money released by the Public Custodian who controlled the assets of German subjects in Palestine, such as the proceeds of the sale of Sarona some time prior to our departure. Who owed what to whom was to be sorted out later.

The men had lots of time, so our little tents were continually being improved. The POW 'found' some rolls of *Dachpappe* (bituminous roofing felt) to cover the floors of our tents and stop the sand getting into everything. Our tent was one of those closest to the water, so Dad built a windbreak using sticks from a nearby bamboo stand. He built tables and folding chairs from old packing crate timber, and soon we had a cosy corner visited by friends and POWs on their way to and from the beach.

96. Kyrenia Castle

97. Elfriede Hardegg, Karl Richter, Rose Imberger, POW, Erika Richter, Siegfried Hahn, POW, Elfriede Doh, Walter Imberger, Manfred Frank

We children and our newly acquired friends had a great time, spending most of the day on the beach in each other's company. The fun started when we queued for breakfast, tin plates in hand, ready to be served porridge or toast and jam. The socializing process continued at every mealtime. We ate in a large *Speise-Zelt* [dining tent], sitting together with schoolmates. School was much more informal than it had been in Wilhelma. The few schoolbooks we had salvaged had to be hand copied and 'roneoed'. Herr Bamberg, our geography teacher, even made a large globe out of plaster, with longitudes, latitudes, continents, mountain ranges, rivers and cities all carefully scratched in and coloured in by us students.

After school, we spent the rest of the day on the beach. It was clean, golden sand and the water of the Mediterranean was crystal clear, azure blue, shallow and ALWAYS inviting! We played or swam in large groups. The sea breeze and sun soon gave us a deep brown tan and the salt and sun bleached our hair to almost white. It looked funny when a dark-tanned face flashed a pair of light blue eyes at you. We had a ball!

OUR GEOGRAPHY TEACHER, HERR BAMBERG, EVEN MADE A LARGE GLOBE OUT OF PLASTER, WITH LONGITUDES, LATITUDES, CONTINENTS, MOUNTAIN RANGES, RIVERS AND CITIES ALL CAREFULLY SCRATCHED IN AND COLOURED IN BY US STUDENTS

100. Sightseeing at Kyrenia

98. Teacher Adolf Bamberg and Irene Eppinger

For the first time in our lives, we were free: enjoying life without camp guards, without barbed wire fences, without curfew, without the need for permission to leave the camp! In short, the bottled up world we had known in Palestine, was suddenly uncorked in Cyprus and we felt the 'bubbles' rushing through our veins.

We could now stroll for kilometres along the beach, down to the distant southern cape or up to the ancient city of Famagusta, explore its sea wall and Crusader fortifications, watch small coastal steamers unload their cargo and dream of sailing away with them to distant places. After our evening meal, we would walk through the neighbouring Greek villages to be greeted by a friendly *kali mera* or *kali nicta* and, on warm summer nights, listen to them singing their lovely melodious songs while sitting in groups outside their houses. At other times we would go to a local cinema; when the obligatory 'God save the King' started, the locals would whistle, stamp their feet and jeer loudly in protest. The Cypriots felt that now it was *their* turn to be rid of the British, just as the Palestinians and Indians had done.

At other times, we made group excursions by horse-drawn cart to the mountains or by rickety old buses to the capital Nicosia or the ancient copper mines that gave the island its name. A whole new world full of positive experiences magically opened itself for us freedom-deprived country boys.

WE ESTABLISHED A GOOD RAPPORT

We stablished a good rapport with the young German POWs, who had been part of Rommel's *Afrikakorps*. They taught us a lot of new games, songs and poems and often invited us to a concert or other entertainment. Some of them had built a small two-man sailing boat out of scrap plywood, which we kids inherited after their departure. I still remember the distinctive smell of the fresh coat of 'red lead' they had applied just before they left.

99. Walter Imberger with a motorbike

This boat was moored to a submerged millstone, which was to be instrumental in overcoming my phobia of swimming. One day, while wading out to the boat, my brother Gerhard yelled, pointing at the millstone, "Look out for that turtle!" He knew the huge carapace of a dead turtle we had found earlier on the beach had scared me. I panicked because, without my glasses, I really thought that it was a turtle, and dog-paddled furiously towards the

101. Preparing a fish for a meal

102. The Eppinger family with friends and POWs

103. POWs and Templers at a table tennis tournament

safety of the boat, only to be greeted by laughter. My lesson was swift, and my phobia disappeared as quickly as that 'turtle' did.

My older brother Herman was a bit of a handyman. Having befriended a few POWs, he decided to try, with their help, to run electricity to our tent. Coming from a rural settlement without electricity, it felt marvellous to throw a switch and see the inside of the tent light up instantly as bright as day! For the first time in our lives, we experienced electricity and radio. Soon illegal electric lights increasingly replaced our dim kerosene lamps, but we still needed the storm lamps to visit the toilets at night to avoid tripping over tent pegs and ropes.

The toilets were the open air 'drop' type, screened by hessian walls. There was one such toilet at each end of the camp. I remember Mum telling us at one time not to use the southern toilets because cases of diarrhoea had been reported in that part of the camp.

I also remember the muffled curses of *Ihr Saubuaba*! [You bad boys!] coming from inside a tent when we kids tripped over tent ropes while playing

104. Karl Richter

105. Walter Imberger

Some romances had blossomed between Templer girls and POWs. One of the POWs could not bear to leave his girl, so he stayed behind in hiding. With her help, he stowed away to Australia in a large trunk – as deck cargo! However, he was soon discovered and deported back to Europe

'chasie' well after dark! Mum would then call out *jetzt hent er aber g'nuag g'schpielt*! [Now you've played enough!]

Once there was a great commotion. My brother Herman, Cousin Hans [Hornung] and a few of the other older boys had made a raft by lashing four barrels to a timber duckboard they had 'borrowed' from the showers. They launched this unwieldy contraption, but soon found themselves carried out to sea by wind and current. As the tents got smaller and smaller, the waves got bigger and bigger. Soon, concerned parents gathered on the beach, fearing for their safety. Thankfully, a fishing vessel heading back to Famagusta harbour realized their plight and rescued them.

The weather in Cyprus was mostly fine, but as the days turned to winter, storms began to buffet our tents; kitchen utensils and mirrors hanging from the tent walls started to bang together, making a terrific din. This did not bother us boys because we accepted it all as part of our romantic new life. Sometimes, when a storm was at its worst, Dad would get up in the middle of the night to drive loose tent pegs deeper into the sand to stop the wind from blowing our tent away. We would lie awake and listen to the wild seas crashing endlessly against the concrete sea wall built by the POWs, and the wind would slap sea spray on to the canvas of our tent. Next morning, after the storm had subsided, we would inspect the driftwood and the flotsam the storm had washed up along the beach.

To farewell the POWs, the camp dwellers assembled on the crest of the dune, waving bed sheets until the ship disappeared over the horizon. The POWs responded in kind.

We spent Christmas in our tents, gathering around a small Christmas tree that Mum had decorated with white beach lilies. After the POWs had departed, we vacated our trusty little tents and moved into their larger ones for the winter because these bigger tents were better sealed and had roof vents that allowed us to use kerosene heaters to keep warm.

Some romances had blossomed between Templer girls and POWs. One of the POWs could not bear to leave his girl, so he stayed behind in hiding. With her help, he stowed away to Australia in a large trunk – as deck cargo! However, he was soon discovered and deported back to Europe. Not long afterwards, he returned to Australia to marry his girl.

Finally, the *Partizanka*

Finally, the second time around, the *Partizanka* took the last of our group to Australia. We were bussed to Limassol because of strife in Famagusta. On board ship, we met up with Aunt Rickele Imberger and the wife and daughters of Christian Beilharz, all of whom had boarded the vessel in Trieste. After an uneventful journey, we arrived in Melbourne on 3 April 1949, almost exactly a year after having left Palestine.

Our departure from Cyprus was wet and windy but, for us boys, the sunny memories of a happy and carefree camp life will remain forever.

Siegfried Hahn (1924-)

My last days in Palestine

Written 2005

On 20 April 1948, the majority of the internees of Wilhelma were taken to the port of Jaffa by bus, escorted by British army units

On 20 April 1948, the majority of the internees of Wilhelma were taken to the port of Jaffa by bus, escorted by British army units. They embarked on the ship *Empire Comfort*, which sailed to Cyprus, after it had picked up our friends from Waldheim and Betlehem in Haifa.

The internees who stayed behind in Wilhelma included a group of about forty people, who had opted to go to Jerusalem, and the seven men who had remained to sell the livestock and equipment that was left behind. They also loaded the trucks for those destined for Jerusalem and helped with the heavy luggage to be sent to Cyprus.

Thus, the last ones to leave Wilhelma, on 24 April, were the Jerusalem group and the seven, who were: Gottlob Löbert, Adolf Bamberg, Wilhelm Groll, Hans Stephan, Walter Imberger, Heinz Vollmer and I; we went to the airport at Lydda to fly to Cyprus. Chaos reigned at the airport when we

106. Wilhelm Groll, Gottlob Löbert, Walter Imberger, Siegfried Hahn and Adolf Bamberg leaving Lydda airport, April 1948

arrived. The hotel where we were going to stay was being evacuated and all the airline staff had packed up to leave. We decided to go to a hotel in Lydda and asked the taxi driver to get us two more taxis from the airport, which he did.

HOWEVER, WORD GOT AROUND IN LYDDA THAT WE WERE STRANDED

However, word got around in Lydda that we were stranded. Mr Haddad a long standing business friend was good enough to offer us accommodation in his house. We waited there for our departure.

It had previously been arranged with the District Commissioner of Jaffa that he would charter a plane to take us to Cyprus. Since we had not heard from him, we decided to visit him in Jaffa. Three of us went to Jaffa in a taxi, which was not going to return to Lydda. While I went to look for something to take us back to Lydda, Walter Imberger and Hans Stephan went to see the District Commissioner, who was not very pleased to see them, because he thought the streets in Jaffa were too dangerous for us. He referred us back to the Lydda District Commissioner for further information.

Meanwhile, I had found a mode of transport that would take us back to Lydda. It was an open truck collecting Arab 'troops' to defend Lydda. We made it back to Lydda safely after we had convinced the 'troops' to hide their rifles when passing Jewish strongpoints.

Finally, on 28 or 29 April, we heard from the Lydda District Commissioner that a plane would be at the airport to take us to Cyprus. Our departure was somewhat delayed by members of the crew who were not going to leave behind the various items of furniture abandoned by the management of the airport hotel.

107. POWs leaving for home in Germany

108. POWs waiting to be transported home

109. POW last farewell

Now it was off to Nicosia. We decided on the way that we were going to have a good time enjoying whatever 'night life' or anything else there was to be had in Nicosia but, after touchdown, we were that tired and keen to see our families again that we hired three taxis to take us to Famagusta, which was only an hour or so away. Not having heard from our families, we did not exactly know where they were. The taxi driver suggested going to the Jewish refugee camp, but we refused, telling him that we were Germans. The alternative was to go to the German POW camp. So off we went and when we arrived at *that* camp we saw our friends and families. We enjoyed a great welcome.

110. A POW boarding ship on his way home 1948

111. Famagusta refugee camp 1948

Adelheid Groll (1904-1985)

Correspondence

27 March 1946 [to Otto Lämmle, POW in USA]

... I still have to tell you that, when on a trip from here to Sarona on 22 March, Mr Gotthilf Wagner was deviously shot and killed on the first bend of the road after the bridge on the other side of the railway line. This cruel blow hit us terribly hard, and the consequences do not bear thinking about. Mr Wagner was going to pay out the contract workers [in Sarona, Camp 4] and for this reason Mr K[arl] Steller, Irmgard Weiss and Miss [Frida] Wagner were with him. The [military] escort sat next to Mr Wagner, for Mr Wagner drove his own car. Mr Weinmann, [Jakob F.] Weiss, Jakob Sickinger, Herr Jak[ob] Weller, Annelies and Mr S[amuel] Faig followed in a taxi. I had seen them all depart in good spirits, and then this horrific murder took place soon after.

On Saturday, Mr Wagner was laid to rest in the presence of all the colonists and the staff of his firm. The people of Waldheim and Betlehem were not allowed to attend

On Saturday, Mr Wagner was laid to rest [in Wilhelma, Camp 5] in the presence of all the colonists and the staff of his firm. Unfortunately, the people of Camps 2 and 3 [Waldheim and Betlehem, 100km away] were not allowed to attend, for safety reasons, it is said ... We have to wait and see how things will now develop without Mr Wagner, we just have to stick together more to make everything bearable. It is a pity we had to leave from lovely Sarona, which made our lot even harder to bear. Yet I assure you again that we will do whatever we can to be equal to all demands...

1 December 1946 [to Otto Lämmle]

... Today I have much to tell you ... although it won't be enjoyable news. A few weeks ago, Mr Parkhouse who, as you know, is in charge of our Camp[s], informed us that we should supply addresses in Germany in connection with repatriation. We, however, had no inclination to be voluntarily deported to Germany; a general protest was raised about this.

Despite some calm weeks, we did not feel good about the matter because we knew rather well what they thought of us. Mr Parkhouse had coldly stated that we, after all, had lost the war utterly, and that 'they' could do with us what they wished ... The result of the talks was that all of us who were no longer wanted here would be repatriated; the old and weak might possibly be accommodated in 'Homes'.

When asked whether there was a chance for the rest of us to go to Australia, the spokesman said that if Australia would have us, his government would have no objection. Since we had heard only bad news about conditions in Germany, we did not fancy to go there ... Yes, my dear Otto, who would have thought that even our small band would have to give up our own land and beloved home. It hurts terribly having to abandon all our beautiful settlements...

IT HURTS TERRIBLY HAVING TO ABANDON ALL OUR BEAUTIFUL SETTLEMENTS...

Also, two Germans from Waldheim were shot dead, Müller and Mitscherlich...

28 April 1948, in Cyprus [to Lina and Otto Lämmle]

Today you shall receive the news of our sudden expulsion from Palestine. Late at night on Saturday, 17 April, we were informed that we had to be ready to leave by Tuesday the 20th. We would have loved to postpone this departure for a week, but since Waldheim had been attacked by the Jews, the government no longer hesitated, and we lived through four terrible days of packing. Much harder was tearing ourselves away from the land we had come to love ... Wilhelm Groll, Gottlob Löbert, Sieger Hahn, Bebs [Walter] Imberger, Hans Stephan, Herr Bamberg [and Heinz Vollmer] stayed behind to look after the bulk of the luggage, and we expect them to arrive here in Cyprus any day now, keen to hear what they will report from dear old Palestine. A group led by Nikolai Schmidt opted to go to Jerusalem to stay in Palestine for good; we hope that they are all well and that they will have nothing to fear from the J[ews].

TODAY YOU SHALL RECEIVE THE NEWS OF OUR SUDDEN EXPULSION FROM PALESTINE

The attack on Waldheim must indeed have been terrible. Mr and Mrs Aimann were shot dead, leaving three children, aged 10, 5 and 3, and Mrs Deininger was wounded by bullets. While Waldheim was thus harassed, the people of Betlehem had taken flight to Nazareth from where the British took them to an army camp at Akko together with the Waldheimers. They joined us on the ship, a British corvette, which reached Famagusta, Cyprus, on the next morning, 22 April.

WE ARE STILL STUCK IN CYPRUS AND, WHILE THIS LASTS, I AM STILL IN PALESTINE WITH ONE FOOT. I JUST CANNOT SWALLOW THAT THINGS HAD TO END THIS WAY ... ALL OF US HAD BELIEVED IN AN ORDERLY PROCESS OF LIQUIDATION, BUT EVERYTHING HAD TO BE ABANDONED JUST BEFORE THE HARVEST

15 August 1948 [to Otto and Lina]

We are still stuck in Cyprus and, while this lasts, I am still in Palestine with one foot. I just cannot swallow that things had to end this way ... All of us had believed in an orderly process of liquidation, but everything had to be abandoned just before the harvest ... Nothing was allowed to be sold beforehand, and afterwards there was no time left for that except at give-away prices. Our bulk luggage has not arrived to this day...

Adelheid left for Australia on the "Al Misr" on 26 January 1949 with a large group of Templers. We are indebted to Dr Charlotte Lämmle for permission to select from her extensive correspondence.

112. German refugees waiting to be transported from Waldheim, 1948

MR AND MRS AIMANN WERE SHOT DEAD, LEAVING THREE CHILDREN, AGED 10, 5 AND 3

Karoline Krafft nee Bätzner (1888-1964)

Letters from Cyprus

Golden Sands, 22 December 1948

Dear Helga, [Helga Brown née Krafft, in England]

We cannot say anything concrete regarding our departure. We were to sail in January 1949 on the *Misr*, an Egyptian pilgrim ship, but heard last night that this was out of the question. Now we are waiting for the next opportunity. You know, don't you, the fine proverb, 'If it's not today, it'll be tomorrow, or the day after, to be sure!' So we hope that it will come true for us, one day. We baked Lebkuchen for ourselves, just a few, because we live very primitively here. We had a small Christmas celebration together even before 37 of our fellow camp inmates and sufferers left for Australia on 16 December; they were from among our oldest, including only a few young people. We had been given the use of a stone barrack belonging to the British army to accommodate our older people. It was also used for Sunday services, school and Christmas celebrations, as well as for our cholera injections and smallpox inoculations. So you see we are ready for departure but just lack the opportunity.

Golden Sands, 22 December 1948

Dear Sister and Sister-in-law,

We are sorry that we could not send the promised Christmas candles. We had bought them, but sending parcels from Palestine was almost impossible during the last few months we were there. The roads were unsafe even in town, so nobody wanted to hang around in Haifa longer than necessary. Since we had to leave Betlehem in a panic, we could only take the most essential things. We had to leave behind so much of what was dear to our hearts. We have been in Cyprus for eight months now and have lived in tents the whole time. Six weeks ago we moved into larger tents, which are more pleasant than our former small tents. We still do not know anything definite about our departure; we keep hearing that there is no shipping space available, or at least only of the inferior sort. Since we are used to waiting, one or two more months do not matter any more, one day it must come true.

Healthwise, we are well. Of course, we have to look after ourselves at our own cost; our young people have taken over the kitchen, so the cooking is to our own taste and there is plenty of fruit. All the same, it is a waste of time; instead of pursuing our own work and earning a living, our assets are being used up, and afterwards nothing is left.

We sit here right on the sea and have enjoyed swimming in the sea from May to November, twice a day. Now it is over, of course, but we go for short walks every day to get some exercise. Mrs Katharina Deininger, whose head was injured during the raid on Waldheim, has fully recovered and also wants to go to Australia with her loved ones. Forty-nine persons have flown to Germany and have arrived there safely within the day. Now there are 225 of us left, and we want to depart from here as a group, if at all possible. Inshallah, may God grant that we, too, will reach our destination, Australia.

Golden Sands, 23 December 1948

My dear Nieces,

When we had to leave Betlehem behind and came here, we would have never thought that Aunt Emma [Bätzner] would not be with us on this day, why, the way she went to swim in the sea every day and then peeled vegetables [in the dining tent]. She hardly ever missed a day of the latter, except for the last five or six weeks of her life. Every time I hear something new, I think I must tell Emma about it. On Tuesday 21 December, we went to visit her grave in the cemetery. Mr Seidler had told me two weeks ago that the gravestone was ready, but something always interfered; if it wasn't the rain, it was the injections and vaccinations (cholera and smallpox) to get us to Australia in one piece. We planted bulbs of beach lilies, which are plentiful around here, on her grave, as well as twigs of oleander and a flowering geranium. Unfortunately, the cemetery is too far away from our camp for me to walk, about 1¼ hours, and driving is too expensive for us. Mr Seidler has taken the trouble to photograph the cemetery and Aunty's grave.

Golden Sands, 29 December 1948

Dear Meta [Beilharz] and family,

You will surely have received our letter with the news of our departure in the first week of January, and perhaps you have even heard that this was postponed for another month. Now we will not write until we are quite sure we're sure. We are supposed to get word on 3 January that we might sail in February. We sure have learnt how to wait here, and we do not get excited any more, indignant at most.

We had a lovely end of school celebration in the hall of our barrack on Christmas Eve. Miss Luise Dreher had gone to a lot of trouble with her pupils, as well as with the mixed choir to rehearse all the songs; five of the littlest ones also sang their Christmas carols. It was a beautiful evening; we even had two Christmas trees. On Christmas Day, Mr John led the congregation. The students played the violin and the flute and afterwards the mixed choir sang. A storm blew up that night, enough to think the tent would be ripped from over our heads. Yesterday the weather was fine again, but cold, especially at night. We have also received *Pfeffernüsse** here and *Ausstecherle**, not many of course; Mr Richter and his helpers had baked *Gutsle** for everybody. In addition, there was a gingerbread heart for each child and a big piece of *Streuselkuchen* for everyone for breakfast on Christmas morning.

**Traditional German Christmas cookies*

P.S. I received a letter a week ago from the Temple Society in Stuttgart, saying that Canberra had approved seventeen more Templers for immigration to Australia. We in Cyprus must now see that we get all the papers for making the application. Police clearances had to be asked for from Berlin. Martha was sponsored by her parents, likewise Friede Weberruss and Georg Weber. Good friends, who are financially better situated than us, provided the Becks and Weberrusses with the money (£100), to be paid back later, of course. Father was not able to sponsor Edith [his youngest daughter], because only the most urgent cases are being considered.

Golden Sands, 30 December 1948

All signs indicate that the five of us will get away from here in February, after all. We were very much shocked by the stowaway affair. You would have heard that one young woman took her boyfriend, a prisoner-of-war, along with her in a trunk as a stowaway on the *Partizanka*. It was, of course, discovered and reported. We don't know yet what the consequences will be.

Golden Sands, January 1949

Dear Maria, [Maria Laube, widow of Friedrich Bätzner and sister-in-law of Karoline Krafft] I wanted to write to you earlier but there was always talk about leaving, so I waited until I would be able to give you definite news. But since we still can't give you a time, I won't make you wait any longer. I wish you and your sister a happy New Year. May it be better than the last one. You ask whether Emma knew that she had to die. I think that she probably felt she did, but she did not say. When we asked her during the last few days whether she had a wish, she said 'no'. In most cases, this disease is very long drawn out and painful; we must be grateful that this was not the case with Emma. I will include a photo of the cemetery and her grave.

Things are not much different for us than they are for you; we, too, had thought we could spend the last years of our lives without material worries, but now everything has turned out so very differently. [My husband] Georg and I will go to his daughter in Australia; they have a room waiting for us. We must be grateful to get such a place, but it is still hard to make do with a room after having owned a house.

The climate is much colder here than in Palestine, it dropped to one degree below zero one night. Everything was covered in frost in the morning and looked very beautiful. We are so spoilt in relation to the cold and are glad when it warms up again during the day.

You ask about Lina Wagner, who is with us here in Cyprus. I thought you knew how the family was torn apart. Of her two sons, Walter and Kurt, the latter was killed in action, leaving a widow and young daughter. Walter has been interned in Australia since 1941 with his wife and three children, the first of whom was born in Jaffa. Gotthilf [Lina's husband] was murdered in Tel Aviv on 22 March 1946. He drove his car to Sarona to pay the Arab workers, but was stopped on the way. Two Jews jumped the car left and right and fired four shots, killing him instantly. His sister and two other Germans were in the car with him, but nothing happened to them. Apart from Gotthilf Wagner, seven Germans were murdered during the last two years, three from our settlements and four others, interned along with us, with not a single one of the culprits ever having been brought to justice. Admittedly, the British were no better off; no one in a leading position – or any one else who happened to be in the way of the Jews – was secure any more. It was no longer nice in Palestine. Murder and mayhem were the order of the day even amongst the Jews themselves. Not a day passed without reports of armed robberies, or worse, in any newspaper. We look forward to living in a peaceful country with law and order once more.

Golden Sands, 16 January 1949

Dear Edith and Hildegard [Krafft],
You may think we are no longer in Cyprus; but we are, unfortunately. Yesterday, news arrived of the 37 who left on the *Partizanka.* They did not have a pleasant passage. Mrs Sawatzky broke her arm, Mr Sawatzky contracted pneumonia, Mr Fritz Katz senior suffered a light stroke, Gerda Wied was swept across the deck by a strong gust of wind and her mother lost her handbag overboard during the chase. These were the side effects that had to be endured. It must have been very stormy. Mrs Steller wrote of waves as high as houses.

Forty-five persons are supposed to be leaving by plane in a few days. We have not opted for that. It is a troop transport plane and the trip is supposed to last five days. We hope and wish that everything will work out and they will all arrive in Australia safely.

On board the Misr, 1 February 1949

Dear Meta,
Just a few lines from en route. Airmail will reach you sooner than we will. We finally boarded a ship for the voyage to Australia in the afternoon of Wednesday 26 January. We left Famagusta at 11pm and arrived in Beirut

at 7am, without having been seasick. Despite a two-day delay, we could not go ashore. Mr Ernst Gassmann came to the ship but was not allowed on board to see us. Mrs Robinson and her mother also came and waved to their friends from below. We left Beirut at 4pm and arrived at Port Said at 9am on Saturday. Forty-five passengers had come on board in Beirut and 450 in Port Said.

Hermine Haar and her husband had come from Cairo to see her relatives but they were allowed to come on board for only five minutes, the rest of the time they stayed in the motor launch and talked to their relatives from there. We entered the Suez Canal at 12 midnight, but took all Sunday to get through the Canal because we had to lie at anchor in the Great Bitter Lake to let other ships pass. After this, we travelled in a convoy to Suez, and are now cruising in the Red Sea, which will take five or six days. Since the sea and the weather are very pleasant, nobody has become seasick.

Our meals are excellent: breakfast with tea or coffee, two eggs, butter and jam, with as much bread as we like. For lunch, there is a two-course meal, followed by cheese and coffee. Afternoon tea is at half past three with biscuits or other bread, and supper at seven with soup, fish, potatoes or rice with meat, vegetables or salad, or both.

Uncle Philipp and Aunt Amalie [Krafft] share a cabin with us. We did not like the arrangement at first, but there was no other way. We partitioned the cabin with a sheet so we could at least dress and undress without embarassment.

4 February

On the evening of 2 February, we entered the beautiful and generously designed harbour of Massawa. We heard we would be allowed to go ashore, but then this was prohibited by the harbour police. Some of the ship's officers went ashore and became involved in a brawl; three of them got away with minor injuries.

On 3 February after breakfast, we left the harbour of Massawa, it was very beautiful to watch. At midnight of 2 February, our clocks were advanced by an hour, which caused many to be late for breakfast. The sea continues to be calm and we are grateful for every day that passes so pleasantly. At 3pm all passengers had to report to the lifeboats with their life jackets. As long as it is only a drill, we dismiss it with laughs and jokes, but woe betide if it should happen in earnest! Even now some people are pushing to be first – how would it be if we were in danger? Heaven forbid.

When we came on deck at 6:30, we sighted ships and distant mountains, as well as seagulls and fishes. The mountains came ever closer and one of the rocks had the shape of a lion, its name was said to be 'the resting lion'. On the other side was a rock that looked like a walrus. At 9am, we entered the Gulf of Aden after having passed through Bab el Mandeb [the Gate of Tears], and soon we will be floating in the Indian Ocean. After lunch we heard that an Italian man had died on board. He was with his wife and two children, as well as his mother and three sisters (all widows) with their children, fourteen persons in all. Since docking at Aden would have involved extensive costs (£700), it was announced that he would be buried at sea at 10pm. The loudspeakers announced: keep quiet and play no music.

5 February

We arrived in Colombo on 10 February without seasickness. Sieger Hahn, our group leader, announced there would be a sight-seeing trip arranged by James Cook Tours. We went on the mountain, and what a disappointment it was; firstly, because it was just a hill and secondly, because all there was to see was a large hotel with pushy souvenir vendors. At the zoo, we saw many animals we only knew from pictures: a zebra, a wildebeest, bears, elephants, lions, pythons, giant lizards, all kinds of fish, a big cage full of monkeys and two crocodiles, for which I felt rather sorry because they were lying in such a small pond.

Driving through Colombo on our way back to the ship was a treat. The lush vegetation, high trees and palms with coconuts on them, the wealth of flowers – it was almost too much to take in. Life in the street was also worth seeing: trams, cars, double-decker buses, oxcarts and lots of little carriages [rickshaws] being pulled by Indians. I would have loved to sit in one and have my photo taken, but we were only with the Jakob Blaichs, his three sisters and Mrs [Emma] Uhlherr and none of them had a camera. We sailed on the next day, and finally arrived in Fremantle in the evening of 21 February. Klara Cluss (Mader) with her husband and two children, and Magda Hahn (Persztik) with her husband and son came on board to welcome us and stay a few hours.

We left Fremantle at 10am on 22 February, headed for our last stop, Melbourne.

At 8am on 28 February, the pilot came on board to guide us through Port Phillip Bay into the port of Melbourne, where we arrived after lunch. It took us a long time to spot Meta in the crowd. Mr Temby welcomed us and told us that we had to go on to Sydney that night. Our tickets, including Meta's, and our passports were handed to us, plus two Australian pounds. It was half past five before we could leave the ship and were free to greet Meta and our other friends. The journey continued by train under Meta's guidance and we were all happy and grateful when we arrived in Sydney.

113. Forlorn refugees waiting for transport

Nikolai Schmidt (1876-1953)

The End of the Templer settlements in Palestine

Preliminary remarks

Nikolai Schmidt assumed the duties of President of the Temple Society after Philipp Wurst had died in the Wilhelma internment camp on 7 February 1941.

Mr Schmidt was greatly restricted in the execution of these duties because, along with all other Germans, he was interned at the outbreak of war. To make matters worse, he was plagued by a painful eye disease which, eventually, led to almost complete loss of sight.

Mr Schmidt collected material for an account of Temple Society history, ably assisted by his wife Babette née Eppinger, and Karl Schnerring. Arrived in Australia, he dictated a description of the weeks and months that marked the end of the Templer work in Palestine.

I express my heartfelt thanks to the last Templer president in Palestine.
Dietrich Lange

EXILED FROM THE HOLY LAND

As I proceed to write about the break-up of our work in Palestine, I feel there is not yet enough distance between us and those sad years of cruel events and hard decisions to describe without bitterness the often ugly occurrences and our deep emotional turmoil.

The Wilhelma internment camp

At the outbreak of the Second World War, all Templers in Palestine were concentrated in the settlements of Betlehem, Waldheim, Sarona and Wilhelma, all of which had been transformed into internment camps with barbed wire and watchtowers.

In addition to our own three hundred souls, the CID (Criminal Investigation Department, i.e. the Police) forced us to accommodate increasing numbers of motley 'Illegals' and Italians. ('Illegals' were illegal immigrants totally unknown to us, often subjects of axis powers caught without papers at the outbreak of war).

In Wilhelma up to fourteen different nationalities were represented by such 'Illegals'. They were not always pleasant fellow sufferers. We had much trouble coping with their messy disorder, their noise and their dirt

In Wilhelma, where most Jerusalem Templers were interned, up to fourteen different nationalities were represented by such 'Illegals' at times. They were not always pleasant fellow sufferers. We had much trouble coping with their messy disorder, their noise and their dirt, as well as persuading the camp administration to take steps to settle disputes or relocate the worst recalcitrants to other camps. We suffered very much because of their yelling and screaming and their dirty habits. They also did not show the necessary care in combating mosquitoes and sandflies.

Much worse than this was the fact that these unwanted groups were competing to decrease our portable belongings. Some had arrived with one rucksack, but left in 1945 with half a truckload of luggage. The Arab workers employed in the camp, as well as the Jewish or Arab guards were willing partners in this lucrative enterprise. It was inevitable that the groups ended up blaming each other.

A high barbed wire fence surrounded each rural German settlement. Jewish or Arab guards manned the gates and kept a sharp lookout from watchtowers

A high barbed wire fence surrounded each rural German settlement, now internment camp. Jewish or Arab guards manned the gates and kept a sharp lookout from watchtowers. A British commandant (usually a sergeant) resided in the camp with some support staff.

The people who had always lived in the settlements had to provide for their own livelihoods – as they had done before the war – from their own pockets and supplies.

The newcomers from the other settlements, on application to the commandant, could obtain rations based on their daily or weekly food requirements, for the procurement of which the Mandate Government had retained the services of a Jewish or Arabic contractor, who purchased meat, bread, vegetables and other provisions. The contractors delivered the required quantities to the camp, but settled their accounts with the government separately.

Thus, the internees living in the camps were split into two different groups: the self-reliant and the recipients of rations. Those who could no longer supply themselves could join the latter on application. In due course, we were allowed to negotiate more appropriate arrangements with the contractor, i.e. instead of bread, he would supply flour, but instead of meat, fat, eggs, fruit and vegetables he paid out the government allocation in cash, because we had these foods ourselves. The settlers of Wilhelma were allowed to kill six animals per month and 'sell' the meat to the 'self-reliant'. According to government regulations, only young steers and dry cows (no longer milk-producing) could be slaughtered.

SOON AFTER THE OUTBREAK OF WAR AND THE ESTABLISHMENT OF THE INTERNMENT CAMPS, SOME WIVES HAD TO SELL LARGE NUMBERS OF THEIR CATTLE. ARAB WORKERS WERE NOT ALLOWED INTO THE CAMP. LEFT ALONE, THE WOMEN COULD NO LONGER COPE WITH THE WORKLOAD

Soon after the outbreak of war and the establishment of the internment camps, some wives had to sell large numbers of their cattle. Their men had followed the call of their national duty and Arab workers were not allowed into the camp. Left alone, the women could no longer cope with the workload.

When in 1941 a large number of internees were deported to Australia, more cattle had to be sold. Milk production fell to one fifth of pre-war levels. The government therefore prohibited further sales and slaughtering, which caused the number of cattle in the stables to rise out of all proportion.

Fruit and vegetables were plentiful in the German gardens. By paying us the government allowance in cash, the contractor was able to do good deals on the side. He obtained these foodstuffs from the government and sold them for a high price on the black market. This was none of our business and we kept our mouths shut, which in turn caused him to feel obligated to us, which made him meet us half way when we needed help.

Attempts to cancel our rations were made a few times. I, for one, had to pay for them for about two years. However, we successfully objected to this withdrawal, because we knew the government had made provision for each and every internee. The profits from undistributed rations would only line the pockets of less than honest officials in the form of cold hard cash.

The relationship with the authorities

WE HAD GOOD RELATIONSHIPS WITH OUR DIRECT SUPERIORS, SUCH AS THE CAMP COMMANDANT. WE, OF COURSE, WERE NOT ONLY NICE TO THEM, BUT ALSO SUPPLIED THEM EVERY WEEK WITH BUTTER, EGGS, CHICKENS, VEGETABLES AND MORE. SOME PAID THE OFFICIAL PRICE FOR THESE AND SOME SIMPLY FORGOT TO PAY

We had good relationships with our direct superiors, such as the camp commandant. We, of course, were not only nice to them, but also supplied them every week with butter, eggs, chickens, vegetables and more. Some paid the official price for these and some simply forgot to pay. We did not remind them. On major holidays, we handed them substantial quantities of food provisions. The guards sometimes treated us roughly. They took special pleasure in reporting us when not all lights were properly blacked out at night. Some were quite mean.

When an internee had to see a doctor in the city, an Elder, an accountant or urgently needed to go to another internment camp, permission from the commandant had to be obtained. This was not a simple matter. The commandant assigned a guard to the applicant, who henceforth 'shadowed' him everywhere, even to meals and to the door of the toilet. During the last years, this shadow was missing; we often would have had to guard him, because the places we had to attend to transact business were predominantly in the Arab sector, where no Jew could go without endangering his life. From 1947 onwards, those of us who had to leave the camp more often carried Arabic papers in order not to be mistaken for Jews.

SOMETIMES, BRITISH OFFICERS VISITED THE INTERNMENT CAMPS TO INSPECT 'THESE GERMAN CRIMINALS' AND WERE FLABBERGASTED EVERY TIME BY OUR PEACEFULNESS AND BY THE ORDER IN OUR CAMPS

HE SPENT HOURS CHECKING OUR BOOKS, THINKING HE *HAD* TO FIND SOME MISTAKES. ONCE HE BECAME BETTER ACQUAINTED WITH US, HE ONLY MADE RANDOM CHECKS AND PREFERRED TO CHAT, ESPECIALLY WITH RICHARD O. EPPINGER, WHO HAD THE BEST COMMAND OF ENGLISH

The first Custodian (of enemy property) we had to deal with was Mr Bailey. He was fair throughout and treated us decently. Unfortunately, this cannot be said of all British officials. The British Secret Service had apparently collected much material against us in its files, which was not surprising, given the hate campaigns being conducted against all things German. We were little bothered by 'myths', too horrible to be believed by rational people. They had, however, some effect on the guards. We could see that some of them were afraid of us. They had obviously been 'warned' about our 'base' and 'bloodthirsty' character, or succumbed to the all-pervasive psychosis of hate.

Sometimes, British officers visited the internment camps to inspect 'these German criminals' and were flabbergasted every time by our peacefulness and by the order in our camps.

One financial inspector (auditor), whose job it was to examine our books, thought at first he had to follow his brainwashed, prejudiced ideas. He spent hours checking our books, thinking he had to find some mistakes. Once he became better acquainted with us, he only made random checks and preferred to chat, especially with Richard O.Eppinger, who had the best command of English.

114. POW Boenke (dentist) and Richard Eppinger (leader of the German refugee camp)

After the murder of Gotthilf Wagner on 22 March 1946, the inspector suggested the Temple Society Central Fund Ltd should assume the administration of the German Community Funds. I declared I was willing if I had permission to sell pieces of land in Sarona or elsewhere. The inspector said he would consult with his committee. He wanted to know exact details about the Central Fund, but never followed up on his suggestion. (There will be more about the German Community Funds below).

Late in 1939, the Custodian had asked Gotthilf Wagner to assume the management of the German orange groves near Sarona. Wagner hesitated. He was afraid the owners would later criticize him. He finally agreed with a heavy heart, convinced that otherwise a Jew, whose management would be more expensive and less reliable, would be entrusted with the job. Wagner thereby took on a big responsibility. Many trees were unsound. The workers could not be supervised, because the groves were outside the camp enclosure. Much thieving was going on and there was no prospect at all for selling the crop to at least partly cover the expenses. Karl Steller supported the efforts of Gotthilf Wagner in a commendable way. To administer the necessary expenditure and possible income, an account needed to be set up which, under the existing regulations covering internees, was subject to control by the authorities.

Mr Stevenson, a member of the government, suggested that a private person, such as Mr Bryant, the director of the Jerusalem Electric Corporation, perform the audit. This was accepted and Mr Bryant opened an account called 'German Community Fund' with Barclays Bank in Jaffa, and another one called 'German Fund' in Haifa.

The above-mentioned files of the CID had swollen to thick bundles. Here we were accused of many lawless and hostile acts: we were accused of being in possession of firearms, of manufacturing our own ammunitions; of militarily training Arab freedom fighters and supporting them with large sums of money, as well as maintaining a secret news service, and more of the same. It was sheer slander, ideal to help promote the planned expulsion from our settlements and from Palestine. In reality, the members of the Temple Society and their Lutheran co-settlers had always striven to be well-behaved, law-abiding guests in a foreign land ever since the establishment of our settlements from the 1860s onwards.

Overeager officials of the CID, presumably goaded by certain parties, kept lobbying the Mandate Government to demand stricter supervision over us. We suspected that the top officials of the government, who knew us well and, in many instances, had lived in our houses, did not take these demands too seriously. However, this being wartime, they finally had to investigate the complaints in their own interest.

THE OVERCROWDING OF THE CAMPS WITH FOREIGNERS AND STRANGERS RESTRICTED THE LIVES OF THE SETTLERS EVEN MORE AND MADE LIFE DIFFICULT. CONSTANT RACKETS, FREQUENT THEFTS, ARGUMENTS AND FIGHTS, DIRTY CONDITIONS AND SWARMS OF MOSQUITOES CONSTITUTED ORDEALS THAT EXACERBATED THE ORDINARY AILMENTS AND HARDSHIPS COMMONLY EXPERIENCED BEHIND BARBED WIRE

Conditions

The long deprivation of freedom in the internment camps would have been easier to endure if it had not been accompanied by so much inconvenience. In addition to their normal peacetime populations Wilhelma, Sarona and Betlehem had to absorb evacuees from the Jerusalem, Jaffa and Haifa colonies. During the hot summer months, we were all forced to move closer together within the available living space. The overcrowding of the camps with foreigners and strangers restricted the German settlers even more and made life difficult. Constant rackets, frequent thefts, arguments and fights, dirty conditions and swarms of mosquitoes constituted ordeals that exacerbated the ordinary ailments and hardships commonly experienced behind barbed wire.

About one hundred Jewish auxiliary policemen did guard duty in Sarona and Wilhelma in addition to several Britons, such as the camp commandant, his deputy, and his driver.

In the beginning, the Arabs working for the settlers were not allowed into the camps. They took over the horses at the camp gate in the morning, worked the fields according to the directions given to them by the German farmers and returned the horses to the gate in the evening. After 1946, the few remaining farmers were allowed to go out to their fields in person, albeit in the company of a guard. It was an odd scene to watch: the armed policeman tramping up and down the length of the field, duty-bound, next to the German farmer. Some made it easier for themselves by watching their farmer ploughing his field from the shade of a tree or from underneath the parked wagon.

Being subject to such military supervision was quite unpleasant on trips to hospital or surgery, or when visiting the toilet. The 'shadow' stopped in front of the door and waited, resuming his guard duty when the person came out again. Every camp also had a Jewish policewoman. I know of no cases, however, where her services were needed during the interrogation or investigation of female internees. On visits to authorities outside the camp, some British officials were considerate enough to keep the escort waiting outside the door.

Towards the end of our time in internment, after 1946, leaders or authorised representatives could leave the camp without guards. We would have had to guard them more often than they guarded us because we frequently had business in the Arab sectors, which Jews could only enter at the peril of their lives.

The large contingent of guards was reduced during these final years. Just two men were in charge of clerical and supervisory duties as well as the military training of the Jewish auxiliary police. Many of these had only recently immigrated, and being a guard was their first job in their new country. Betlehem and Waldheim had mostly Arab guards with usually three British superiors.

At the outbreak of war, German men of military age had been taken to a prison camp near Acre. There, among other prisoners, languished 541 Germans. Some of them were returned to the four other camps (Wilhelma, Sarona, Betlehem, and Waldheim) to help with the work. Only 65 [Templer] prisoners were left in the Acre camp in the summer of 1941, when they were transferred to Camp 13 near Jaffa.

An inspector of the CID checked on the commandants of the four internment camps every month. The internees also had to line up then. He knew many of us, not so much from his files than personally from pre-war days. We had no reason to complain about him.

Our financial inspector usually came once a month as well. The officers of the Custodian – his office employed about eighty of these loafers – rather liked us

Our financial inspector usually came once a month as well. The officers of the Custodian – his office employed about eighty of these loafers – rather liked us. We saw them often during their visits. Sometimes, higher British officials also conducted camp inspections.

Charitable activities

The secretary of the Spanish Consul-General in Jerusalem also visited our camp once a month. After the outbreak of war, first Switzerland, then Spain had assumed responsibility for looking after the Germans' interests. Two of the five Spaniards we encountered in this way really did their utmost to make our lot more bearable.

A committee of an English charity sent some of their ladies, three times, asking lots of questions and busily taking notes. However, we did not need their help. The German Reich transferred funds to us via the Spanish Consul, but it was the 'Illegals' who mainly benefitted from this money.

Representatives of the International Red Cross visited us twice a year. We had a very good relationship with them. On their instigation, we collected much money from the internees to support prisoners-of-war in Africa. 'Sister Hanna' in Egypt eagerly helped with the distribution of parcels. We have given in excess of £P2000 to the Red Cross for such purposes [the Palestine pound equalled one English pound].

When we started a relief action for Templers in Germany, our first gift consignments went through the Red Cross. Subsequently, our relief operations were channelled through Switzerland, the USA, and even South Africa. We paid hundreds of Palestine pounds for postage alone. We regretted that we could not free more funds for parcels. Since the government controlled our funds, we could not withdraw money as we wished.

We began to look around for help in the spring of 1946. The Mandate Government remained tight-lipped as to what their plans were for our future

Trying to hang on

When, after the collapse of Germany, our internment continued, we began to look around for help in the spring of 1946. The Mandate Government remained tight-lipped as to what their plans were for our future. We therefore wrote to all places from which help might be expected. We described our situation to the Unitarians, to the Red Cross in Geneva, to prominent parliamentarians and respectable private persons in London. We always stressed that Palestine was the home of our choice, and that we had come here for religious reasons, but that the government wanted to send us off to Germany as soon as ships became available. Some of the above offices replied to our cries for help with the assurance that they would be of assistance but, obviously, nothing was done.

When I was in Jerusalem to see my eye doctor, I also spoke to the Lebanese Consul to suggest he might induce his government to help us move to our land near Amik in Lebanon. We even sent a lawyer to Lebanon to explore the possibility of our resettlement there. He reported that the biggest obstacle was the French Custodian, who was still in charge of all 'Enemy' property and unless there was a peace treaty between France and Germany, there was hardly a prospect for the release of the Amik land for settlement purposes.

Years earlier, a man from South Africa had suggested re-settlement in that country. We turned to him now, but received no reply.

No help was forthcoming. We therefore fought in vain for the continued existence of our settlements and the right to free disposal of our land and property

Two further attempts failed as well. We had asked a member of the 'Arab High Committee' about possibilities of settling in Arab countries, and in June 1947, we submitted a request to the Anglican Bishop of Jerusalem to put a word in for us when the last commission charged with regulating the Palestine problem arrived in the country, (probably the so-called Paton Commission). Help was promised in both instances, but either no steps were taken, or they remained without effect; in any case, no help was forthcoming. We therefore fought in vain for the continued existence of our settlements and the right to free disposal of our land and property.

I have mentioned the establishment of the 'German Community Funds', and how they were subject to government control. In the beginning, the finance inspector (auditor) appeared very frequently, but came more irregularly later on. He had to check the books of receipts and expenditure of the four internment camps. Each camp was allowed a certain amount of cash, but was not allowed to touch the bank account without the inspector's permission. Sales outside the camps, such as cattle sales, needed his permission. Some sales, already arranged, did not eventuate, because the buyer had disappeared by the time the permit was issued, or the market had deteriorated to a point where the seller would have sustained a large loss if he had sold at the low prices offered. Mr Bryant, the inspector, was therefore willing, in urgent cases, to grant the camp commandant the right to issue permits. Until the end, not a single unlawful payment was transacted on our part. In this way, we gradually achieved good co-operation with the finance inspector.

Gotthilf Wagner had tried more than once to have the growing losses arising from the management of the Sarona orange groves covered by the Custodian. Unfortunately, he was not successful in this. The payment for these expenses continued to come out of the German Community Fund whether our comptroller of finance liked it or not. At the last moment, however, the Custodian agreed for the Temple Society Central Fund to make these payments and agreed to the sale of single pieces of Sarona land; but alas, it was now too late for that – nothing could be done any more.

THE CIVILIAN AUTHORITIES OF THE MANDATE GOVERNMENT WITHDREW FROM ACTIVE ADMINISTRATION. WE CAME UNDER THE JURISDICTION OF MILITARY ADMINISTRATION. THIS GAVE THE CUSTODIAN A POSITION OF MONOPOLY

In 1946, the civilian authorities of the Mandate Government withdrew from active administration. We came under the jurisdiction of military administration. This gave the Custodian a position of monopoly, which empowered him to do as he wished with our properties. Everything now became more complicated, more unpleasant, more nerve-wracking and more loss-making. One example stands for many: because of foot and mouth disease towards the end of the war, many cows had perished; others were 'dry' and did not become pregnant any more, so were now useless eaters. According to the authority's regulations, no cows were allowed to be sold or slaughtered. The stables were becoming crowded and feed was scarce. We applied to the Custodian for permission to slaughter sixty unproductive cows. A representative of the Custodian appeared at last and declared that, because he knew nothing about animal husbandry, he wanted to send for a veterinary surgeon. The vet agreed it would be absurd to maintain useless cows on expensive feed. This did not seem convincing enough to the representative of the Custodian. He consulted an official of the health department who ascertained that overcrowding of stables was indeed unhealthy. However, everything remained the way it was. Not until I was able to see the Custodian in person, as late as August, was the permit to slaughter issued. In the meantime though, lots of people had been killing animals without permits and, to make matters worse, meat was being imported from abroad. Prices had dropped. A cow worth between one hundred and two hundred pounds before, would now barely fetch sixty.

This development, lasting months, had led to a situation in our camp where some cattle just 'disappeared'. Without bothering to wait for official permits, some people bribed the commandant for a permit. Even crops in the fields, standing grain, were sold on the black market. Who would police it? Obedience to law and order deteriorated day by day and a feeling of impending doom was rife. News from Germany told of want and hunger. Most internees tried to get money wherever they could to finance sending food parcels to Germany. The Red Cross was very helpful in implementing this. We could legally transfer money to the Red Cross to have them send the consignments of parcels. Some Jewish agencies offered their services in this respect as well.

Unfortunately, unsavoury elements were selfishly active in the dispatch of our parcels. One smooth talking 'Illegal', a police informer for the

British, had lived in Waldheim for a long time. He reputedly had betrayed a German paratrooper after he had jumped out of his plane. He provided permits for the sale of cattle and equipment and suggested to use the money for sending parcels to Germany. He and another 'Illegal' from Wilhelma amassed large sums of money, travelled to Paris, and from there by luxury car to Germany, where he had the Templers acknowledge the receipt of his consignments. When the latter opened the parcels, they found they only contained useless, cheap women's underwear.

Selling Sarona?

This 'Illegal' had one more elaborate plan which, however, did not come to fruition: while his parcels operation was under way, he approached the settler F. with the idea to sell Sarona. F. discussed it with Gotthilf Wagner and me. We advised F. to show interest, but to be very cautious. During the course of the developments, he learnt that government officials in high places would agree to the plan if there were something in it for them. F. was soon summoned to the CID in Jerusalem where an official took him to his private home to negotiate with him. F. was most fiercely threatened if he would not keep silent.

Some difficulty, however, must have arisen. The 'Illegal' who had started the whole affair booked a plane trip, and the official who was privy to the secret was transferred to a different department. Thus failed the first attempt to sell Sarona.

Soon it was attempted in a different way. The Custodian, we learnt, had passed on sizeable pieces of Sarona land held in trust to the City of Tel Aviv. Gotthilf Wagner submitted a letter of protest on Sarona's behalf. The letter was never replied to.

WE JUDGED OUR SITUATION AND OUR FUTURE TO BE MORE AND MORE UNFAVOURABLE AND DANGEROUS. THIS VIEW WAS REINFORCED WHEN THE MURDER OF GOTTHILF WAGNER DROVE HOME THE POINT THAT THE NEW OWNERS OF PALESTINE WOULD, BY HOOK OR BY CROOK, DRIVE US OUT OF THE LAND OF OUR CHOICE

This experience only added to our worries. We judged our situation and our future to be more and more unfavourable and dangerous. This view was reinforced when the internees of Sarona were relocated to Wilhelma and when the murder of Gotthilf Wagner drove home the point that the new owners of Palestine would, by hook or by crook, drive us out of the land of our choice.

It had been clear to me for some time that our stay in the Jewish sector of the country was about to be terminated, and more of us might possibly share the fate of Gotthilf Wagner. I therefore established contacts with rich Jews in early 1946 and reached the following verbal agreement. The buyers would pay between 1500 and 3000 pounds per dunum (1000m^2), as per exact title details, by bank draft payable in Switzerland, in the USA or even in Jaffa (because of the Custodian) for the handing over of the land and a receipt signed by me and three Sarona land owners. Each of the buyers wanted to pay me a cash deposit of one or two hundred thousand pounds on the spot, but I insisted that they first obtain the approval of the government. However, they could not get this approval.

In May 1946, I went to Jerusalem myself for negotiations regarding this issue. I cited the reasons forcing us to sell Sarona as follows: the land is surrounded by Jewish-owned land, we had not been able to cultivate it for over a year, our Arab workers refuse to work on it because they feel endangered, and most of the crops are stolen before harvest. The government officials agreed that these were valid reasons to sell. However, when the buyers wanted to follow up on their submitted applications, the government fed them excuses. Both departments, Custodian and Control of Finance, kept procrastinating. Jewish newspapers warned, 'Speculators want German land', but the Mayor of Tel Aviv stressed that the "German land belonged to him and whoever did not heed this will be 'blacklisted'."

After a few weeks, two persons appeared at the upper camp gate of Wilhelma and sent me word that surely I had read in the papers that they were forbidden to buy German lands. They were sorry, but remaining alive was more important than a good land deal, so they had to pull out. I thought it was a pity, for I had already envisaged myself depositing five million pounds in foreign banks. Thus ended the second attempt to sell Sarona.

We had initiated legal action against the Custodian, because he had given parts of our Sarona land to the City of Tel Aviv. To pursue this action, Richard O. Eppinger drafted a submission to the Chief Secretary. Among other things, we requested information as to whether we were able to leave the country, and if so, how this was to be effected, and in what form we could take our property with us. We handed this letter to the District Commissioner in Ramleh, Mr Stevenson, in person. He promised to pass it on to Jerusalem. Regarding the dispossession of the land, he thought we had a right to adequate compensation by the City of Tel Aviv. He would keep us informed of further developments.

Bombs in Jerusalem

A few days later, explosive devices hidden in milk cans destroyed the southern wing of the King David Hotel. The southern wing contained the secretariat of the Custodian. The Chief Secretary, the recipient of our submission, narrowly escaped being killed
.

During the following week, the District Commissioner invited Richard O. Eppinger and me to a conference in Ramleh. He confessed that he had not yet passed on our submission, because the Chief Secretary had been snowed under with work, and would be out of town in a few days. He asked us for our consent to hold back the submission for the time being and pass it on at a more suitable time. Apart from this, he tried to console us with the typically English ambiguous phrase: "I will do my best". Regarding the dispossessed land, he said we would probably have no other course of action than to try reaching a decision by pursuing legal avenues. He was willing to be of assistance, he said, and sent us a copy of his application relative to this matter.

Some time earlier, I had already requested powers of attorney from our Sarona settlers in Australia to represent their interests. They had now been released from their internment camps and were allowed to settle in Australia. This would improve our chances at law.

We now retained two Arab lawyers regarding the Sarona land dispossessed by the City of Tel Aviv ('vested in the municipality of Tel Aviv'). Now documents had to be produced for the three pieces of land so far dispossessed, to ascertain which Sarona settlers were the owners of the land and what size area it was. It also had to be stated whether the people concerned were 'enemies' or 'enemy subjects'. People who had left Palestine on or before 1 August 1939 had been labelled enemies by the government. All others were said to be 'enemy subjects'. Confiscated enemy property now or in the future was subject to transfer to the reparations fund and was lost to the owner.

We received no reply from Tel Aviv to our request for compensation submitted by our solicitors. We made two more presentations, spaced three weeks apart. Finally, our solicitors were called for negotiations. They were offered one hundred pounds per dunum. The talks were discontinued because they could not possibly agree to such a ridiculous price.

Shocking news

The chief of the CID and the commandant of Wilhelma appeared in my room and disclosed to me that we had to leave the country and would be deported to Germany within six weeks

Much more incisive problems threatening our very existence were soon to command all of our attention. The chief of the CID, Mr Sherringham, and the commandant of Wilhelma appeared in my room and disclosed to me that we had to leave the country and would be deported to Germany within six weeks. Only the sick would be allowed to remain.

For the first time in my life, I suffered from shock. I collapsed into my chair after the first words, shaking and as white as chalk. I could neither move nor talk. A group of fellow internees, who had been in my house when the British officials arrived, were equally discouraged and had lost all their faith in the future. (They were Johannes Wagner, Probst Döring, Fritz Katz, and several Wilhelma settlers).

Admittedly, we had harboured secret fears of deportation, but had always reassured ourselves with the idea that justice would prevail as it did after the First World War. This last hope had now been shattered by just a few short words.

If we were not allowed to stay in this country, which had become our second homeland and which our fathers were at such great pains to make a success, we replied to the British officials that now perhaps we were at least justified in hoping to emigrate to Australia

If we were not allowed to stay in this country, which had become our second homeland and which our fathers were at such great pains to make a success, we replied to the British officials that now perhaps we were at least justified in hoping to emigrate to Australia. The Germans already there, having been deported from the Palestine settlements, had now been released from captivity and were allowed to freely integrate into the Australian economy. This was news to the British bureaucrats. Mr Sherringham looked up in surprise, if not indignation, and rumour had it that this news went off like a bomb in the British secretariat, where they could not understand that these 'wicked' Germans had been released in Australia.

Now that it was official, one can imagine the effect this planned expulsion had in the various internment camps. Most had probably gradually realised that our stay in Palestine would come to an end sooner or later, but secretly everyone had hoped we would get permission to stay, as we did after the First World War. Now deep despondency descended on the people because of the latest decisions by the Military Government.

Nobody knew anything definite about our imminent departure. Would we be allowed only a little hand luggage, as was the case in the deportation of six hundred settlers in 1941, who could take only as much as they could carry, or should we pack larger items such as bedding etc? Would we be allowed to sell off our portable assets, such as cattle and agricultural equipment, to the Arabs? Would there be only a limited amount of cash available for each person on the day of departure? These questions were keenly discussed in the families, among friends and in the street – without coming to any conclusion, I might add.

I was repeatedly granted permission to consult my eye specialist in Jerusalem. Naturally, I tried to learn something about our future on these occasions.

Since the Temple Society Central Fund, before the war, had bought a large tract of land in Lebanon for settlement purposes, it seemed a logical conclusion that we might find a new home there. I paid the Lebanese Consul a visit for this reason. He could not promise much. The French Custodian had confiscated our land there and it was very questionable when he would release it, if at all. There was also a rumour that Turkey would impose heavy taxes on new foreign settlements. It was feared that Lebanon would follow their lucrative example.

We even considered a move to Jordan. Presumably, we would have been granted permission from the Jordanian government to establish German settlements there; perhaps they would have even given us land, but where would we have found markets for our produce?

As early as 1946, we had begun to take stock of all the German properties in Sarona. Buildings, gardens, the winery and other facilities in the settlement were listed according to size, condition and value. Two delegates from the City of Tel Aviv and two representatives of Sarona had begun with this work. Political unrest between Arabs and Jews put a premature end to this undertaking.

The confiscation of German lands

The confiscation of about one third of German land and property by the Mandate Government began as early as 5 September 1939, and was continued by the Custodian, who was appointed by the government on 1 November 1939. This land and property belonged to Germans who, on the dates mentioned, were no longer in the country and had been designated enemies for the purposes of the Mandate administration and the Allied powers. The remaining two thirds of the land and property belonged to the Germans interned in Palestine. They were deemed to be 'enemy subjects'. Their properties were not confiscated until 3 November 1947.

This very confiscation was revoked on 3 May 1948 by the Mandate Government. Theoretically, enemy subjects could now sell their properties, or have them sold by an agent on their behalf. The revocation order, however, could not be publicised in the prescribed manner, because of the extensive political unrest and the resulting difficulties with printing. For this reason, the revocation remained largely unknown and was often denied, precisely because of this disrupted procedure. In any case, the revocation had no practical value for the Germans of Palestine, if only because the new state of Israel immediately confiscated all German land and property and placed it under the control of an Israeli Custodian.

All these processes were not very well known, let alone familiar, to the interned Germans in Wilhelma and elsewhere. We also believed that the confiscation was far from being the last word spoken. Therefore, I urged our two Arab solicitors independently of each other to keep pursuing our interests at government level. I was very happy when both were able to tell me in December 1947 that things were looking good: the properties owned by companies, i.e. legal entities with suffixes like 'Palestine Limited', had already been released.

I then saw to it that all areas of land belonging to companies registered as 'limited' were included in lists and documented by block and parcel numbers. I was very pleased to see that the S.G., the *Siedlungs-Genossenschaft* [an agricultural cooperative] had more than 2000 dunums of land registered in its name. The size of our other 'limited' companies was not to be sneezed at either. Unfortunately, it was once again all in vain.

British officers and public servants were being tortured or killed in ambushes or bomb explosions, but Jewish terrorists were not prosecuted

The expiry of the British Mandate

The British Mandate Government declared on 1 December 1947 that it and all of the British military forces would leave Palestine on 15 May 1948.

We immediately tendered a submission to the government that we would need to leave the country even before the British, because the acts of terror had become more appalling daily. British officers and public servants were being tortured or killed in ambushes or bomb explosions, but Jewish terrorists were not prosecuted, let alone punished, whereas Arabs taking revenge on Jews were most severely punished, as we had heard time and again.

The Jewish resentment against 'foreign settlers' exploded. At dawn, the Haganah attacked the settlement of Waldheim. Two people were shot dead

The Jewish attack on Waldheim

The Jewish resentment against 'foreign settlers', meaning Germans, stirred up and fanned since 1928, exploded on 17 April 1948. At dawn, the Haganah attacked the settlement of Waldheim. Two people were shot dead and the rest were treated brutally and declared prisoners. The guard posts of Waldheim had been subdued, but were able to notify the military authorities in Haifa of the attack. Soon, a strong British army patrol arrived and enabled the people from Waldheim to flee to Acre under their protection.

Alarmed by the Waldheim raid, the settlers of neighbouring Betlehem fled to Nazareth by horse and cart. After a short time, they joined their fellow sufferers at Acre. They were told they would all be taken to Cyprus on a British warship.

The news of these events reached us in Wilhelma in the afternoon of 17 April 1948. The commandant announced forthwith that we also had to leave our settlement. A British Navy corvette would take us on board at Jaffa and take us to Cyprus with the others.

All settlers honoured my wish to meet for one last time in the crowded *Saal*. The commandant announced our expulsion and how it was to proceed

We leave the Land of our Second Home

The time allowed for packing and clearing our houses was very short. It therefore seemed futile to call the settlers to one last gathering in the community hall. Hardly anyone would have been able to concentrate. However by Saturday, the most urgent things had been done and all settlers honoured my wish to meet for one last time in the crowded *Saal*. The commandant announced our expulsion and how it was to proceed.

I thanked the people of Wilhelma on behalf of the Jerusalem settlers who had enjoyed the hospitality of Wilhelma for many years. The last Templer congregation on the Plain of Saron was closed by singing together with deep emotion the hymn, *Befiehl du deine Wege und was dein Herze kränkt, der allertreusten Pflege des der den Himmel lenkt.* [Commit whatever grieves you into the gracious hands of Him who never leaves you, who Heaven and Earth commands.]

A corvette took the refugees from Wilhelma, and from Acre to the island of Cyprus. The last ones left from there in March 1949

Everyone left the settlement except for seven men. A corvette took the refugees from Wilhelma, and the ones from Acre, about three hundred souls in all, to the island of Cyprus. The tent camp of 'Golden Sands' near Famagusta was their destination. It was to be a long wait until finally about two hundred of them were able to proceed to Australia and the rest to Germany. The last ones left the camp as late as 9 March 1949.

The seven men who had stayed behind in Wilhelma had the task to protect the vacant houses from theft and raids until guards of the new masters of the country could take over. They managed to sell some furniture and farm equipment, albeit at throwaway prices. Much was stolen in spite of their keen vigilance. After seven days, this team of watchmen was able to join the settlers in Cyprus by taking a plane from Ramleh.

A small group of German settlers stays put

About fifty old and sick settlers had been granted permission to remain in the country for the time being. They rode in cars to Jerusalem via Latrun and Ramallah, sometime between the dates of 19 and 24 April 1947. The ten-hour trip took them through areas where Jews and Arabs were violently fighting each other. The refugees repeatedly heard bullets whistle past their ears. The destination of the refugees was the Templer settlement at Rephaim near Jerusalem. British civil service and army personnel had so far occupied most houses there but now all these people had left and the houses were empty. We had no keys to our very own houses. If we wanted to go inside we had to 'break and enter' to gain access to our properties.

What a lamentably neglected view of our formerly so attractive and cosy homes presented itself to us. Traces of hurried departure by the tenants and evidence of bad neglect could be seen everywhere. There was dreadful dirt and filth all over the place and the keys for the inside doors were lost – some even had the locks missing. Downhearted, we went through the rooms in silence, down to the basement, into the carpenter's shop, to the toilet – sadly, it was the same everywhere.

We had telephoned the St Charles Hospice [hostel] from Wilhelma to ask for accommodation. Something must have gone wrong with the telephone message; the Hospice had only two rooms available. However, Mother Emiliana had people move closer together. As we arrived from Wilhelma only in small groups and the British kept vacating more rooms as they left, twenty persons of our group could get into the Hospice by the end of the week. The remainder took up residence in the vacant settlement houses as follows:

- The families of Nikolai Schmidt and Jakob Imberger in our own house;
- The family of Hermann Imberger and Mrs Anna Rohrer in Hermann Imberger's house;
- The Faigs in their own house;
- The Stellers and Miss Wagner in the Fauser house;
- Karl Schnerring in Hermann Schnerring's house;
- Emma Imberger, Frieda & Martha Schmalzriedt, Mrs Bertha Knoll, Mrs Moll, Miss Maria Weiberle and Mrs Weber with daughter Hilde, in the house of Emma Imberger.

Life was no longer comfortable in Jerusalem. The noise of the battle between Jews and Arabs was rumbling all around us day and night, sometimes nearby, sometimes farther away. In April, the Jews attacked the Katamon, but the Arabs succeeded in splitting up the Jewish forces. Next, the Arabs planned to drive the Jews out of their hiding places with explosives, but failed because the British declared a neutral zone between the battlefield and the Old City, cutting the Arabs off from their base. British armoured cars were sent between the warring fronts. Now the guns fell silent. During the night though, the Jews received reinforcements and were able to occupy the upper part of the Katamon. The beginning of the conquest of South Jerusalem had succeeded.

Our solicitor and I went to the Custodian two days after our arrival in Jerusalem. He disclosed to me he had given all files over to what was left of the government, but was willing to give me a letter of recommendation. My solicitor then arranged an audience with this torso of a government for 23 April 1948. I went there in the company of two solicitors and presented our problems and matters of concern, asking that I and Richard O. Eppinger be paid half a million Palestine pounds each as an advance on the compensation for, or sale of, the German-owned land in Palestine. I further requested the sum of £P150,000 in cash, which the Custodian had mentioned in February 1948 as being income on behalf of enemy subjects. Two British officials seemed inclined to agree with my pleas but wanted to see proof. I had carried the necessary documents with me. Obviously, other British authorities were not so ready to pay. Still, after a week I was handed a payment of £P4000 and, on 11 May, I was informed that £P60,000 had been deposited to our credit at the Ottoman Bank. We managed to have both amounts transferred to a bank in Amman, Jordan. Three of us signed the acknowledgment of receipt of these payments: Schmidt, Eppinger, and Steller.

We were greatly worried about the money from the sale of Sarona. There were rumours circulating that two million pounds had been paid by cheque and that £P200,000 were on deposit somewhere for damaged houses.

A delegate of the Australian government, Brigadier White, visited us in May 1948. He was to report to his government about the German settlers and their property. We – Nikolai Schmidt, Hermann Imberger and Karl Steller – supplied him with extensive written descriptions. I urged him to demand as much money as possible from the government remnant as an advance payment for the assets owned by German settlers in Palestine for quick transfer to Australia, because the continued existence of our settlements seemed impossible. Therefore, the settlements should be liquidated quickly. Perhaps there was a possibility of saving the Templer colony at Rephaim, in case it was true that Greater Jerusalem would be declared an international zone. I also conveyed to Brigadier White that the majority of the Cyprus group were hoping for Australian immigration permits.

To our surprise, Brigadier White emphasised firmly that the Australian government would not tolerate our style of agricultural settlement. They had, he said, not fared well with projects of that kind in the past. After three days of talks, he flew to Cyprus.

To our surprise, Brigadier White emphasised firmly that the Australian government would not tolerate our style of agricultural settlement. They had, he said, not fared well with projects of that kind in the past

While so far, the fighting between Arabs and Jews was mainly restricted to the city fringes, chaos was now threatening to engulf the city proper in uncontrollable turmoil, waiting only for the departure of the British.

My wife and I had managed to obtain passes that allowed us to cross the various zone boundaries in the city, so we could stock up with food for a few months.

We first felt the effect of the approaching economic upheaval when our water supply line began to fail sporadically. Our cisterns had let us down; they contained only brown undrinkable sludge. We filled all available vessels with water while the waterline still functioned.

We had implored the representative of the International Red Cross to place the German Hospice belonging to the Borromeo Sisters under its protection. (The Hospice was situated in the German colony of Rephaim). We asked the Sisters to fly the flag of the Red Cross alongside the Papal flag. We also asked whether, in an emergency, they would grant asylum to all fifty-one of us German refugees.

On 13 May 1948, Hermann Imberger and I intended to call on the Commander-in-Chief of the British forces in respect of the outstanding rent for our houses. He had set up his office in the old *Institut* of the Temple Society. We were told by an official to come back next day. Next morning we had to wend our way between the trucks of a long column lined up in our main street. At the *Institut*, we were met by chaos, caused by hurried departure. All doors were wide open, gaping cabinets and open drawers everywhere, empty boxes, the floor covered with papers and packing material. No living soul was to be seen. We rushed back on to the street just in time to hear the shrill whistle that gave the signal for the convoy to move. The British Army was leaving the city and the country. It was the fourteenth of May 1948, the eve of the new State of Israel's first day of existence.

We were met by chaos.The British Army was leaving the city and the country

Survival under terror

The last of the vehicles were not yet out of sight when the first 'grave robbers' and pickpockets were seen sneaking about. This made us return to our houses as quickly as possible. As I entered my house, one of these fellows shouted at me, wanting to know what business I had being here. Ignoring him, I went in and was soon sitting at my writing desk again. However, when the gunfire and the rumble of explosions were coming closer and closer, I hastily packed my briefcase with whatever I could find and hurried to the Sisters of Borromeo, where my wife and my sisters had already sought refuge with all our supplies.

In order to report about the fate of the fifty-one refugees from Wilhelma I must ask the reader to backtrack a few days with me.

When we first arrived at the German Hospice on 19 April 1948, the building was largely occupied by British Army officers and personnel. Only two rooms were available for us. But, as the British were in the process of departure, more rooms became available during the next few days so that most of the people who had come from Wilhelma could eventually be taken in. Some found a place to stay in the other houses of the settlement.

Everyone accommodated themselves in their rooms as best they could under the circumstances. The life we were forced to live here from now on was certainly not going to be cosy. The Arab inhabitants of most of the houses on the Plain of Rephaim and in the surrounding hills were in the process of fleeing. The events at nearby Deir Jassin had shocked and frightened them. During the absence of their menfolk, all women and children of Deir Jassin had been murdered most cruelly by Jewish partisans and terrorists. One hundred and seventy bodies were said to have been found in a cistern, seventy more mutilated and lying at the side of the road. Such stories were driving people to flee in mindless panic. Anyone who still found a seat on a bus at the high price of eight pounds was considered lucky.

When we walked through the empty streets between the deserted houses, we were haunted by an oppressive feeling. All shops were closed and barricaded, their owners gone, perhaps forever. Only the poorest of the poor had remained.

We had, as mentioned, succeeded in buying some food conserves, so we had enough to eat for a few months. The people living in the houses of the settlement suffered water shortages. The previous occupiers of these houses had allowed the cisterns to become polluted. They only contained a brown, unpalatable sludge. We found a little water in tanks that had been connected to the water supply, but the line was already cut and the supply had dried up.

The Hospice and the other houses of the colony, situated between the fronts, were now in the middle of the battlefield. Stray bullets frequently crashed into the walls of the Hospice. The gunfire then moved past us to the East in the direction of the railway station and beyond. On the Saturday before Pentecost, they were fighting for control of Abu-Tor, of Nebi Dahud, and the Gate of Zion. Gunfire was still to be heard on the Plain of Rephaim as well.

During the night, many Arabic refugees had climbed over the outside walls of the Hospice and had tried to find shelter in the rooms, the salon, the passages, in short in every tiny spot they could find. A few of the Sisters were busy at the gate warding off even more refugees. A Jewish army patrol arrived in the afternoon for guard duty at the Hospice. Its captain ordered all men to assemble in the dining hall for questioning. Those older than sixty years of age were sent back to their rooms, some others were arrested. Of two hundred and fifty Arab refugees in the Hospice, seventeen were arrested and taken away. In addition to the disturbing noise of the battle on the Plain of Rephaim, we now had to endure the thuds of hobnailed soldiers' boots, which made our stairs and passages shake day and night.

WE HAD TO ENDURE THE THUDS OF HOBNAILED SOLDIERS' BOOTS, WHICH MADE OUR STAIRS AND PASSAGES SHAKE DAY AND NIGHT

A search for weapons in the rooms produced no result. On the other hand, some insisted that objects resembling mines had been found in the garden.

THE 1948 WAR

It was a most unholy Pentecost holiday that dawned on the next morning. We stayed put in our rooms most of the time. In the evening, we heard that Jewish fighting units had penetrated the Old City of Jerusalem. The sound of uninterrupted gunfire from that region seemed to confirm this. The fire even increased in intensity. We heard that a Jordanian fighting force, the Arab Legion (or division) had arrived near Kalandia via Wadi Farra and Nablus to reinforce the advance of the Arabs.

The Haganah guards left the Hospice before dark, because they had no provisions and because the Red Cross emphatically demanded their departure.

On the next day, the Neve Jacov was shut down and on Wednesday we heard the rumble of big gun fire from Nebi Samuel and Neve Jacov coming closer and closer. The Jewish Haganah troops had a five day lead on the Arabs because the Arab Legion was not allowed into the country before the fifteenth. The Arabs encamped in the area surrounding Jerusalem posed no serious danger to the Jews. They did mount many small attacks but were poorly organised and lacked persistence.

Only a few thousand men from the Arab Legion were deployed in the Jerusalem sector. The Egyptian troops, deployed against the Jews for the first time near the Ponds of Solomon on 22 May 1948, also lacked decisive action. They were deployed against Ras Betshalah later on. I found it surprising that the Haganah did not capture the guns of these Egyptian troops by a coup de main. The forty thousand well-organised and well-trained Haganah troops would have posed a serious danger to the Arabic front if they had attacked in bold sorties, but soon bigger and bigger contingents of the [Arab] Legion poured into the Old City, and on 27 May 1948, King Abdullah of Jordan signalled by visiting the Dome of the Rock that he was willing to maintain Arab control against the Jews of at least part of the city. We keenly watched these belligerent events, of course, and collected all reports about them. Almost every day, Haganah men knocked on the gate of the Hospice but the Mother Superior would not grant entry to anyone bearing arms. Our women frequently dared to sneak over to our houses in the colony and were able to salvage many items. On such occasions they observed how all kinds of riffraff, men, women, and children, were hauling from our houses anything that seemed worth their while.

The Haganah troops had strict order to confiscate only weapons, if any, and provisions or bedding. It was, however, inevitable that locked cupboards, chests of drawers or strong boxes were broken into by force and ransacked. Even though our women were frequently threatened and chased away by such plunderers, they still managed to salvage some of our things here and there. Lucky for us and our possessions, the raiders could get no petrol for their vehicles, so their rapacity was somewhat slowed down and kept in check.

THE WOMEN ALWAYS CAME BACK QUITE SHAKEN FROM THEIR TRIPS TO OUR FORMER HOUSES. A DEAD DOG, KILLED BY A BULLET, LAY IN OUR HOUSE AND THE PAPERS AND PHOTOS THROWN ALL OVER THE FLOOR WERE BESMIRCHED WITH HUMAN FAECES. A HORRIBLE STENCH EMANATED FROM AN OVERFLOWING WC

The women always came back quite shaken from their trips to our former houses, of which we had grown so fond. The places formerly known for their order, cleanliness and comfort, now presented a picture of terrible dirt and devastation. A dead dog, killed by a bullet, lay in our house and the papers and photos thrown all over the floor were besmirched with human faeces. A horrible stench emanated from an overflowing WC.

On 3 June 1948, nineteen Padres from the Dormitio arrived at the Hospice. They had sat in their basement during the battle of the Old City, while Israeli Haganah men installed machine guns in the window recesses of the Dormitio, firing them to try to find their range. For the time being, the Fathers were accommodated at the Catholic Sisters', but then directed to the vacant Bäuerle house.

On 8 June 1948, eighty-one year old Mrs Magdalene Wächter died of a heart attack. After some difficulties had been overcome, we were able to bury her in our cemetery.

One of the Fathers of the Dormitio was severely wounded by a shell fragment in the garden of the Hospice on 10 June 1948. He was quickly taken to a sick bay, but died while being operated on. He was buried at St Pierre's.

THE LAST DAYS

THE ARABS HAD NO SKILLED SOLDIERS, ONLY POORLY TRAINED AND MORE THAN SCANTILY ARMED PARTISANS. UNLIKE THE JEWS, THEY HAD NO FACTORIES; THEY HAD TO PROCURE ALL OF THEIR ARMS AND MUNITIONS FROM ABROAD AND SOMEHOW SMUGGLE THEM INTO THE COUNTRY

The neutral powers had negotiated an armistice, which began on the next day, 11 June 1948. That sealed the defeat of the Arabic cause, for only a bold and furious attack by all available forces could perhaps have brought them victory. Their situation was much less favourable than that of the Jews. The Arabs had no skilled soldiers, only poorly trained and more than scantily armed partisans. Unlike the Jews, they had no factories; they had to procure all of their arms and munitions from abroad and somehow smuggle them into the country. They were probably exploited by swindlers from time to time. We could tell the miserable quality of many detonators, because ill-timed fuses and ricochetting missiles had endangered us many times.

As time went on, we began to worry about our food situation. Fruit had not been available for a long time, and all kinds of kitchen herbs were substituted for vegetables. Earlier on, we could buy eggs and chickens from passing Fellah women but such vendors had stayed away of late. There was barely enough milk for our old people. Eventually, a distribution point for provisions was established in a garage near the Hospice. Some things were available there, albeit at high prices. The Hospice kitchen was supplied from there as well. In spite of that, our menus became more and more primitive: sticky rice, low-grade flour, beans and more beans, lentils with a little oil or dripping and dried fruit for dessert. In time, we even became used to the very peculiar taste of the cistern water.

During the truce, our women could salvage some more things from our houses. Eventually, the men went along as well and nailed the front doors shut, but Jewish refugee families had already moved into many of our houses. They were not afraid of further raids, however; it was more important to them to be near the above-mentioned food distribution point.

Back in May, we had already taken precautions with respect to our drinking water. We had observed that Jews were pumping the water from our cisterns. That is why we set up a powerful electric pump to pump the water of all cisterns within reach into the cistern of our house. At one time, surprisingly, we received food parcels from the Old City.

In July, our food rations began to improve. We even received oranges. Life seemed to become more normal in other ways as well. A Greek man opened a primitive grocer's shop in our vicinity.

The Hospice, however, was still situated between the fronts. When the Padres or the Sisters wanted to go to town, they had to use the bus zig-zagging along the only road that led across the Katamon into the Jewish quarter of the city. It was noticeable that there was less gunfire after November 1948. Were both fronts getting tired?

The civil servants of the new state of Israel were friendly and kind. The laws and regulations in force under the Mandate were upheld. Non-Arabs were treated well, so we had nothing to complain about. Lately we received excellent bread as well. The rations were still rather small, but the old were sharing theirs with the young. The only thing we wanted now was to go home. That would only be possible when there were no longer two fronts.

On 1 December 1948, the noise of the battle stopped, after one attack had followed the other for months. Neither party had achieved decisive success. In July, the Jews occupied Malha and Ain Karen. Ramat Rachel near Mar-Elias was captured five times by Egyptian troops and was five times lost.

In the Jewish sector of the Old City of Jerusalem, shortages of water and food were beginning to be felt more acutely. The Jews succeeded, however, in building a road from Hulda to Jerusalem and in breaking the Arabic roadblock near Bab-el-Wad, and since a road from the Jewish settlement of Rehovot to Bab-el-Wad already existed, the way from the coast to Jerusalem was clear. The Arabs, it is true, held their position at Latrun but could not block the road to Jerusalem from there; all they could do was to disrupt the traffic.

We at the Hospice soon had to endure an invasion of mosquitoes. Many cisterns in the German colony had been broken open and partly emptied by pumping the water out. The remaining puddles of water and mud provided a favourable breeding ground for mosquitoes.

An extraordinarily poor populace now began to occupy our houses, as well as others, on the Plain of Rephaim. It began with an invasion of about two thousand Jews from the Old City. They were followed by the Jewish refugees brought into the country from Yemen, Morocco and the Balkans. Even the Arab proletariat living here previously was not as dirty and as discontent as these were. On some days, we could observe an influx of hundreds more. Water carts in the streets dispensed small portions of the precious liquid to the refugees.

HOW WAS THIS TO CONTINUE? THE ARAB VILLAGES ALL AROUND HAD BEEN DESTROYED, THEIR INHABITANTS MURDERED OR DRIVEN AWAY. THE ORANGE PLANTATIONS NEAR JAFFA AND SARONA, WERE NOW COMPLETELY GIVEN OVER TO NEGLECT, NO ONE PICKED THEIR FRUITS

How was this to continue? The Arab villages all around had been destroyed, their inhabitants murdered or driven away. Would they ever be allowed to come back? It was not much better on the plains of the desert. The large orange plantations near Jaffa and Sarona, which had only barely been maintained during the war years, were now completely given over to neglect, no one picked their fruits.

We tried, once, to collect rent from the Jewish refugees living in our houses. They replied that none of them were renting, the houses had been allocated to them by the state of Israel. Some of them had actually been looking for work and had soon found well-paying jobs. After a few days, though, the police prohibited this.

THE END

We lived through long and monotonous months at the Hospice from spring 1948 to the end of 1949. That taught us clearly that our stay in this land, which had become our home, was now more in question than ever before. Our fellow colonists, deported to and interned in Australia, had been released from captivity and allowed to integrate into the Australian economy, while the Cyprus group had dispersed to Germany and Australia. We had maintained lively contact by mail with both groups.

In view of these conditions, we were not surprised when, on 14 November 1949, some of us received notice to leave the country. The reason given was membership in the Nazi Party. We understood that to protest against this expulsion would be useless, so the persons concerned began to pack their things. For the moment, it affected the families of Hermann Imberger and Nikolai Schmidt. A few days later, several others were also implicated.

This was the beginning of a time-consuming task for us. We needed various documents for this emigration. Every relevant office delayed the completion of our applications or relegated us to other offices. It meant we had to wait, wait and wait again, and then deliver longwinded explanations. It took five months to collect all papers and visas. On all these endless errands, it helped that almost all Israeli civil servants spoke German. Some, who were particularly strongly aligned with the Jewish cause, used an interpreter to have our concerns translated into Hebrew, even though they had a good command of German. So much time had been wasted by these energy-consuming visits that we missed the deadline of our departure. We now had to hire a solicitor to help us apply for an extension of time.

A group led by Samuel Faig and Karl Schnerring were able to leave the country in December 1949. They boarded a ship in Haifa and reached Melbourne by a detour via Smyrna, Cyprus, Naples and Genoa on an Italian steamship.

The second group, consisting of eight persons and led by Hermann Imberger, embarked in Haifa on 4 April 1950, and arrived in Melbourne after a similar odyssey.

On 12 April 1950, my wife and I (Nikolai Schmidt) flew from Lydda to Sydney. Four more persons flew to Sydney a little later on, and three women and one man flew to Munich.

The last group to leave the country did so on 20 July 1950. Five persons led by Jakob Imberger boarded a ship in Haifa bound for Australia. Eleven German refugees remained with the Sisters in the Hospice in Jerusalem.

So ended the enterprise of our settlements in Palestine that had begun in such earnest faith and with such high expectations.

Postscript

As I leave our home of many years, I want to convey my last greetings and best wishes to all those who have become aware of the values it has imparted to us. We wistfully remember the land of our birth, the land where we spent carefree childhoods, where we were blest to experience happy times, where the bonds of community have matured and bore such excellent fruit, where we have grown up in freedom with commitment to our beliefs and where, most of all, we would have liked to stay for the rest of our lives.

From this land, which now has acquired an entirely new name and whose inhabitants mistakenly had wanted to blame us for many ills, I call out one more time: here we have learnt to distinguish between the glass and the gold; we have learnt to value community life higher than the mundane, which often is so highly rated by the selfish, and we have learnt to obey and honour God through His voice and His presence, which helped us to serve the people made in His image in pure, active love and to become more fulfilled in the process.

If humanity abandons the Master's uniquely true message – which draws human beings to religion and makes them good, true and fair – deep abasement of individuals and communities will result.

Let us make our inner light shine, so that we may be directed on to the right path and that peace and happiness will grow.

Let us take leave, then, of this episode of religious history and let us rest assured in the hope that it has not been in vain.
May God grant it. -Nikolai Schmidt, 11 April 1950.

115. Some of the last Templers in Jerusalem, April 1948
L - R, top row: *Samuel Faig, Jakob Imberger, Nikolai Schmidt (President of the Temple Society)*
2nd row: *Karl Schnerring, Mathilde Weigold, Dora Faig, Luise Schnerring, Rosa Imberger, Babette Schmidt, Charlie Schnerring, Heinrich Jung*
3rd row: *Agathe Lange, unknown , Karoline Weeber, Paula Paulus, Repha Franz, Sophie Schanz*
Front row: *Lydia Weller, Pauline Ruff, Friedrich Klink*

PART TWO

Other Perspectives

Paul Sauer (1931-)

The loss of the agricultural settlements

The bloody confrontations between Arabs and Jews continued to escalate

By early 1948, the majority of the Templers interned in Palestine were no longer under any illusions about remaining in Palestine. The bloody confrontations between Arabs and Jews continued to escalate. On 27 February of that year, Jakob Weiss wrote from Wilhelma to his cousin Jon Hoffmann in Stuttgart: "I am surprised that there are still some who are 'clinging' to Palestine ... You say that, in view of the troubles in Palestine, you are very grateful for N(ikolai) Sch(midt)'s reassuring letter. I really cannot imagine what N. Sch. may have written that reassured you. One cannot but shake one's head. Anyone who is at all realistic knows that the barbed wire is no better than a line drawn with chalk. The Jewish guards, who were initially posted there to prevent us from escaping and were later retained for our protection, provided at least symbolic protection and moral support; we were under Jewish protection, we were entrusted to Jews. That was

(Left) 116. Guards in Waldheim 1948

all. Now, fearing the Arabs, these Jewish guards have asked to be relieved of this duty and have been replaced by a handful of Arabs. Despite their good intentions, they are unable to protect us. In fact, not one person in this country is fully protected, not even the H(igh) C(ommissioner). We may well say, we are alive by the grace of God ..." Jakob Weiss deplored that the Templers had not, from the outset, i.e. since the end of the Second World War, handed 'all their affairs' to the Australian Government, i.e. that they had not decided in favour of emigration and subsequent settlement in Australia and had not entrusted the handling of their financial affairs in Palestine to the Australian authorities. "At least we would have been better off and would now be safely in Australia, instead of remaining in this inferno which blazes higher each day and perhaps will also consume us in the end!" Weiss expressed his fears of what might happen after 15 May 1948, when the British Mandate over Palestine was to end. He feared that chaos and anarchy would break out among the people of the Holy Land.

Nikolai Schmidt continued to warn against abandoning Palestine lightly. On 8 March 1948, he expressed the following view in a letter to friends in Australia and Germany:

"It is quite impossible for everyone to leave. There are too many old and infirm amongst the remaining members of the Society: 145 people over 60 years, which is half of the local group. Some are totally bedridden. This group needs care as well as money. Australia has no attraction for some people who have only distant relatives there; they would be a burden, rather than a support, to those making a new start ..." Even Schmidt, however, could no longer close his eyes to the fact that the Templers no longer had a future in Palestine, whereas Australia offered them a real chance to rebuild their community.

The Mandatory Government, as only now became apparent, had long ago revised its decision of November 1946 to deport the internees to Germany. It now asked the Templers to choose between Australia, Kenya, UK, Germany or Palestine for their resettlement, which was to be financed with their own resources. Their properties continued to be administered by the Public Custodian, but could be sold upon obtaining a special permit. The Government left the internees in no doubt that they had to depart by 15 May 1948, if they wished to avail themselves of British assistance, which was essential for their safety. The matter was most urgent.

On 11 March 1948, Nikolai Schmidt sent a cable to the representatives of the Temple Society in Australia, stating that 90% of the internees intended to go to Australia, but in view of the lack of shipping berths and the still outstanding entry permits, they would accept a temporary stay in Egypt. Schmidt requested that a binding undertaking be obtained from the Australian Government immediately to grant the internees entry. He had decided to stay in Palestine for the time being "... the most important reason being, I think, that I cannot flee the country, even if it were to my advantage. I have worked here for too long and have experienced too much to be frightened off by shootings and bombs. No, the place, the Holy Land, has never rated very highly with me; it is unholier than any other place, because there is nothing here but hypocrisy and other ways of defrauding God. God who

... does not want to be worshipped but wants people to live their lives in a manner according to His will, and who abandons everyone who does not seek Him ..." Schmidt hoped that by remaining in Palestine he would be in a better position to settle matters in a way that would still benefit the Society.

March and the first half of April 1948 passed in agonising uncertainty for the internees. They did not yet know whether Australia, the land of the future, would open its doors to them before the rapidly approaching end to the British Mandate. Suddenly, however, on 17 April 1948, brutal violence brought things to a head. At four o'clock in the morning of that day, the inhabitants of Waldheim were abruptly awakened from their sleep. Shots were fired from all directions into the small village, which was guarded by a British sergeant, two British policemen and six Arab auxiliary police, but was practically unprotected against armed raids. Soldiers of the Jewish Secret Army, the Haganah, forced their way into the houses and searched for weapons. 65-year-old Katharina Deininger, who was already in the shed milking the cows and tried to shut the door during a brief pause in the firing, was severely wounded in the head by a shot which had evidently been aimed at her. Her daughter Hedwig and her future son-in-law, Kurt P. Seidler, found her lying in a pool of blood and took her to the basement.

In the kitchen of the Staib house, members of the Haganah shot dead 63-year-old Karl Aimann and his 42-year-old wife Regina in front of their children Gisela, Helmut and Traugott, whose ages ranged from three to ten years. Aimann, a very quiet, deeply religious and apolitical man, had most certainly not offered resistance to the intruders. Like the other inhabitants of Waldheim, he did not possess any weapons. It appears that the Jewish killers had made a fatal mistake. The Staib property was located near the barbed wire fence, close to the so-called Betlehem Gate. From this gate, one of the Arab or British guards had presumably fired a few warning shots at the beginning of the raid. Irritated by this, the Jews had assumed that the shots had been fired from inside the Staib house. They had quickly forced entry into the building and killed the Aimann couple without mercy.

Hulda Stoll, an unmarried elderly woman, who lived in the same house and, alarmed by the shots, had rushed into the kitchen, escaped a similar fate only through her resolute manner. After the heavily armed Jewish soldiers had occupied the village, the residents were driven from their houses to the community dairy and there locked into two rooms, men and women separately. Seidler managed to draw the attention of the Haganah unit's leader to the seriously wounded Katharina Deininger, and he arranged for her to be taken to the hospital in Nazareth. After several hours of detention in the dairy, the prisoners were escorted to the Deininger family's barn. There they were forced to listen to a speech by the Haganah unit's leader, who pointed out to them the heinous crimes the Germans had committed against the Jews, and then declared that all the settlers were Nazis. He even went so far as to make the grotesque claim that in one of the houses in the settlement soap had been found marked 'made from Jewish fat'. He further stated that his people would have found it easy to shoot all of them dead; the Jews, however, were more civilised than the Germans and, therefore, they would release them. Six of the younger men were singled out and taken to the upper storey of the Deininger house by two armed men. There they were forced to undress completely in order to be given a thorough body search. The armpits were subjected to a particularly careful scrutiny. Also the heels and soles of their shoes were examined closely. The Haganah were probably trying to trace members of the SS, thought to have gone into hiding in Waldheim.

During the body searches, in which each one in turn was ordered into an adjacent room, they were again subjected to the most violent reproaches for the terrible atrocities committed by the Germans, as Kurt Seidler, one of the young men involved, later told. Subsequently, the six men were returned to the other prisoners, who were obviously relieved that those subjected to the 'inspection' had got off so lightly. They had feared for the lives of the six men, who also had naturally expected the worst. Two young camp inmates, one a Romanian, were ordered to dig two shallow graves in the Waldheim cemetery where, in the presence of only the closest relatives, the bodies of the Aimann couple were buried, wrapped in sheets. At night, all the men were locked into the hut, which previously had been reserved for the Arab guards. The women and children remained in the dairy. The Jewish soldiers fetched blankets and bedding for them from the houses.

The next morning, a British army unit arrived in Waldheim by truck. The British had already been informed of the raid on Waldheim on 17 April by the Camp Commandant of Betlehem, who had gone to Haifa via Nazareth by motorbike, as telephone messages could not be sent because the lines to the German settlements were cut. The inhabitants of Waldheim were allowed twenty minutes to enter their houses and collect their most essential belongings. They found their houses in wild disarray, with everything having been rummaged through. Most valuables, as well as money had disappeared; some clothes and linen had also been stolen. Members of the Haganah searched the suitcases, bundles and other baggage, which the people of Waldheim brought to the trucks, and money, documents, official papers and various books were seized. The British ignored these encroachments; they allowed the Jewish soldiers a great deal of latitude. The British took the former internees to the army camp of 'Sidney Smith Barracks' at Acre. They treated them very kindly, provided them with toothbrushes, razors and other items of daily use that were missing, and even invited them to visit cinema screenings. After a two-day stay in the wooden huts of the military camp, they were taken to the port of Haifa, where they boarded the vessel *Empire Comfort.*

The settlers of Betlehem were more fortunate than those of Waldheim. For days, they had been expecting the occupation of their village by the Haganah – a wide variety of rumours circulated – and, as a precautionary measure, they had already packed. Then, in the early hours of 17 April, when they heard heavy machine-gun fire from the direction of Waldheim, they hastily loaded their horse-drawn carriages and fled to Saffuriyeh near Nazareth. The Haganah found an almost deserted settlement (three settlers had stayed behind). The British accommodated the inhabitants of Betlehem in the 'Sidney Smith Barracks' as well.

The raid on Waldheim was the signal for the British to complete the evacuation of the perimeter settlements immediately and to take the internees to safety. Convoys of trucks escorted by armoured vehicles transported the internees from Wilhelma, as they had previously done at Waldheim. Apart from a group of around 50 – led by Nikolai Schmidt and Hermann Imberger, they were mainly elderly and infirm people who had been granted permission to stay in the country for the time being and found refuge in the Jerusalem Templer settlement – the former inmates of the Wilhelma camp were taken to Jaffa by a roundabout route on 20 April 1948. The abovementioned *Empire Comfort*, a converted corvette, under the protection of a British warship, awaited them there. The ship set course for Haifa. On the morning of 21 April, it berthed in the port near the German settlement, where the internees from Waldheim and Betlehem were to embark. Chaos reigned in Haifa. There was constant shooting. Bullets whizzed over the ship. Some of the settlers, especially many of those from Waldheim, were frightened and expected trouble. Everyone was relieved when the ship finally left port around 5pm. Not long afterwards, Jewish forces took the port. In the morning of 22 April, after an uncomfortable, stormy passage, the *Empire Comfort* dropped anchor in the port of Famagusta, on the island of Cyprus. Six men had stayed behind in Wilhelma under the direction of Gottlob Löbert. They were entrusted with the sale of the remaining cattle of around 300 head and, once having completed that task, were to give all their attention to arranging the transportation of the large items of luggage which had been left behind (each adult had been allowed 40kg of hand luggage and each child 25kg). Through the good offices of the District Commissioner, they followed the others to Cyprus by air a few days later.

From *The Holy Land called (1991)*

117. Entering the port of Famagusta

Danny Goldman (1945-)

Waldheim, April 1948

The warriors' silence, and the courage of frankness

This document was made possible through the cooperation and history-consciousness of many good people in Israel and abroad, among them: Dov Meyer, Aryeh Dressler, Nogah Binstock, Shirley Reuveni of the IDF Archive, "Benya" Zarchi, Meir Amit, Kobi Fleischmann, Shraga Peled of the Haganah Archive, Batya Leshem of the CZA, Judith Ivri. Data donors with Templer ties from abroad: Horst Blaich, Martin Higgins

This paper is dedicated to the courage of honesty and frankness of those fighting men of Golani, who took a step forward

Katharina Deininger, 65, was the only person awake in the early hours before dawn, April 17, 1948. She was humming quietly her favorite tune while milking the cows in the dusky cowshed, next to her home.

The rest of the people were asleep, in the quiet and bashful village of Waldheim, on the green hills overlooking the Valley of Jezreel.

No one saw the blurry silhouettes of the armed *Haganah* troops stealing their way into the village through the woods; they were equipped with automatic rifles and followed by machine gun-mounted armored trucks; they were a part of the *Golani* Infantry Regiment, troopers in the *Dror* and *Nafat Levi* Battalions.

The peaceful community of Waldheim was about to be changed forever.

Waldheim was one of seven thriving German communities, founded by *Die Tempelgesellschaft** in Palestine, a group of Germans originating in the region of Württemberg; they migrated to Palestine in order to fulfill and implement their Christian religious beliefs, and to create an economic and social environment for themselves for a better life, spiritually and economically.

Led by Christoph Hoffmann and Georg David Hardegg, they founded their first colony in Haifa, 1869; Waldheim was an extension of the Haifa colony, which was doing very well, but had exhausted all its agricultural land reserves. In 1906 and 1907, upon the realization that no more expansion was possible in Haifa, the Haifa settlers purchased land on the northern

* Waldheim was founded by a group that had left the *Tempelgesellschaft* [PH]

edge on the Jezreel Valley. Two communities were born: Betlehem (not to be confused with the historic Bethlehem), and Waldheim. Betlehem was populated with Templers, and Waldheim with *Kirchlers*, a group that had separated from the main Templer body under the leadership of Georg David Hardegg (former associate of Hoffmann), in the 1870s. Although the two groups held different religious views, there was an on-going affiliation between them, including marriages and business partnerships.

The late 1940s found the Holy Land in turmoil; WWII was over; the British Mandate in Palestine was approaching its end, the Palestinians and the

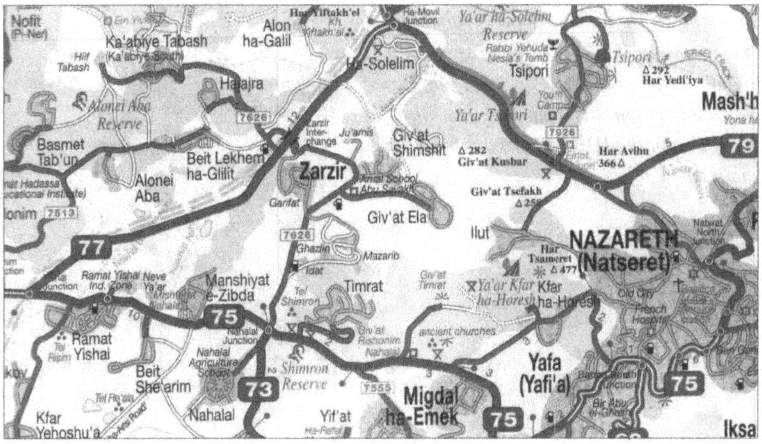

118. Recent map of Waldheim – Betlehem region. Source: Belinski, Elena (Cartographic Editor), 2007. Israel Road Atlas, Tel Aviv: Mapa Publishers

Jews engaged in hostilities that broke out following the November 1947 UN resolution on an independent Jewish State along with a neighboring Palestinian State. Both parties were trying to establish facts on the ground, so that when the British would finally leave, each group would have scored the most, in terms of control of lands, strategic points, such as British strongholds and military camps, highways and other infrastructure.

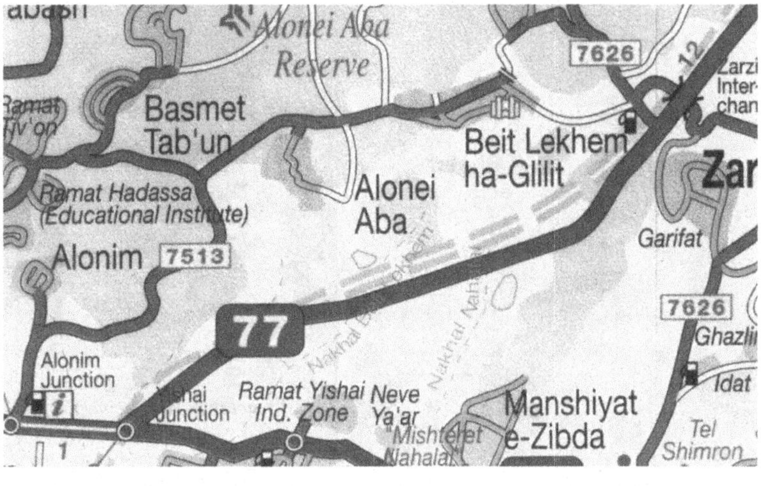

119. Road 77 goes to Tiberias, road 75 goes to Nazareth, about 10km east of Betlehem (as the crow flies). The settlements of Waldheim and Betlehem were renamed Alonei Aba and Beit Lekhem Ha-Glilit. The location of Nazareth is provided for ease of orientation. The access road (7513), leading into the settlement, was paved by the Templers

This was the situation in April 1948, when British forces were loosely controlling various areas in Palestine, Waldheim included. The IDF [Israel Defense Force] was not yet in existence as such; it existed as an 'army yet to be formed', actually an emerging militia, which was already structured in an army-like organization, the *Haganah*. The main aim of the *Haganah* at this point was 'Plan D', established on 10.3.1948, meaning "[…] taking over the territories of the Jewish State, and defending its borders." The Golani brigade was designated as part of the Plan.[2]

120. Waldheim, general view, 1940s
This print was found along with others by an unknown Haganah trooper, probably during the April 17 (1948) operation, and found its way to the IDF Archive. The Templer photographer is unknown. The other images from the IDF Archive are from the same batch

In the book edited by **Benjamin Etzioni**, published in 1959 by the official IDF publishing house *Ma'arachot*, there is a short passage concerning the taking over of Waldheim and Betlehem:

121. A tractor in Waldheim. Probably one of the first in Palestine. Source: IDF Archive

[...] The status of Waldheim and Betlehem, the two German colonies situated to the north of the Western Valley, was still unclear, since they were under British control. But the assistance that these villages provided the Arabs during the days of the 'Events' was known, and their existence was, therefore, a high risk 3. From the military standpoint, there were no particular problems in taking them; it demanded, however, substantial daring, taking into account possible confrontation with the British military and police. But the operation did succeed, and the two colonies were taken by the combatants of the 'Dror' [the '14th' Battalion] and 'Nafat Levi' battalions on 17.4.48, the German inhabitants were evacuated under British custody to Haifa and from there abroad [my translation D.G.].

This concludes the official documentation on the moves of the *Golani* brigade on the night between 16 and 17 April. There is no mention of the killing of two Germans on that morning: Karl and Regina Aimann.

IT WAS ABOUT 4:00 WHEN KATHARINA DEININGER, IN THE DUSKY COWSHED, THOUGHT SHE HEARD SHOTS OUTSIDE. A BULLET HIT HER IN THE HEAD, KNOCKING HER DOWN TO THE SHED'S FLOOR, UNCONSCIOUS. A POOL OF BLOOD WAS RAPIDLY FORMING, WETTING RED HER SILVER HAIR

It was about 4:00 when Katharina Deininger, in the dusky cowshed, thought she heard shots outside. She rose hastily from her milking stool, which fell aside as she rushed to the shed's gate, attempting to close it. She was slow, too slow. A bullet hit her in the head, knocking her down to the shed's floor, unconscious. A pool of blood was rapidly forming, wetting red her silver hair.

By then the entire village was in commotion. Shots were fired by the raiders in all directions with the automatic rifles, echoing and reverberating in the nearby forests. The small British force securing the village was helpless.[4] They were outnumbered by the raiders, and soon offered no resistance. It was already silverfish gray daylight.

According to eye-witness reports and personal accounts from Waldheim and Betlehem in the Templer archives in Stuttgart and Melbourne, and related in Paul Sauer's book, this was the point of "the fatal mistake". When the shooting started, some of the British guards fired from a position next to the house of the Staib family, where the Aimann couple and their 3 children had taken refuge. The house was spotted as a target, and later stormed by the Jewish raiders. They found the Aimanns hiding in the house, and shot the couple, "in front of the children".

122. The Deininger house, Waldheim, unknown date. Image courtesy of Horst Blaich, Albert Blaich Family Archive, Melbourne

123. The Staib house in the 1950s, by courtesy of Sam Staib, Tübingen, Germany. The house in Waldheim still exists, as do most of the other houses

Bruno Weinmann, an Australian citizen of German descent, and related to the Aimann family, wrote a report about the affair and interviewed (June 2006) one of the three children of the Aimanns, Traugott, who was about ten years old when the incident took place. Traugott remembers the event very vividly. The following provides a first-hand eye-witness testimony as to what actually happened in the Staib house. In the early hours of the morning, he was awakened by sounds of gunfire from outside the house and located somewhere near the perimeter wire of the settlement. He had been sleeping with his younger siblings, Helmut and Gisela, in their bedroom that was connected via a door to the front room that was in turn connected to the exterior by another door.

He entered the front room and was immediately ordered by his father to take a gramophone record from the wind-up record player and to dump it in the toilet because it bore the grooves of the German national anthem of Nazi era with the words *Deutschland über alles* and he understood that his father did not want Jewish raiders to find that in their house, even though it was the property of the absentee owners of the house. He returned from the toilet to the front room to join his parents and siblings and from here his father ordered the children into their adjoining bedroom.

He followed both siblings into the bedroom but although they both fully entered that room, he did not and reached only the front room's edge of the bedroom door and heard loud knocking on the door that opened onto the street, and stopped short of entering the bedroom.

He saw his parents approach the door side by side to open it and saw his father open it widely. He immediately heard many gunshots that must have come from the two gun-bearing men who he saw standing side by side outside very near the opening and opposite his parents.

He saw his parents drop in their tracks and fall backwards, deeper into the room; their feet little more than the door's swing width from the doorstep. There was much blood on the floor and he could see no bullet holes in the bodies because the clothing obscured the puncture wounds. He assumed that his father did not die immediately because he moaned, but thought that his mother died immediately because there was no sound or movement from her.

Traugott noticed both gunmen immediately enter the room while shouting loudly, incomprehensively and perhaps in a language he did not understand. He noticed that now an upstairs internee resident,[5] middle-aged Hulda Stoll, had entered the room via the stairs and in a loud and intimidating voice addressed the gunmen. He noticed that her outburst did not draw any gunfire on to herself.

STOLL ORDERED HIM TO BRING HIS FATHER WHO LAY MOANING AND WAS STILL ALIVE A DRINK, BUT THE GUNMEN WOULD NOT LET HIM FETCH IT. HE AND THE OTHERS WERE HERDED AWAY FROM THE GUNSHOT VICTIMS' BODIES UNTIL ALL WERE ESCORTED FROM THE ROOM

Stoll ordered him to bring his father who lay moaning and was still alive a drink, but the gunmen would not let him fetch it. He and the others, now prisoners in the room, were immediately herded away from the gunshot victims' bodies until all were escorted from the room. During that interval, the gunmen refused to apply medical help to his moaning father and nothing came of Stoll's assertive plea, which he heard, to the gunmen to get medical help for his father.

He and the other three prisoners in the room were ordered by the two gunmen to leave the room whilst avoiding the bodies lying on the floor and they escorted them out of the still open door past which the bullets had sped. He noticed that on reaching the street there was more Jewish soldiery to escort them to a place where they would hold prisoners.[6]

The suffering and humiliation of the German settlers was far from over on that miserable day. Once the takeover was complete, an officer of the raiding force assembled the Germans in the community dairy,[7] where they were locked up for some hours; one of the settlers managed to persuade the Jewish commander to send the wounded Katharina Deininger to a hospital in nearby Nazareth. The settlers were then moved to another spot, a barn, where they had to listen to a long speech, declaring that (according to Sauer) "[...] all settlers were Nazis." Some of the younger men were subjected to a body search, probably aimed at locating possible SS tattoos, but none was found.

The bodies of the Aimanns were buried the same day in the Waldheim cemetery, wrapped in sheets, in the presence of just the closest relatives.

124. Waldheim dairy (1940s), courtesy of IDF Archive

125. Waldheim (Alonei Aba) dairy (2000) Image by D.G. The structure is currently used as a minimarket and small winery. Part of the cooling tower on top is still visible

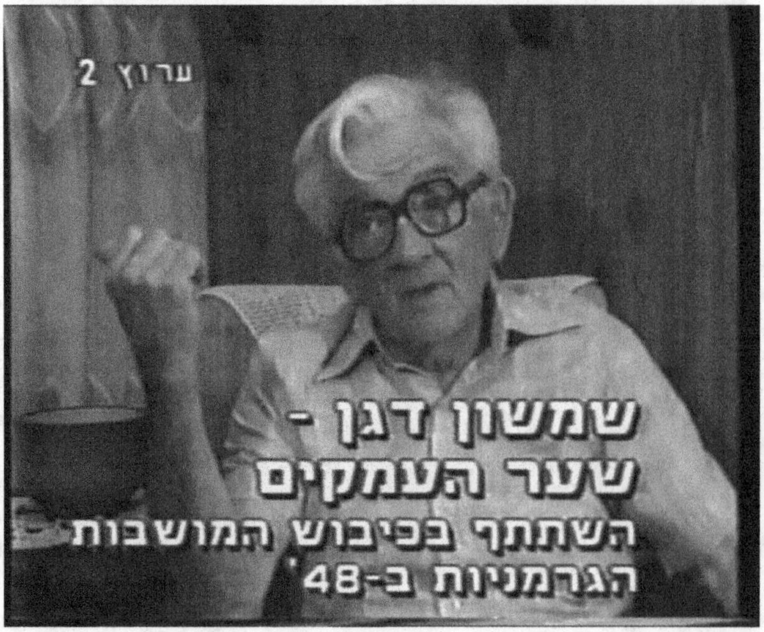

126. Simshon Dagan, Kibbutz member, Sha'ar Ha'amakim Still image from Binstock documentary. Dagan: "[...] We lost Aryeh Givati, killed by a land mine on the IPC road. The mine was prepared or assisted by Waldheim people [...] they [?] told me: make a speech to the Germans, tell them that we know exactly who they are, and we are not like them hiding behind someone's orders. But because we were instructed by the [Jewish] Agency not to hurt you, we are letting you go"

THE NEXT MORNING THE GERMAN SETTLERS WERE EVACUATED BY THE BRITISH MILITARY. FRIEDRICH KATZ, THEN MAYOR OF WALDHEIM, RECALLS IN HIS TESTIMONY IN WEINMANN'S REPORT WHAT FOLLOWED

The next morning the German settlers were evacuated by the British military. Friedrich Katz, the then Mayor of Waldheim, recalls in his testimony in Weinmann's report what followed:

At about 8 o'clock in the morning of April 17, 1948 the internees were allowed to re-enter their houses and found everything in great disorder and all their valuables and good clothes and personal belongings gone. They were given 20 minutes to pack what was left of their belongings and take what they could carry in their hands. Then everybody was ordered to an assembly point where all their bags and bundles were searched again and money, handwritings, documents and several books were taken out of them. All the internees were subjected to a body-search. One of the Haganah officers then made a political speech in German and said, amongst others, insulting things about the Germans. Six young Germans were picked out by another officer and marched off under armed guard. They were brought to a room from where one was taken in to the office to another room and thoroughly searched, asked questions, made to undress to the waist and scrutinized for certain signs.

At about 11 o'clock the internees were taken over by the British Army and brought in army lorries together with their luggage, under escort to the military camp 'Sidney Smith Barracks' near Acre. They were kept there by the army for 2 days and taken by the British Army, on 21 April 1948 in the morning to the Haifa harbour and taken on board the ship 'Empire Comfort'. The ship sailed about 5 o'clock in the afternoon and reached Famagusta (Cyprus) in the morning of April 22, 1948. The internees were then brought in army lorries to the holiday camp 'Golden Sands' near Famagusta where they were accommodated in sand dunes under tents.[8]

TILBURY WAS ALSO APPREHENDED BY THE GOLANI RAIDING FORCE, BUT WAS ABLE TO COMMUNICATE WITH THE RAIDERS, ONCE THE FIRING DIED OUT.

A complementing account of the event is provided by Alan Tilbury. Tilbury was also apprehended by the Golani raiding force, but was able to communicate with the raiders, once the firing died out (this is on 18 April, morning hours):

Having, with my two British Constables been confined for some time in the cold store at the creamery [dairy], *we were taken outside and moved to an olive grove, when in due course some commotion became apparent on the road outside the Commandant's office. I was eventually taken up there, where I saw what appeared to be two British Staghound armoured cars, with the crews sunning themselves on the tops of their vehicles, eating oranges and chatting to members of the occupying force. I was taken to a man dressed as a British army officer, and initially assumed that he was a member of the Haganah impersonating one.*

He in turn was by no means sure who I was in my Palestine Police uniform. After some conversation it appeared that he really was a British army officer, who had received a radio message from Haifa HQ, telling him to go to Waldheim (which he believed to be a Jewish kibbutz) and (or so he thought) to recover a missing British army vehicle! When he arrived at the main entrance to Waldheim he was initially denied entry but eventually allowed in. His friendly untroubled approaches to the occupiers, and the relaxed

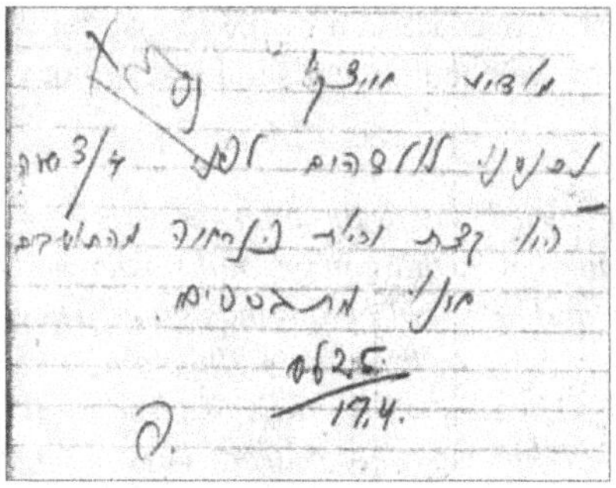

127. *First document. Courtesy of IDF Archive, no reference*

behaviour of the Staghound crews, must have at first seemed odd to those who had been attacking the place only that morning!

I went back to Haifa with the Staghounds to report the situation, and the following day returned to Waldheim with the British Army convoy sent to evacuate the inhabitants, as recorded in Sauer.[9]

How is it, that this highly charged affair is not accounted for in the formal sources of Israel's history? This is, by any standard, a severe incident; two foreign nationals, non-combatants, are being killed by semi-official militia. Someone has to be able to explain this; Israelis are known for their 'history consciousness', documenting and filing everything there is to document and file, almost compulsively. Is there a 'conspiracy of silence' here, an intended cover-up, something to 'sweep under the carpet'? I have made up my mind to do a field search, and to pursue this issue further.

In the IDF Archive, historical data is open to anyone, and there is no secrecy classification on materials from that period. The documents of the 1948 war are digitized, and the monitor was soon blinking with these documents, which, to my surprise, showed no information on the Aimann killings.

The first document is a note, probably a radio or field telephone message, dated 17 April at 06:25.

Relayed by Itzik: *We have entered Waldheim 45 minutes ago. There were some shots fired, probably by the inhabitants. We are establishing a foothold.*

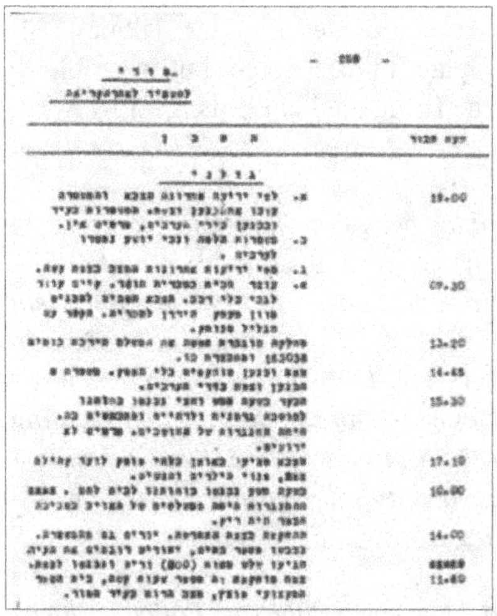

128. *Second document. Courtesy IDF Archive, reference number 464/54/2. The document says that at 09:00 "our forces" entered Betlehem and found it empty. It goes on to describe "resistance from enemy strongholds in the vicinity"*

The second document is a page from the operations log of the Golani Brigade. The date on the document is April 16, which is probably a mistake. The page is marked "Secret, destroy after reading", probably meaning to destroy copies of the original page. Here the information is even shorter. The message was received at 15:30, and contains only few lines:

This morning at five-thirty our forces entered the German colony Waldheim, and are establishing a foothold. There was resistance by the inhabitants. Details are unknown.

The third document, and maybe the most interesting one, is a record of a communication from a commander in *Carmeli*, another Brigade of the *HISH*, (abbreviation for 'Field Army'), to a commander in Golani. It is dated April 17, 10:00, and says:

A telephone call from Haifa. To: Golani, From: Carmeli. In connection with the seizure of Waldheim by your men, the Haifa Police is waiting for instructions from its HQ. The Army moved for the location, not in order to act, but in order to find out.

Some interpretation is required: the "police" and "army" referred to are the British police and army. The *Carmeli* commander is actually calming down the *Golani* commander that the British police is somewhat con-

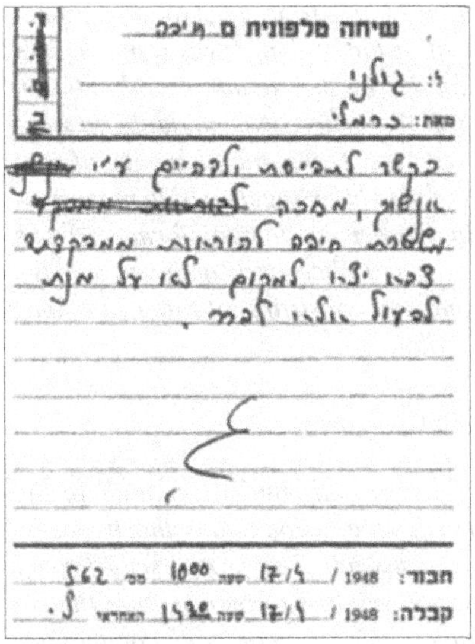

129. *Third document. Courtesy of IDF Archive, reference number 128/51/37*

fused, "waiting for instructions", and that the Golani commander need not be alarmed by the British military moves, these are investigative measures only. As related by Sauer and Tilbury (above), when the British Army arrived at Waldheim, already taken by Golani, all they did was evacuate the Germans to Haifa the next day.

I called Meir Amit, trying my luck to set up an interview to find out first hand from the person who actually commanded the operation. Amit was very cooperative and friendly, but reserved. "Why would you want to know about the military aspects of the [taking over of the] colonies, your research deals with architecture?" he asked, as an experienced Intelligence person. I said, "You are right, it is a little removed from architecture. But the point is that from time to time while doing the research, I come across such interesting historic episodes, which have a right to exist as such, and there is a need to shed light on these; I understand that you were directly involved in the operation (I mentioned the 2 Germans killed) and you may be among the few that can illuminate this affair. There is very little record of this affair." We set the interview for a week later in his office.

130. *General Amit and Yigael Yadin, "1970s"*
Source: Israel National Photo Collection. Amit is considered one of the most talented generals in IDF, having a rich history of combat experience, and later in high command positions. In the 1950s he became head of Training Command, followed as head of Operations Section, managed the 1956 war, promoted to head of Central Command, and in 1961 head of Military Intelligence. In 1963 he left the military to take the position of head of Mossad, and in 1968 retired to civil service. Served as Minister of Transportation and, at time of writing, is in private business. Yigael Yadin was the Chief of Staff during the 1948 war

131. Kibbutz Alonim, November 2000. Image by DG

Amit: *I can contribute to your report all I know from a personal perspective. In the first place, I was a resident of the region. I was a member of Alonim from 1939. I arrived at Alonim during the 'seam' period between the end of the 'Events' and the start of WWII. There was no doubt on what side the Germans were. They sided with the Arabs, for a number of reasons. In addition, there was a branch of the Hitler Jugend youth movement in Waldheim, formally. I was active in the security domain, formally I was involved with the JSP, the Jewish Settlement Police, and commander of the regional 'Mobile Guard', I had a company consisting of three platoons, from Alonim, Kfar-Yehoshua, and Nahalal.*

Question: Was this a British organization?

Amit: *No, this was the Haganah. I was formally the commander of the 'Mobile Guard', which was under British supervision and authority, or by British 'eye-shutting', call it any way you want. This was a semi-formal body. The 'Mobile Guard' platoon was composed of people from the region settlements. Simultaneously, I functioned as a company commander in the Haganah, under the surface.*

Question: This was in 1939?

Amit: *Starting in 39, through the 40s. There was constant tension between the Arabs of that region and us. And there were quarrels. They were uprooting our trees, stealing our livestock, all sorts of things. It even reached a point where they tried to attack the* [Alonim] *settlement, and here we have already acted in the format of 'getting out of the fence', which started then, not only measures of defense, but also retaliation; all in all we managed to have the situation under control. The Germans were constantly on their* [the Arab] *side.*

Question: What were the implications of this? How was this expressed?

Amit: *I'll tell you the implications. They provided them with shelter, an administrative backup, but the Germans themselves were not active. They provided a solid base behind the scenes; call it any thing you want. But: during the war years 1942-1943* [1939-1948 PH] *the British put the Germans in detention camps. Some Germans were even shipped to Australia. This situation lasted until the end of the war, 1945-1946* [1948 PH]. *By the end of 1947, when the UN acknowledged a Jewish State, the intensity of the Arab aggression had increased. In this period, between November 1947 and May 1948, there was a struggle for the control of the roads [...] in March 1948 there was an attempt by the Kaouggi*[11] *militia to attack the settlement of Mishmar-Ha'emek, in order to gain an open axis between Genin and Haifa. My company was involved in the fighting.*

In the same period, right after the fight over Mishmar-Ha'emek, Waldheim and Betlehem were perceived as unreliable, since there was there a population, a youth movement, which was affiliated with the Germans; the Moufti [spiritual leader] *of Jerusalem had previously established contacts with Germany, so it was decided to take over these colonies. This was by late March 1948. I was assigned as a company commander to take these*

132. Nahalal police station, November 2000. Image by DG

two colonies. We knew that the Arabs in Tab'oun were cooperating with the Germans, the British were, I would say, neutral in respect to us, and we all knew that they were about to leave Palestine on May 15. They were about to evacuate the Nahalal police station, not far from there; the British would always create a situation in which that facility is handed over to the Arabs and not to us. Therefore we had an interest that the German colonies be taken, because they were close to the main axis which leads to the Nahalal Police.

Question: Was the interest to take Waldheim and Betlehem connected to the next interest to take the Nahalal Police?

Amit: *To create a situation that, when the British leave, we would have quick access to the police. The tendency of the British was in general in favor of the Arabs. Police stations which they evacuated towards May 1948, were evacuated in such a way that the Arabs could take them before we could.*[12]

The taking over was relatively easy. I had a company composed of three platoons: from Nahalal, from Alonim, and from Kfar-Yehoshua and Sde Ya'akov [...] There was no German resistance. There were a few Arabs that were shooting; the Germans, in my opinion, did not. But there were two things, which I would term 'problematic', from our point of view, in spite of the fact that we knew that the colonies were a hornets' nest. In Waldheim, two men from the Nahalal platoon entered a house; they shouted to open the door, the people in the house opened, or did not open the door, I do not know. I do not know whether they kicked the door open; inside there were a man and a woman. Before they could even say "good morning", they shot them.

Question: You mean, it is not clear exactly what the reason was for shooting the Germans?

Amit: *Not clear, and also following an investigation, still not clear. Their version was that the Germans made "suspicious moves". But my personal opinion is that in the heat of breaking in, this by the way was on the second floor, they went up the stairs. Before they asked, before they warned, before they searched, before there was any resistance, they shot. This was one 'problematic phenomenon'. They were reprimanded and received a treatment* [punishment] *pertaining to this matter.*[13]

A second 'problematic phenomenon', which was repeated in Waldheim and Betlehem, was the matter of looting, mainly of tools. Ploughs, disks, tractors, anything they could lay their hands on, they took away home.

Question: In the report following the operation, which you wrote, and filed at the IDF Archive…

Amit: *Please send me a copy of that report...*

Question: Gladly. There you write that you are disturbed by the subject of looting…

Amit: *I was deeply disturbed, and regarded this as a failure, a matter that is expressive of much more than the actual taking. I can give you an example from another situation; later I was asked to dispatch a platoon to take over Arab-A-Zbeich, next to Segera. This was a small Bedouin village on a hill. The platoon took it, started to indulge in looting, and paid no attention to what was going on. The Bedouins made a counter attack and drove them away. I say we have not learned the lesson from Waldheim and Betlehem, and this deeply annoyed me, this matter [...] this was the last time. Under my command, throughout the War of Independence* [1948 War], *and even after that, this subject of looting, of Maher Shalal Hash Baz*[14]*, would not exist with my men any more. I have reacted to this with severity. I am not talking only about the moral issue. The practical – operative side was being impeded. We have learned the lesson for both cases.*

Bear in mind one more thing: those who participated in the operation were real partisans. The company was not homogeneous. The controlling of the company was difficult, because it was not homogeneous, and the rural, local affiliation overrode the regional. On the other hand they were outstanding men, during the entire war our company was considered the best in Golani [...] but composed of individualistic persons, and somewhat, I would say, undisciplined, as in the cases of looting.

Question: On the night between 16.4 and 17.4 you were the company's commander. Were you present on premises?

Amit: *We were located somewhere below Basmet Tab'oun* [a nearby village], *from there we split* [into two platoons]. *I was there, and later joined the forces. Immediately following the events in Waldheim, I went there. Immediately.*

Question: The morning after?

Amit: *No, already that night. I was present in all locations. I had very good platoon commanders. I fully backed them up, except for these two points, which were deviant, I would say.*

Question: I was told by Dressler from Betlehem that there were two brothers from Nahalal. Zarchi. One was killed later...

Amit: *Chummi, Nachum Zarchi. He was killed later, and the older brother... yes, both were...*

Question: Could it be that one of them was the one that...

Amit: *Chummi. He was killed when we descended to the Negev. He was an outstanding person, Chummi. A gifted person.*

Question: Dressler told me that Chummi's brother, Benjamin, received from Chummi the German flag that he found in the house where the Aimanns were killed. He kept the flag for more than 40 years, and finally handed it over to Dressler. Dressler himself donated the flag to the Schumacher Institute in Haifa...

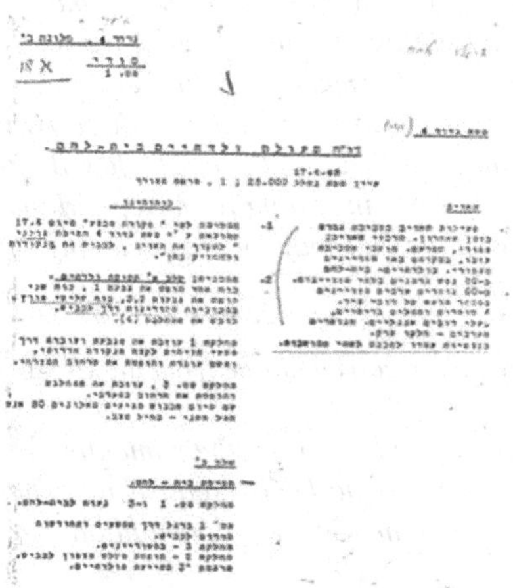

133. Amit's report on the Waldheim/ Betlehem operation
Source: IDF Archive, courtesy A. Dressler. The date is April 17, 1948, just a few hours after the operation was completed, and classified 'Secret': In his conclusion, Amit remarks that "[...] it is imperative that a strong and disciplined force be organized in order to control the issue of enemy property. In this domain we were not able to assume control", meaning that he is disappointed with the issue of looting. I gave Amit a copy of this report

Amit: *This is true. One of the excuses of the two men was that when they opened the door they saw this Nazi flag, this in turn had increased their blood pressure. I don't think that this is actually what happened. In my opinion they simply acted instinctively.*

Question: What, a sort of overflow of adrenalin?

Amit: *Yes, in the course of... later they found the flag in the house. I was not there when it actually happened, but this is my impression. A German publication...*

Question: Sauer, an established German historian wrote that the Haganah men thought that they were being shot at from that house; they identified the house as a target, and when it was possible, they broke into the house and shot. Carmel says that probably the name Aimann was taken by mistake for Aichmann, and that's why they were shot. There are a number of versions...

Amit: *Look, I don't know, my version is much more simple, that in the heat of the operation they climbed the stairs, broke the door open, and shot before they could say 'good morning'. This is what I remember and my impression. Dressler has plunged deeply into this affair [...] I know Dressler [...] the young lady from Sha'ar Ha'amakim I have not met, but saw her film. She researched the affair too. This is all I can tell you, I regret that I cannot add any more.*

Thank you, General Amit.

In the CZA (Central Zionist Archive) I scanned the daily newspapers, which were published the day following the operation. To my surprise I found that all but one, relate the same version, almost with the identical texts. This, for example, was the message in the *Al Hamishmar Daily*:

The German colonies Waldheim and Betlehem are in the hands of the Haganah.

Afula, Saturday. [...] Waldheim and Betlehem were taken over this morning by the Haganah units, following a fight against the Gang [Arab militias] *Personnel, who had infiltrated the settlements [....]. In the last few days an intensive movement by alien Arabs in the vicinity of these two colonies* [were observed], *with the aim of infiltrating them. The few British policemen in charge of the property were intending to leave, and the Arab auxiliaries defected with their weapons already by the beginning of the week.*

The Germans remaining in the village had received notice from the [Arab] *gangs that they would have to leave.*
The infiltration by the Arab aliens was an indication of their intention to take over these two colonies, located behind of the Jewish settlements. The takeover by the Haganah was intended to eliminate this potential danger [....]
[...] The storming of the Haganah units on Waldheim and Betlehem came as a surprise to the [Arab] *gangs, who intended to invade today.*
[...] The Germans present in the villages were taken out of their homes and imprisoned in a central location under Jewish guard. The Germans resisted the arrests with firearms, and a young male and female were killed [...]
Searches conducted in the houses by the Haganah revealed a quantity of documents, testifying to their close association with the Nazis, even during the war [World War II], *when they were detained in their locations* [my translation D.G.].

All the rest of the daily newspapers convey the same information. The *Davar Daily* and the *Palestine Post Daily* report that this information was released by an "Official Report" or "Haganah Bulletin". No reporter was actually present there at the time of the operation (this point will be addressed later).

The report in the Palestine Post, however, illuminates the operation from a totally different angle, which is worth considering. Besides providing the usual information cited above, the Palestine Post of the same day reveals that:
[...] the Jewish National Institutions have been negotiating with the Palestine Government for the purchase of the property, according to the Haganah Radio. Recently the government intimated that is was unable to conclude the negotiations, and with the impending evacuation of the British, and the Germans still at Waldheim, Arab gangs planned to assume control.
Earlier in the report the unknown reporter does not neglect to mention that:
[...] The action was taken when it was learned that Arab gangs were pre-

paring to occupy the 9,000 dunams [1 dunam=1000 square meters], *controlled by the* [British] *Custodian of Enemy Property.*

Perhaps this suggests a part of the issue of the purpose of taking over the colonies. With the British Mandate nearing its end, the conflict between the two major groups in Palestine of April 1948, Jews and Arabs, each group was determined to establish 'accomplished facts' as fast as possible. The property had already been seized by the British as 'Enemy Property', and was administered by the British Custodian, a British agency. The negotiations with the Jews reached a dead end. The only way to gain control over the land was by use of force. The concentration of "Arab gangs" around Waldheim and the decision of the Haganah to run the operation, were, perhaps, of the same motivation: a race to gain control over that considerable piece of land.

Nogah Binstock, a member of Kibbutz *Sha'ar Ha'amakim*, shares, at least in part, the same observation. Binstock made a video documentary on the affair (1989). I met her and her husband Benny at their modest flat. I was interested to find out why she made that video in the first place.[15]

Question: Why have you decided to do it?

Binstock: *It all started with this, that members of Sha'ar Ha'amakim took part in the operation, including my father. On the other hand, I married a person from Germany, his father was Jewish, a holocaust survivor, and his mother a German, Christian. And this association with Germany... when I needed to make a film as a final project for my* [cinematography] *studies, it dawned on me that this was the thing to do. This examination of our relationships as Israelis* [with the Germans], *and the question of our right to behave in such a way that these things will guide us... this is why the title of the film points at its character: 'We Are Not Like Them';*[16] *this is a quote from what a member of Sha'ar Ha'amakim said to the Germans during that operation. He meant: 'we are not like the Germans, we will not behave like the Germans', but on the other hand, there were acts in the operation, like the looting, which do not represent moral conduct.*

As if part of the justification was that we do it to them because they are Germans. This is not all the justification, because probably everyone possesses these feelings.

I tried to examine whether they were Nazis or not; how they were perceived by the Jewish Yishuv [community], *how did they perceive themselves. I tried to examine this affair from all kinds of angles, and somehow to examine if there was a justification for this kind of conduct.*

Question: This film, is it your personal, private effort, stemming from the fact that you had some kind of involvement...

Binstock: *On one hand, out of my involvement came the idea to do the film. But later, when I thought why do I want to show that film, what is it good for? I found out that I have hit the target: to actually examine ourselves. If somebody has done this and that to you, does it justify that you conduct yourself immorally.*

134. Hans Meyer, a Swiss national who lived in Waldheim. Source: Still image from Binstock's film: "[...] the swastika flags were the national flags [...] they started the activities of the NS youth movement, but it never had a Nazi character [...] the Germans were blamed probably because of the tools the Arabs used. When the Arabs did their night [sabotage] *operations, they used the Germans' tools [...]; tools left on site caused the Jews to believe that the Germans are involved. But this is not true. We have always told them not to hurt the Jews"*

Question: So on one hand this is a historical depiction, and on the other hand this is an observation into one's self...

Binstock: *This is absolutely subjective. I have, in fact, described the events according to the information I have received, but I have constructed the film based on my personal attitude. It is possible that should I have received more data, I would have done this differently. This is, in fact, a Rashomon,*[17] *everyone sees it from their own angle. I have tried to look for a wide spectrum, the German side too. I found Hans Meyer, who was evacuated with his parents, also in the Deininger book there is a first-hand testimony of a person telling what he has been through. These are not just inventions, because when I have interviewed some of the people who took part in the operation, the same data surfaced, sometimes from a different angle... in the film you see and hear what they all say, and the viewer has to make his own judgment.*

Question: How did you make the film, technically?

Binstock: *It had to be a team. The film is mine, because the idea is mine, and all the research work is mine.*

Question: Did you talk to the remaining Zarchi, whose brother was in the operation?

Binstock: *No. I talked to others.*

Question: Why, he did not want to talk?

Binstock: *I just did not have enough time to reach them. The Project was limited in time, I have contacted a lot of people, but not all the contacts were developed into an interview. For example, I heard about Moussa Peled, who was in the operation, and was uneasy about the looting, and demanded from the men to open their bags and pour the looted contents on the road. I wanted to hear the story from him, but could not make the contact. He was too busy.*

Question: I read here in a critique of that film, published after the broadcasting, written by Avi Bettleheim, titled 'Retroactive Shame': "[...] during five effective minutes of interviews, out surfaces a retroactive shame and covers the faces of the Haganah veterans. If it takes for the shame 40 years to take its place, than we have no chance." – What actually does he mean by that?

Binstock: *That it came too little, too late. That we actually avoid dealing with these issues.*

Question: Following the film, what are your conclusions as to the relations between Jews and Germans in Palestine of 1947-1948?

Binstock: *They were the last Germans here. Almost all the Germans were already deported by the British, mainly to Australia, or exchanged for Palestinian Jews in Germany, in a POW* [civilian internee exchange, PH] *ex-*

change transaction. The last Germans were in Waldheim, and the Jewish Yishuv regarded them as Nazis.

Question: Rightfully?

Binstock: *The Yishuv was motivated by hatred of Germans. Actually those who were in Waldheim were only the old and the children. Men of* [military] *service age were almost not present there. They were all in Germany, and some of them took part in the war. And there was also the matter of the 'Events', and people were* ***saying*** [Binstock's emphasis] *that the Germans have assisted the Arabs in land mining etc. But when I checked this out, it turned out to be not factual. The Arabs who worked for the Germans have used their tools, and hence the false evidence of German assistance to the Arabs. On the other hand, it is possible that some Germans actually collaborated with the Arabs. Certainly not all of them. Probably, there were some Nazis who hated Jews, and some Nazis who substituted nationalism for religion. Some sided with the NS Party (for them Hitler would be the savior of Germany), but not necessarily with the anti-Jewish policy.*

135. Adina Levine, settler from Nahalal. Source: Still image from Binstock's film. Levine: "[...] I must say only good things about our Templer neighbours here at Nahalal [...] I have good memories from the time before the Nazi regime [...] They were visiting us, bringing with them their guests [...] they would bring home-baked bread on the last day of Passover [...]"

Question: Is your impression that the Waldheim-Betlehem population was maybe partly pro-Nazi, but not anti-Semitic or anti-Israeli?

Binstock: *Yes. Although I assume that here and there, there were anti-Semites. But surely not all of them. For example, one Nahalal resident testifying in the film about very good relations with the Germans, that they were visiting, bringing bread as a present on the last day of Passover, etc.*
But the moment the war started, all connections ceased. Before the war they had commercial connections, and also, the Jews who have settled in the Valley have learned a lot from the Germans, how to make agriculture, and how to survive in that climate [...] On the other hand, the Jews were jealous of the Germans, because over there at the German colonies, everything was well-established, stone houses, everything neat and aesthetic, and here at the Jewish colonies everything was 'in diapers', and this was one of the drives to take the colonies, because they coveted the land and the property.

136. Hagai Binyamini, settler from Nahalal. Source: Still image from Binstock's film. Levine: "[...] Their estates were very neat, stone walls, flowers, clean court [...] all we had was made of sheet metal, wires, old pipes [...] I understood the German order and efficiency. If they work so systematically, no wonder they almost conquered the world [...]"

Question: Was this jealousy **and** revenge?

Binstock: *Yes. And also the very real consideration that once the British left, if the Jews would not take over the colonies, the Arabs would. In the final analysis I wanted to learn what the proportions were; whether this was one big operation. Actually this was an easy operation. A sort of a 'in a jiffy' type of operation. For the Germans it was very traumatic, but for our men it was something 'in between' other operations... something minor of a sort, they 'hopped in' on a Saturday, got into the colonies, the brave went first, and the rest came in later and started looting. Then all started looting. It was interesting to check on this, because there were some holocaust survivors among them. There is a person in the film who talks about himself, that on one hand he behaved like the others, and on the other hand, felt very uneasy about it, because he was a holocaust survivor.*

Thank you, Nogah.

Perhaps the most knowledgeable person about the Waldheim Affair was Aryeh Dressler, in his 80s when interviewed in October 2000. He died in 2006, resident of Betlehem, and one of the first Jewish settlers there, after the Germans' evacuation. He built his own house, and had not taken a Templer house, although having been offered one. Dressler, an immigrant from Austria, was fluent in German, and hosted from time to time visiting Templers coming to Betlehem. I knew that he had extensively researched the Affair, being a 'history buff', and when we met, I was amazed to find a private historical documents archive of considerable size.

Question: The night between 16 and 17 April 1948…

Dressler: *Before* [the operation] *there was the battle of Mishmar Ha'emek. Actually Meir Amit was there, it was a unit composed of people from the neighboring settlements. Most of them were in the Mishmar Ha'emek battles* [4.4.1948 to 15.4.1948, ending only 2 days before the Waldheim operation], *and there it was decided that Waldheim and Betlehem be taken.*

Question: What was the reason?

Dressler: *The reason was that everything that the British were going to leave behind, either them* [the Arabs] *or us wanted to take, whoever would get there first. In Zipori the Kaouggi militias were waiting. It was feared that they might take Waldheim and Betlehem first. Also, the future fate of the Germans was unclear. There were still 400 Germans left in Palestine. Just before the war, about 340 Germans in Palestine were mobilized into the German military...*

Question: Wasn't that in contradiction to their religious beliefs that they do not fight? [Editorial note: there was nothing in the Templers' religious beliefs that would have absolved them from their national duty during both world wars].

Dressler: *We ask the same question; the older Templers were reserved about this approach. The British did not know what to do with the remaining Germans left in Palestine. The Templers initiated this idea: they came to the British and proposed that the British form 4 detention camps inside the Templer communities, so that they continue to live in their communities, quietly, and keep on farming.*

Question: Are you saying that the detention camps was actually the Templers' idea?

Dressler: *Absolutely. The British accepted this idea, detained them in their own settlements, under supervision, barbed wire fences, with guards.*

Question: Were the Templers adhering to their obligation and did not escape?

Dressler: *Yes, there was not a single case of escape or leave without permission, or contact with German Intelligence agents who were operating in East Palestine.*[18]

Question: What kind of interest was there for the Templers in Palestine to identify with the general consensus in Germany during the 30s?

Dressler: *The veteran Templers were actually reserved about this. Those Templers, who were drafted into the German Army, were sent to serve in the Brandenburg Division, which was responsible for the management of occupied territories. The German military was looking for trustworthy people who had command of foreign languages and were capable of handling occupied territories. 90 Templers were killed in action during the war. In 1941, hundreds were sent to Australia; they stayed there until the end of the war, most of them became Australian citizens. They have managed to blend into the Australian economy, because they were diligent and useful.*

Question: Is it true that the Aimanns were shot because their name was confused with Aichmann?

Dressler: *This is inaccurate. There was here a Swiss non-Templer family, Meyer, who later moved out to Haifa, they claimed that the Aimanns were shot for that reason. In my opinion this is not true. Whoever fought there were Sabras* ['born in Israel', in Hebrew slang] *that already knew what happened in Europe during WWII. They killed the two Germans as a simple act of revenge. No one admits this, but in my opinion, this is what happened. Sauer has maintained that the raiders thought they were being shot at from the Staib house* [see image 123]. *The man who shot* [the Aimanns] *was from Nahalal, and he was killed months later in action.*

Question: What was the status of Amit in that operation?

Dressler: I am not sure if he was present during the entire operation on premises, it is possible that he arrived in Waldheim only towards the end.

Question: Who was the person in charge in the Waldheim portion of the operation?

Dressler: *There was a man from Alonim, but he already smiles a lot, smiles too much...*

Question: In press clips I read from the day following the operation, it says in the Palestine Post that the Haganah Radio announced that the negotiations between the Zionist bodies and the British Mandate authorities on the purchase of Waldheim had failed.

Dressler: *I will show you documents, what Moshe Sharet writes...*

Question: Allow me to complete the question. If you add to this the message that Arab forces had already been spotted in the region, and that somebody was concerned that they would take the colonies before the Jews would, is it probable that someone was concerned about not being able to take the colonies?

Dressler: *Starting 1945-1946 the Jewish Agency demanded that the British authorities evacuate all the Germans from Palestine. The British authorities have not accepted this approach. Further, the* [Jewish] *Agency has demanded that all German colonies be transferred into Jewish hands.*

Question: What do you mean, 'transferred'? Do you mean 'given away'?

Dressler: *Yes, given away; because the Jewish community contributed to the war effort 30,000 soldiers, which were now discharged, and must be settled. This was the axis of the negotiations, but the British have not consented. They claimed that the German population has not done anything wrong to the Jewish Yishuv, they were living here quietly, what do you* [Jewish Agency] *want from them?*

Question: Do you regard the operation of Waldheim-Betlehem, as an attempt to take over [their] land?

Dressler: *It was clear that the moment a Jewish State be declared, any Jewish Government would not allow them to continue their stay here. Why wait until then? Let's take it before the Arabs do.*

Question: Another interesting item I found in the press clips of those days, is that all papers relate the same item almost exactly, except for the Palestine Post. Does it mean that this was…

Dressler: *A pre-cooked announcement of the Haganah. No reporter was present on site during the operation.*

Question: In the Haganah announcement it says that "[…] Young German male and female resisted with firearms". According to Sauer they were in their 40s and 60s and far from being armed…

Dressler: *Something like this, yes. This was 'problematic' that they were killed. So they gave the excuse of resistance.*

Question: What documentation do you have at home that covers the events of April 17, 1948?

Dressler: *I have the report which Amit has filed following the operation; the source is from the IDF archive; and the correspondence covering the lands issue.*

I could not resist the urge to call Benjamin Zarchi, in Nahalal. I was reserved about this; it took me weeks to make up my mind. With a shaking hand I dialed the number. I introduced myself and explained that I wanted to talk about the events of 1948. I said I wanted to come over to his house and talk.

"Why come over, just ask me over the phone" he said, "I can tell it all over the phone and save you the trip", I said I would rather meet him, I wanted to tape the conversation, so it would all come out as accurate as possible. "OK, Friday morning, 10:00" he agreed.

Zarchi, or as his friends call him 'Benya', turned out to be much more co-operative than I thought. He knew I was going to ask about his late brother; we talked for an hour. The following are excerpts from this conversation.

Question: Your boyhood years you spent in Nahalal. Then came the years of the 'events'; of what I heard from people of the region, they say that Arab settlements were harassing Jewish settlements by blocking roads, uprooting plants, and even laying land mines; what have the Jewish settlements done to safeguard themselves?

Zarchi: *First, all were members of the 'Haganah'. The most annoying was the thefts. The Arabs were really poor, malaria-stricken, and in miserable living conditions. Look at the Bedouins of today who live in 3-level houses. Then, all they had was five goats and two cows; they had a lot of respect for us because we had overcome the malaria. The first years we suffered from a lot of thefts. The mines started appearing in 1936. Probably the source was Betlehem. There we knew of a perky NS core, which collaborated with the* [Arab] *militias. They laid land mines all over the Valley and this was terrible. In 1939-1940, after the outbreak of WWII, in Nahalal there was a battalion of Australian Mounted Infantry, which was planning to take Lebanon and Syria. We were sending in our boys as rangers, early every morning to check the roads for mines.*

137. British Army evacuating a victim during the riots of 1936-39, Jezreel Valley. Source: Collection of Rafael Salus, Kibbutz Hefzi-Bah, digitized by Bitmuna and filed in the Haifa University Library Historical Images database

Question: This was in cooperation with the Australians?

Zarchi: *Yes, they found a land mine between Nahalal and Kfar-Yehoshua. A giant mine. I was present when the mine was disarmed. The Australian demolition officer told us that these batteries were made in Germany, and not available in Palestine.*

Question: Are you saying that the mines found and disarmed were made in Germany?

Zarchi: *The mechanisms and the batteries were German. The mine* [shows a size of 30 cm diameter] *was made of cast iron, with canals* [grooves] *like old hand grenades. The ranger noticed it and uncovered the mine. Other mines were not uncovered, and people were killed.*

Question: On April 17, 1948, were you with the company of Meir Amit?

Zarchi: *No. I was mobilized later, on May 15. I was veteran of the* [Jewish] *Brigade. My brother Chummi was already mobilized, my father was too weak to do the farming and the entire work-load was on me. I continued working until we were all mobilized. A bus came over and took us all to the army.*

Question: I understood from other people that your brother was killed in action later.

Zarchi: *Yes. He fell in the Horev Operation, on December 21, 1948.*

Question: Was he in the Waldheim operation, under Meir Amit command?

Zarchi: *Yes.*

Question: He comes back from the operation, brings you a German flag which you keep in the closet for over 40 years…

Zarchi: *Stashed in the closet. I forgot all about it. One day I re-organized the closet and found it. I met Aryeh Dressler in a weekly history session, told him about the flag, and asked him if he wanted it. He took it. But you probably want to ask me about something else. You are beating about the bush. Tell me, what do you want to know?*

Question: I want to ask: Chummi took part in the operation. I have heard from people, that he was one of the persons who entered the house where the Germans were, and shot them. In the Binstock film, an interviewee says that by doing the shooting, Chummi sort of expressed the feelings of the rest of the men; what has Chummi told you about this particular event?

Zarchi: *He did not want to tell me. He would not talk about this. He gave me the Nazi flag; what I know is this: [a.] in our family, on both sides, the father and the mother, there was a large family in the Ukraine. From refugees arriving from there we found out that our father's brother was shot and killed in Odessa. He, his wife and a sister of my mother were shot with her kids in Dniepropetrovsk with the Nazi occupation, and one more sister of my mother was shot in Babi-Yar with her husband and two kids. All this was known to Chummi. He used to talk about this very excitedly. Apart from this, [b.] there were land disputes with Arabs, and the Arabs told Chummi that 'soon enough Hitler will come over and kill you all and we will take over your land', this was in 1944.*

The flag, I do not know whether it was found in the same house where the Germans were shot. When they broke in, he and another person, I don't know who he was, the German told them something they did not understand; a short burst of automatic fire, and the German was killed; that's all I know.

Question: Chummi himself, he never talked about it?

Zarchi: *Did not, and I didn't want to ask. Myself, I fought the Germans in Italy, and was wounded. I was brought into a field hospital and next to me there was a captured German, wounded. I thought to myself, damn it, could be that the night before, the fight was between us two. But this was the British Army; there was 'an understanding' that what was, was. This was the British style: when you fight, you fight, and later, history be the judge. If I try to reconstruct this, I can't... partly because I loved Chummi, and partly because I had an uneasy feeling that he was shot; so, others told me. I received the flag, locked it in the closet, and that's it. That's all I can say.* [Pause].

The background was clear, excitement and lack of control. It is possible that he found the flag in the house. I am not sure about this.

Question: This affair of the German colonies, not only the April 17 operation, but in general, there were here Jewish settlements. Were there any relations with the German colonies?

Zarchi: *At first there were good relations. On Saturdays we used to ride to the colonies, mainly in order to learn their agriculture. We tried to develop relations with them. They would keep distance. We bought cattle from them. But the cattle were of low quality and the cost was not reasonable. The Germans would come over from time to time, but they regarded us as Horanies.*[20] *The conditions here were rough. It was unpaved, dusty, dirty, thorns... over there it was all spic and span, every German family had an Arab family to serve them. The Arab servants were living outside the colony, in a shanty-town* [expresses the term in Arabic].

Question: I would like to ask you, as one of the veterans of Jezreel Valley. The Valley is such a spot, that funnels in all these cultures, the Palestinians, the Jewish settlement, the German settlement, and the British, who were ruling the land. What do you make of this, what are your observations on this peculiar intersection?

Zarchi: *With the Arabs we have had good relations, more or less. There were here the Bedouins, who later have served in the IDF. One Amos Yar-*

koni, a Bedouin kid from a small village near Nahalal, he was a robber and a killer, but very smart. He used to come over and eat with us. He was the only kid the Bedouins sent to school. He used to ride his donkey all the way to school in Nazareth. Moshe Dayan, also from Nahalal, had an Arab friend from here, who was later killed by the Arabs. The British always saw us as 'natives'. But we had good relations. With the Germans, there was this young man from Nahalal who lived with them for a number of years, in the 30s. He brought from there all sorts of innovations in agriculture, and new farming methods. Our first cow, we called her 'firsty'; we bought from the Germans. In Ganeigar, there was also a German settlement. The Arabic name of the village was 'Gingar'. Over there we found exquisite stone houses. I am not sure that the houses still exist today. Talk to Meir Shamir, from Ganeigar, he knows a lot about it.

Question: Can I take your picture?

Zarchi: *What for?* [shows signs of uneasiness].

I sat at my desk reading over the information I collected. What to make out of all this? The trigger to look into the affair was part of my effort to understand the Templer phenomenon, the historical connection between the Templers and the Yishuv; this was the beginning move of the dissertation I was starting to write about the Templer architecture back in 2000. A knowledgeable friend told me about the dramatic events on the night between April 16 and 17, and my personal curiosity to attempt an understanding of the events became a journey in time, into the days of 1948. This was, no doubt, a turbulent point in time for all the parties involved in the region.

For the British, these were the last days for their thirty years of ruling the region. They were getting tired of their stay in Palestine. They were haunted and hunted by the Jewish underground, the *Lechi*, and the Resistance Movement [a short-lived coalition of all the Jewish undergrounds in Palestine], counting their casualties, and, responding to the public opinion in England, were about to bring to an end the Mandate given to them by the League of Nations following WWI. They were doing so unwillingly; they recognized the value of a British foothold in the region for their own interests. But all the same they realized that the clash between the two main communities in Palestine, the Jewish and the Palestinian, was inevitable and beyond their ability to manage. They were beginning the process of winding down, which only accelerated the drive of the two communities to grab as much as possible in terms of taking over of strategic points. The British military's conduct during the events of April 17 in Waldheim and Betlehem is an indication of their general control capabilities for that particular period: they acted passively, did not intervene in the operation, some of the Arab auxiliary were defecting, and Arab militia was flowing into the Jezreel Valley.

The main actors in this drama were the Palestinians and the Jews. Each group did its best to gain as much of the British Mandate as possible during these twilight days. The Haganah was in the process of transformation into a regular army; they were highly motivated, they understood that it was not enough to defend their homes and settlements in the Valley, but needed to act on a larger scale in order to establish a manageable map of the future Jewish State. The Haganah was receiving orders from the Jewish Agency, actually the managing body of the Jewish community in Palestine. There was no Jewish Government, only the 'Agency'. It is safe to assume that at least part of the reason for running the operation of April 17 was a direct instruction from the 'Agency' to do so. A number of documents found in the CZA by A. Dressler support this assumption, described henceforth.

The first document is dated March 28, 1946, three weeks before the operation. This is a letter signed by Moshe Shertok (who later changed his name to Sharet and became Minister of Foreign Affairs and Prime Minister). The title he uses next to his signature is "Executive of the Jewish Agency". The letter is addressed to The Anglo-American Committee of Inquiry in Jerusalem. The main message of the letter is a request on behalf of the Jewish community, urging the Committee to transfer the property of the German colonies into Jewish national ownership. Below are some selected segments:

[...] The Jewish Agency has addressed the British Government, requesting that the German Colony in Palestine be liquidated and that its property be transferred to Jewish national ownership on account of the reparations which, in the Jewish Agency's view, Germany owes to the Jewish people [....]

[...] German residents of Palestine now in Germany should not be allowed to return; that those interned abroad should be repatriated to Germany and not to Palestine, and that those interned in Palestine should be sent to Germany.

[...] The property, consisting in the main of the four villages of Sarona, Wilhelma, Waldheim and Betlehem, and the suburban quarters of Jerusalem, Haifa and Jaffa, is intended to serve primarily for the resettlement of Jews from Europe who were victims of the Nazi regime and of Palestinian-Jewish ex-servicemen who helped to defeat it [...][21]

Shertok says also in this letter that this request of the Jewish Agency started as early as May 1945, with a memorandum submitted to "His Majesty's Government".

The second document is dated May 31, 1946. It is addressed to Moshe Shertok, and signed by R.P Platt [Under Secretary, responding on behalf of the Chief Secretary], probably of the same Committee, refusing Shertok's proposal, on the account that "the lands are fully occupied". Shertok wanted to lease the agricultural land, and at this point backed up from his claim to property ownership. Following are a few selected segments:

... you proposed that the agricultural land of the German colonies in Palestine should be leased to groups of demobilized soldiers [...] to inform you that your proposal has been carefully examined [...] but it is regretted that the fact that the lands in question are already fully occupied, precludes its implementation.[22]

Shertok did not give up. The third document is a letter to the Chief Secretary of the Government office; he insists on "preferential treatment" on behalf of the discharged Jewish Brigade veterans:

[...] We should be grateful if we could be informed by whom these lands are occupied. We assume that the Government recognizes the right of demobilized soldiers to certain preferential treatment over other possible tenants who made no contribution to the war effort, and we are anxious to learn whether this principle has been adhered to with regard to the lands of enemy subjects.[23]

There is no further data on the issue of lands, which is the axis of the above correspondence. But from what has been presented so far, these documents show that the Jewish leadership had a deep interest in acquiring the German property, and was in a rush to score achievements, before the property would be handed over to the Arabs; it also is in line with Dressler's assessment (see above) that a future Jewish sovereign government would not accept German settlements in Israel, which declared independence only one month after the operation.

The last document is a telegram,[24] which was sent from abroad to the offices of the Jewish Agency in Tel Aviv on 11.4.1948, just a few days before the operation. The text is coded in such a way that only those involved can make sense of it.

For Granowsky[:] [later changed his name to Granot, chairman of the KKL management] *first as I have notified you yesterday the* [British] *Government agrees to transfer the gentiles* [the Germans] *to Cyprus stop now it turns out that we have to arrange the transport*[25] *stop we called the Zim Haifa Corporate* [Israeli freight fleet] *which is ready to make available for us the Kedma* [ship name] *for the above purpose stop the expenses of the transport will be deducted from the cost of land stop the fact that we take care of transport may affect the Gentiles* [the British and Germans] *as to the price of the perimeter*[26] *and maybe as to the price of Wilhelma stop a talk with them scheduled for Tuesday morning*[27] *stop very urgent that you notify us if there are no counter arguments to this plan stop second let us know also if considering all arguments it is desirable to raise at this talk the question of Waldheim and Betlehem at least the question of leasing [...]*[28]

Relations between the Jewish and the Templer communities in Palestine were deteriorating rapidly immediately following WWII. As described in Kanaan, (1968), The Palmach, the best military arm of the Haganah, performed a number of provocative operations in order to make the Germans understand that they are undesirable in Palestine. The assassinations of Wagner, a German industrialist from Jaffa, and the two Germans from Waldheim, Mitscherlich and Müller (both assassinations were carried out in 1946), were such provocations designed and carried out by the Haganah. In his book, Kanaan quotes Igal Alon, then the head of the Palmach, as saying:

138. 'Hitler Jugend' event in Waldheim/ Betlehem. Source: IDF Archive. According to Dressler, the Golani troopers burned most of the documents they found. However, some survived, like the batch of photos in the IDF Archive. In that batch there are some pictures of 'Hitler Jugend' events taking place in Waldheim/Betlehem, which were interpreted by the Haganah as Nazi, anti-Semitic activities

[...] Upon the suggestion of the Palmach HQ, the upper command [of the Haganah], *with the approval of the Yishuv Institutions, has decided to prevent the release of Germans detained in the Land* [meaning in Palestine, in the perimeter compounds]. *It was decided to warn them and prove to the* [British] *Government that they will not stay alive in this country. But the British police tried to trick us: instead of releasing the Germans normally, it allowed them to run their business and farm their fields in Sarona, Wilhelma and Betlehem, under police guard [...] in spite of this excellent protection, the implementation of the plan has commenced. On the first days of August* [1946] *a hit team of Palmach members [...] killed the active Nazi, the German industrialist Wagner, without wounding his British body-guards*. On September 17,* [1946] *a unit of the first battalion of the Palmach carried out a similar operation against Nazis from Waldheim [...]*[29] [my translation D.G.]

According to Sauer (1985), these operations proved to serve their purpose, as far as the Jewish interest was concerned. By the end of 1946, the Templers agreed to sell the lands of Sarona to... none other than the Jewish Agency.

Arabs were killing Templers too, probably for the same reasons. In 1910, A German was murdered in Neuhardthof near Haifa,[30] two more Germans were killed in the 1920s in the same area. Templer settlers suffered heavily from theft and crop uprooting initiated by Arabs. Besides, the Templers, as European immigrants, were regarded by the Arabs as 'Alien Corn', just as the Jews were. They were identified by the Arabs of the 1940s in Palestine as an element which has to be discarded from the region.

And back to Waldheim, the morning of April 17. That operation was well planned not only militarily. Once the operation was over, the local newspapers were provided with a press release that bears very little correlation to the actual facts. Since no reporters were on site during the operation,

* Wagner was killed on 22 March. He was with one police guard and three German passengers. No one was an 'active Nazi' in 1946 [PH].

the Agency could supply any information it pleased. The press release described the Aimanns as "Young male and female" (which they were not), claimed that they resisted with firearms (which they did not), and that documents were found that linked Waldheim with the Nazi regime.

This press release was, to say the least, an exercise in disinformation, a tactic which is used by all military organizations, and complements the actual act of combat.

The German settlers of Waldheim were, in my observation, victims. They were crushed by forces greater than they could handle, and became secondary actors in the great drama of the war of 1948. A dream of modest, peaceful, prosperous and simple life ended with their deportation out of their homes, villages and communities. The deserted and neglected church in Waldheim and the beautiful houses there are mute testimony to the sad fate of the settlers and the events that took place and spelt the end of an enterprise of courage, pioneering, diligence, wisdom and faith.

Notes

[1] *The author would like to thank Dov Meyer, the late Aryeh Dressler, Nogah Binstock, Shirley Reuveni of the IDF Archive, 'Benya' Zarchi, Meir Amit, Kobi Fleischmann, Shraga Peled of the Haganah Archive, Batya Leshem of the CZA, the late Judith Ivri, Alan Tilbury, Bruno Weinmann. Data donors with Templer ties: Horst Blaich, Martin Higgins. This paper is dedicated to the courage, honesty and frankness of the fighting men of Golani, who took a step forward and were objective enough to stay with the facts for the sake of historical documentation.*

[2] *Sluzki (1973), pp. 1955-1959. The area of the proposed Jewish state was determined by the map of the 'Partition Plan' (29.11.1947) that divides Palestine between Arabs and Jews. Other elements of 'Plan D' were: achieving a territorial continuity of all the Jewish areas, taking over mixed settlements, taking over main transportation arteries and strategic points controlled their vicinity.*

[3] *One German national from Waldheim has, according to Kanaan (1968), collaborated with the Arabs during the Arab Revolt, 1936-1939. The term 'Events' was used by the Jewish community to describe the waves of riots carried out by Arab Palestinian militias against the Jewish population and settlements in Palestine, mainly in 1921, 1929, and 1936-1939.*

[4] *There was a modest presence in the villages of a British security outfit, consisting of (in Waldheim, according to Sauer) "[...] a British sergeant, two British policemen and six Arab auxiliary police". The TACs (Temporary Additional Constables, the Arab policemen), were unarmed and other British forces were a few hours away, according to Alan Tilbury, the British officer in charge of security in Waldheim on April 17 {Tilbury to Higgins, 2007}.*

[5] *Some German colonies were managed as internment compounds, as the Germans were considered enemy nationals and monitored by the British authorities. Stoll was an internee, as all Waldheim residents, sharing with the Aimanns the Staib house for residence.*

[6] *Testimony of Traugott Aimann, in Weinmann (2007).*

[7] *Meir Amit was the company's commander. See milestones in his career in the caption* "on page 173".

[8] *Katz, Friedrich, Report on the Haganah Attack on Waldheim, unpublished written statement dated April 17, 1948, TGD Archive reference 207-1880. The data provided here is from Weinmann's Report who is quoting Katz.*

[9] *Tilbury to Higgins 2007.*

[10] *Schiff and Haber (1976), pp. 399-400.*

[11] *A Lebanese officer (born 1897), in 1936 headed a militia of volunteers who infiltrated Palestine. Became head of 'Arab Rescue Army' during the 1948 war, a move that was initiated by the Arab League. His militia is estimated at 6000 men. In the battles of Mishmar Ha'emek, days before the operation, Kaouggi lost most of his men. The Arab Rescue Army finally disbanded in October 1948, and Kaouggi escaped to Lebanon. He published his memoirs in 1973. {Schiff and Haber (1976), pp. 442, 457}.*

[12] *This statement is challenged by the Tilbury paper (2007), where Tilbury states: "I question whether Arabs would have attacked the* [German] *settlement as long as there was any kind of British presence there; and I really do not think there was the slightest possibility that, on evacuating Waldheim and Betlehem, we would have deliberately done it in such a way as to facilitate an Arab takeover. However, I can see that from a Haganah perspective the risks of waiting on events would have seemed unacceptable."*

[13] *Another motive for the shooting was proposed by the late Prof. Alex Carmel, an expert on the history of German settlement in the Holy Land. Weinmann met Carmel in Israel in 1996, who told him that in the 1960s he (Carmel) met the second shooter in Marseilles, who told him that they received orders to enter a specific house and shoot the male occupant, mistakenly assuming that the man is Adolph Aichmann, and that those who issued the order for the shooting mistook the name Aimann for Aichmann, one of the main figures in the Nazi scheme to exterminate the European Jewry {Weinmann 2007 document}. Carmel did not disclose that in the 1960s he was a Mossad investigator who was recruited to track down Nazi war criminals, and that his meeting with the shooter in Marseilles was probably a part of his investigative efforts. Aichmann (some spell Eichmann) was captured by the Mossad in May 1960.*

[14] *Amit was quoting form Isaiah, 8:1-3, "quick to the plunder, swift to the spoil."*

[15] *Interview with Nogah Binstock, October 2000.*

[16] *The title was changed by the Broadcasting Authority, to "The Seizure of the German Colonies", because the original title was thought too provocative. The actual words are quoted from a speech made by a Haganah officer to the captured Germans, and actually reflects what Binstock was asking: 'were we?'*

[17] *Binstock was referring to a film by Akiro Kurosawa, Japan, 1950, in which a crime was committed, but told by four persons, each expressing his own version of the crime. The viewer has to make his own judgment as to what actually happened. The film is based on two stories by Ryūnosuke Akutagawa.*

[18] *Dressler was referring to the episode of the German agents parachuted into east Palestine in 1944, probably for intelligence and sabotage purposes. They were caught and detained by the British.*

[19] *Dressler's correction after reading the draft in 2000: "Not hundreds but: 665 Germans, out of which 536 were Templers".*

[20] *Hebrew slang for 'stupid, uneducated, uncivilized, poor, wears worn-out cloths', {Dan Ben Amotz and Netiva Ben Yehuda, The World Dictionary for Spoken Hebrew, Jerusalem: Levine - Epstein (1976), p. 88}.*

[21] *CZA reference 510-33, retrieved by A. Dressler.*

[22] *British reference DEM/141, retrieved by A. Dressler from CZA.*

[23] *British reference Pol/102/46, retrieved from CZA by A. Dressler.*

[24] *CZA reference 610-83, retrieved by A. Dressler.*

[25] *The transport to Cyprus of the German nationals. This means that there already was an understanding between the Agency and the British that the Germans be transported out of Palestine. Indeed this is what happened, the Templers from Waldheim and Betlehem and all the rest of the Templer residents and other German nationals were shipped to Cyprus two days after the operation.*

[26] *Probably the lands of Sarona, the Templer colony in Tel Aviv, as all the other German settlements are mentioned explicitly by name. Sauer relates how the term 'Concentration Camps' was replaced by 'Perimeter Camps' (p.194), which was probably a generic name for all internment camps built by the British.*

[27] *That particular Tuesday was four days before the operation. The Haganah would still have time to get ready for the operation should this Tuesday meeting prove fruitless for the Agency.*

[28] *This is consistent with the letter of Platt (see above).*

[29] *In a recently released television documentary (Leonid Horowitz and Ita Gliksberg 2007), the hit team members of the Wagner assassination exposed themselves for the first time after all these years, detailing the event. The film was a release of the IBA (Israel Broadcasting Authority) dedicated to the Templer enterprise in Palestine, especially in Sarona.*

[30] *Sauer (1985) p. 114.*

Sources of the historical data used in this article

Albert Blaich Family Archive, courtesy of Horst Blaich, Melbourne.

Alan Tilbury to Martin Higgins and Danny Goldman, February 2007.

Ben-Artzi, Yossi (1996). From Germany to the Holy Land, Templer Settlement in Palestine, Jerusalem: Yad Izhak Ben Zvi, (Hebrew).

Sauer, Paul (1991). The Holy Land Called, Melbourne: The Temple Society of Australia.

Binstock, Nogah. The seizure of the German Colonies, documentary video, 1989.

Carmel, Alex (1990). The German Settlement in the Holy Land by the end of the Ottoman Era, Haifa: Haifa University (Hebrew).

Etzioni, Benjamin (editor) 1957. Ilan Vashelach, the Battles Route of Golani Regiment, Tel Aviv: *Maarchot Publications,* MOD (Israel's Ministry of Defence) (Hebrew).

IDF Archive

Kanaan, Haviv (1968). The Nazi Fifth Column in Palestine 1933-1948, Lochmei Hagetaot: Hakibbutz Hameuchad Publishing House (Hebrew).

Leonid Horowitz and Ita Gliksberg (2007). The Templers, Secrets in Tel-Aviv, a television documentary, Tel-Aviv: Israel Broadcasting Authority.

Schiff, Zeev and Eitan Haber (1976). Israel, Army and Defense, a Dictionary, Tel Aviv: Zmora, Bitan Modan Publishers [Hebrew].

Sluzki, Yehuda (1973). Haganah Chronicles Book, Tel-Aviv: Am-Oved, volume 3 [Hebrew].

Wassermann-Deininger, Gertrude (no date). We Have No Lasting City, own publishing. This is translation of the title 'Wir Haben Hier Keine Bleibende Stadt'. A testimony related by Kurt Seidler, pp. 69.

Weinmann, Bruno, Report on Alleged Murders of Karl and Regina Aimann, unpublished document, March 2007.

Alan Tilbury (1929-)

Commandant in Waldheim

Written 2007

An officer of the British Palestine Police in Waldheim at the time of the attack adds another perspective.

During the more than half-century since I left Waldheim, I had almost no contact with anyone who even knew of its existence, let alone of anything about the events of 17 April 1948.

It was a considerable emotional experience for me to read Danny Goldman's article on 'Waldheim 1948' and extracts from 'The Holy Land Called' by Paul Sauer about this eventful period so long ago, and I am gratified that many of the questions about the events of that time have been answered. My overriding comment must be to say how impressed I was to see the amount of work that Danny had put into this fragment of history, his 'history-consciousness' and concern to establish precisely what happened on 17 April 1948 – and especially how it came about that Karl and Regina

Aimann, two elderly non-combatants, were killed. I hope the following observations are of interest.

Security at Waldheim

Waldheim was atypical for an establishment controlled by the Palestine Police both because the PP's *raison d'etre* was to guard a civilian population, and because guard duties were carried out entirely by Arab TACs (Temporary Additional Constables).

Following a government decision that the TACs would not receive compensation for loss of employment once the Mandate expired, many of them absconded with their weapons throughout the country. Police HQ in Jerusalem responded by issuing an instruction that all TACs be disarmed. In the case of Waldheim, the implementation of this instruction meant that (with the exception of my own rifle) the entire guard force at Waldheim was unarmed. Naturally, I raised this special problem with my superior officers, who were sympathetic but found it impossible to get any sense out of HQ (which was already in the process of winding down).

After lining up to hand in their weapons – against the backdrop of a deteriorating security situation throughout the country – more and more of the TAC guards at Waldheim simply began to vanish, usually at night. As a form of backup, two British constables from a nearby police station were transferred to Waldheim. However, by 17 April, security at Waldheim had effectively ceased to exist – except in the symbolic sense that three British policemen were stationed there and British forces were still present in northern Palestine, albeit some hours away.

Uncertainty [on the part of the attackers] as to the state of our defences might account for the volume of gunfire that occurred, with [Haganah] machine guns blazing down the middle of the streets for what seemed like a considerable time. I made contact with the invading units with a view of meeting their commander to explain to him that this was unnecessary. In the event, I was not introduced to him – I wonder whether it was Meir Amit – until after the firing had stopped.

THE FACT THAT ONLY FOUR WEEKS BEFORE THE EXPIRY OF THE MANDATE, THE GERMAN INHABITANTS OF WALDHEIM WERE STILL LIVING THERE IN DANGEROUS CIRCUMSTANCES REPRESENTS A SERIOUS FAILURE BY BRITAIN IN DISCHARGING ITS DUTY OF CARE TO THOSE INHABITANTS

I would just add that, in my view, despite the many problems facing the British authorities at the time, and even (as I have read) of earlier uncertainty about the views of the Templers themselves, the fact that only four weeks before the expiry of the Mandate, the German inhabitants of Waldheim were still living there in dangerous circumstances, and with no scheme as yet made known regarding their evacuation, represents a serious failure by Britain in discharging its duty of care to those inhabitants

The case for the attack

Waldheim was certainly situated in a very strategic location, overlooking Jewish settlements in the valley. Meir Amit states that the seizure of Waldheim was a direct result of 'authenticated information' that the Arabs were getting ready to base themselves there (and at Betlehem).

I cannot understand the significance of the 'last document' quoted by Danny (on page 172) to the case of Waldheim – perhaps nothing was resolved in the time available.

I question whether Arabs would have attacked the settlement while there was any kind of British presence there; and I really do not think there was the slightest possibility that we would have deliberately evacuated Waldheim and Betlehem in such a way as to facilitate an Arab takeover. However, I can see that from a Haganah perspective, the risk of waiting for events to happen would have seemed unacceptable.

WALDHEIM SHOULD NOT HAVE BEEN LEFT IN THE STATE IT WAS SO CLOSE TO THE 15 MAY DEADLINE

It comes down to the point I made above that, in the light of the circumstances of the country at that time, Waldheim should not have been left in the state it was so close to the 15 May [expiry of Mandate] deadline.

The Aimann killings

I heard of the killing of the Aimanns at my initial meeting with the Haganah commander on the morning of the attack, when he explained that shots had been fired at the attackers from the first building on the Betlehem side of Waldheim, and that the attackers had been returning fire.

I was not told – and I did not know until I read Danny's article – that the Aimanns had been found hiding in the basement and had been shot in front of their children. This element of the incident makes it more difficult to dismiss Aryeh Dressler's view (on page 165 of Danny's article), that the killing was an act of revenge. His view has resonances with the then recent fate of two German men from the settlement who, having failed to return to the settlement from a pass parole visit to Haifa, survived only for a very short time before being murdered in a ritualistic and brutal manner in what was clearly a response to what had happened in Europe.

I HAVE ALWAYS THOUGHT IT MOST LIKELY THAT THEY WERE ARABS FROM THE NEARBY HAMLET, SOME OF WHOM AT LEAST WOULD HAVE OWNED FIREARMS

Whatever the complete truth in the case of the Aimanns, I think the incident originated because in the early stages of the attack some shots were fired at the attackers from people taking cover behind the Staib house. I have always thought it most likely that they were Arabs from the nearby hamlet, some of whom at least would have owned firearms. Unfortunately for the inhabitants, the Staib house was the nearest Waldheim house to this hamlet.

Subsequent British action

The British Constable and his driver stationed at Betlehem, hearing the firing from Waldheim, undertook a difficult motorcycle journey to Haifa on rough tracks over the hills and, arriving there early in the morning, alerted the ASP – still in his pyjamas – to the situation.

What happened next was quite bizarre. Having – with my two British Constables – been confined for some time in the cold store at the creamery, we were taken outside and moved to an olive grove when, in due course, some commotion became apparent on the road outside the Commandant's office. I was eventually taken up there, where I saw what appeared to be two British *Staghound* armoured cars, with the crews sunning themselves on the tops of their vehicles, eating oranges and chatting to members of the occupying [Haganah] force. I was taken to a man dressed as a British army officer, and initially assumed that he was a member of the Haganah, impersonating an officer.

He, in turn, was by no means sure who *I* was in my Palestine Police uniform. After some conversation, it appeared that he really was a British army officer, who had received a radio message from Haifa HQ, telling him to go to Waldheim (which he believed to be a Jewish kibbutz) and (or so he thought) to recover a missing British army vehicle! When he arrived at the main entrance to Waldheim, he was denied entry, but was allowed in eventually. His friendly, untroubled approach to the occupiers, and the relaxed behaviour of the *Staghound* crews, must have seemed odd to those who had been attacking the place only that morning!

I went back to Haifa with the *Staghounds* to report the situation, and the following day returned to Waldheim with the British Army convoy sent to evacuate the inhabitants, as recorded in Sauer.

139. British Police officer Alan Tilbury with his staff in Waldheim

140. The Waldheim refugees ready to be transported to Cyprus by the British Government 1948

Paul Sauer (1931-)

Forced stay in Cyprus

On 22 April 1948, upon the arrival of the *Empire Comfort* in the port of Famagusta, British army trucks stood by to take the Germans from Palestine to the holiday camp of 'Golden Sands', situated in sand dunes on the beach. On the left side of the asphalt access road were many small tents and on the right side large Indian double tents, called tepees, which provided accommodation for German prisoners-of-war. The new arrivals were allotted the small tents equipped with two, three or four iron army bedsteads. A huge tent served as a 'dining room'. A newly erected hall, constructed of cement bricks, contained shower cubicles – one section being reserved for the women and the other for the men. The first job for the refugees from Palestine was to fill the empty palliasses with straw, which was piled in large heaps.

The 'Palestiners' soon settled into their new circumstances at the 'holiday resort' of Famagusta. For the first time in nine years, they were not supervised by police guards; at long last they were allowed to feel free again, even though the tutelage by the British authorities continued. Sergeant Walker, the former Camp Commandant of Wilhelma, was appointed Liaison Officer by the Commission of the Palestine Mandatory Government in Nicosia. He was held in high regard by the Templers, as he had always been friendly and obliging, and knew them well. Walker explained to the Germans from Palestine that their stay in Cyprus was only a temporary measure and they were there as guests; the camp site of 'Golden Sands' which had been selected for them was one of the healthiest locations to be found on the island. They were expected not to engage in any employment, so as not to deprive the island's inhabitants of their livelihoods. The group called 'German Templers' was placed under the authority of Sir Godfrey Collins, Commissioner for Jewish Refugees of the Mandatory Government of Palestine (which was in the process of being wound up), as it had been decided not to create a separate administrative section for such a numerically small group. Sir Godfrey Collins was in charge of the financing of the German Templers' stay in Cyprus and of the continuation of their voyage; he did this with means at his disposal from the Public Custodian of Enemy Property in Palestine.

It soon became apparent that the 'temporary stay' in Cyprus would be for an indeterminate length of time, whereupon the Germans from Palestine took the administration of the camp entirely into their own hands. Camp Leader Richard Otto Eppinger was assisted by his deputy Walter Albrecht. Werner Struve took on the office of community treasurer and bookkeeper. The administration followed a very tight budget. They had at their disposal a per capita daily allowance (first 3, and later 7 shillings) made available by the Liaison Officer from money obtained from the Public Custodian. The job of postmaster fell to Walter Imberger. Sister Maria Wagner cared for the sick. The orphaned Aimann children were looked after by Kurt P. Seidler, who became their guardian. Luise Dreher was in charge of the camp school. She was ably assisted by Hulda Struve – who taught senior History classes – Adolf Bamberg and Walter Imberger, as well as Grete and Werner Ehmann. The spiritual leader of the Templer group was Imanuel Katz, a Community Elder, who had been entrusted with this task by Nikolai Schmidt before their departure from Wilhelma. Apart from Katz, Heinrich Sawatzky, the oldest of the Templers (born in 1861), as well as Eugen John led the services. The pastoral care of the small Protestant group was entrusted to Missionary Heinrici. The Sunday services were conducted in part by the Templers and in part by the Protestant church members. On 3 October 1948, the Templer Community – which called itself the Temple Society Refugee Branch – celebrated their traditional Dankfest [Thanksgiving]; three children were presented. Since, on arrival in the camp, the settlers' group had arranged that the 51 non-settlers, despite their protests, were given their own camp section, the Temple Society Refugee Branch formed a self-contained group filled with a spirit of communal harmony.

The 'idle life' did not appeal much to the majority of the camp inmates. In a letter of 25 July 1948, one of them complained that it would be very difficult to become used to working again. Through intensification of the camp services, those responsible sought to create activities for the people fit to work. Great emphasis was placed upon social life and entertainment. A song evening was held once a week for young and old, with the emphasis on German folk songs. Soon friendly relations were established with the German prisoners-of-war. They paid frequent visits, and the prisoner-of-war Commandant noticed with satisfaction that the fellow-Germans from Palestine exerted a decidedly favourable influence upon his men. Some Templer girls became friendly with prisoners-of-war, and several of these friendships developed into life-long unions. There was general regret when, in early September 1948, the prisoner-of-war camp was disbanded and the soldiers were repatriated. The Germans from Palestine were now able to move into some of the larger tents. In view of the approaching winter, with its severe storms and heavy rain, this was a definite advantage. Already during the night of 11 October, a severe storm damaged some of the tents. During the ensuing winter months, the wet and cold weather badly affected the refugees. They were not able to protect themselves adequately against the inclement weather.

The Cyprus group, in its hope of an early departure to Australia, was subjected to a long trial of patience. As early as 8 May 1948, the Australian Government's representative, H.T. Temby, visited the camp in order to gain a reliable picture by interviewing the refugees from Palestine, and to make preliminary arrangements for their immigration to Australia. He also flew to London in order to discuss the means of transportation with the British Government. On 16 July he was back at the camp. At the end of July, in Platres, camp leader Eppinger and his deputy Albrecht held negotiations with Temby, the Australian Brigadier White and a representative of the IRO (International Refugee Organisation). This did not result in concrete possibilities for the transportation to Australia of the Cyprus group. The situation had not altered by the time White and Temby departed on 4 August. Initially, London and Canberra reserved the right to decide upon the means of transportation of the Germans from Palestine to Australia. The choice of the ship and time of departure rested with them. Only gradually was participation in locating a suitable ship conceded to the Germans. They negotiated with British, Dutch, Norwegian and other shipping lines. However, the ships they tracked down were all rejected by the British authorities. They were usually described as 'not up to British standard'. Three Templers, who had arrived in Cyprus from Germany by plane, were in the camp waiting to continue the trip to Australia together with their fellow-Germans who had fled from Palestine.

The first group able to depart consisted of 49 persons who had chosen repatriation to Germany. They left Nicosia on 21 October 1948 on a Danish plane. Finally, after weeks of bargaining with the Commission and with London, it was decided: the Yugoslav ship *Partizanka* was to take on board the first group bound for Australia. On 16 December, they embarked at Limassol. The next day brought great excitement. A stowaway, a former prisoner-of-war, had been smuggled on board in a packing case. This incident placed a strain upon relations with the British authorities. The Liaison Officer blamed the German camp leadership for 'infamous intrigue and deception', although the latter had had no knowledge of the affair. As a result, it became even harder than before to gain British acceptance of ships the camp leadership considered suitable for transporting the refugees from Palestine. On 11 January 1949, the 37 German passengers from Palestine arrived in Sydney on the *Partizanka*. Mr Temby welcomed them whilst they were still on board ship. The Australian newspapers made much of the incident of the stowaway, and generally presented it in a favourable light, rightly viewing it as the love story of two young people, without any political background.

The remainder of the Cyprus group was obliged to spend Christmas in the camp. Christmas Eve, so Hulda Struve wrote to her children in Germany, had been beautifully organised by Miss Luise Dreher: "The children and the mixed choir, the violinists, flautists and accordion played beautiful Christmas music. Poems were recited and plays performed. We were like one large family celebrating together, so that, for a while, we forgot all earthly sorrow. There were two Christmas trees, one on either side of the stage, trimmed with decorations we made ourselves out of tins, matchboxes, nuts and silver foil. Also the snowflakes made from cotton wool looked very nice. The children received biscuits and gingerbread hearts with their names on it. We adults were also given ginger nuts and shaped biscuits for the festive days."

A week later, the New Year's Eve celebrations commenced with a short service. Richard Eppinger recalls that afterwards they sat together in the unheated large stone hut drinking hot tea and eating open sandwiches. "At a later hour, even *Glühwein* (mulled wine) was served." Amusing sketches performed by the young people captivated their audience and provided a carefree atmosphere. They looked forward to the New Year 'with more confidence', Eppinger wrote, "although there was no cause for hope".

On 26 January 1949, 45 camp inmates led by Werner Struve left Nicosia by aeroplane bound for Australia. A few days later, after several stops, they arrived safely in Sydney, where they were welcomed with great joy by friends and relatives. The same day as the air travellers departed, a further 170 members of the Cyprus group boarded the Egyptian pilgrim ship, *Al Misr* berthed in the port of Famagusta – the camp leadership had fought for weeks to gain permission to travel on the *Al Misr*. The remaining 77 'German Templers' had to bide their time in the camp of 'Golden Sands' for almost another month-and-a-half, until at last for them also the final barriers blocking their journey to Australia had been removed. On 9 March 1949, after vacating and handing the camp over to the British authorities, they boarded the *Partizanka* and met up with nine of their fellow countrymen from Germany, who were already on board, bound for the same destination. After a voyage of three weeks, they reached Melbourne on 3 April 1949. Mr Temby made a point of welcoming the last members of the Cyprus group onto Australian soil.

141. Entrance to the cemetery in Famagusta

Two members of the Temple Society and two of the Protestant Germans from Palestine died in the camp of 'Golden Sands'; they found their last resting place in Cyprus. In the years to follow, happy events and experiences were uppermost in people's memories. The unfortunate circumstances of life in the Cyprus camp, such as the wearing wait for their departure to Australia and the tutelage by British authorities in running the camp, were relegated to the background. The young generation in particular, having grown up behind barbed wire, thoroughly enjoyed the freedom on Cyprus and the opportunity to move around the island unhindered without danger to life or limb. The beautiful scenery and the many stone relics, bearing witness to a great historic past, were engraved on the minds of the majority of the refugees from Palestine. Not least, however, it was the close community life, living as one large family, which the members of the Cyprus group recall gratefully.

From *The Holy Land called*

142. Confirmation group in Cyprus Camp, 30 January 1949
From left to right: Walter Kazenwadel, Hans and Richard Hornung, Elder Imanuel Katz, Irene Eppinger, Hilda Katz

Danny Goldman (1945-)

The Famagusta Templer

REFUGEE CAMP

Excerpts from 'Famagusta's Historic Detention and Refugee Camps'

Alcatraz, Devil's Island and Fort Denison in Sydney Harbour are just a few locations where islands were used for the detention of political and criminal prisoners. The island of Cyprus was no exception; after the British took it over in 1878, they used it as a detention and refugee location for at least five different groups: Turkish POWs during WWI, German POWs in WWII, and illegal Jewish immigrants (to Palestine) between August 1946 and February 1949. The fourth and fifth groups were hosted by Cyprus as a courtesy and not as detainees: these were the remaining troops of General Baron Pyotr Wrangel, of the 'White Army', defeated in 1920 in Russia by the Bolsheviks,[1] and German nationals (Templers),[2] evacuated from Palestine in April 1948. All these groups were in the custody of the British in Famagusta.

This paper describes the camps in Famagusta, the circumstances that brought camp residents to Cyprus, aspects of life in the camps, relations between the local population and the detainees and attempts to locate relics of the camps. It is a story that must be told, as the relics of the camps are disappearing and the ex-internees are growing old.

The British took over Cyprus in 1878. At that time, the Porte [Ottoman Empire] and the British signed an agreement (the 'Convention of Defensive Alliance' or the Berlin Agreement) whereby the sovereignty of Cyprus would remain Ottoman, while the British assumed the responsibility for the administration of the island. This marked the beginning of an eighty-two-year British presence and de facto rule of Cyprus, exactly the same length of time as Cyprus had been ruled by the Venetians (1489-1571). The British received Cyprus from Sultan Abdul Hamid II, 'to be occupied and administered by England'.[3] The official reasoning behind this arrangement was the provision of an area for military staging and, in case of Russian aggression towards the Ottoman Empire, possible British intervention. The real British interest, however, was to obtain a strategic outpost in the region which was becoming increasingly significant to them. From Cyprus, they could monitor military and economical movements in the Levant and the Caucasus.[4] They could also use the island as a military post in case of trouble in the Suez Canal (opened 1869), where they had extensive interests. The involvement of the British in Cyprus only deepened with time and, by 1925, Cyprus was declared a Crown Colony, and the position of the High Commissioner was replaced by that of a Governor.[5]

One of the least known groups to be hosted in the camps of Famagusta were the Templers, who were Christian German colonists from Palestine, evacuated by the still-in-control British in April 1948, when hostilities between Jews and Palestinian Arabs were already in progress, preceding the war of 1948. The *Empire Comfort* arrived in Famagusta on April 22 with the Templers on board, who were taken to a camp located next to the harbour, known (at that time) as 'Golden Sands'. Today, this is where the strip of hotels is located south of the Old City of Famagusta, now a closed military zone pending a solution of the current Cyprus conflict.

143. 'Golden Sands', 1948
Source: private collection of Irene Eppinger-Blaich, Bayswater, Australia.
The photo provides information about the location of the camp, the proximity to the sea, and how the area looked before the massive build-up of hotels in the 1960s. The solid buildings were used by camp personnel, the tents by the refugees. The large tent is the mess hall. There are no fences or watchtowers. The photo shows where the first Templer camp had been, between the beach and the last solid building. They had moved into the larger tents to the right after the German POWs were repatriated in September 1948. In all probability, the photo was taken secretly, as the British were sensitive about their installations being photographed

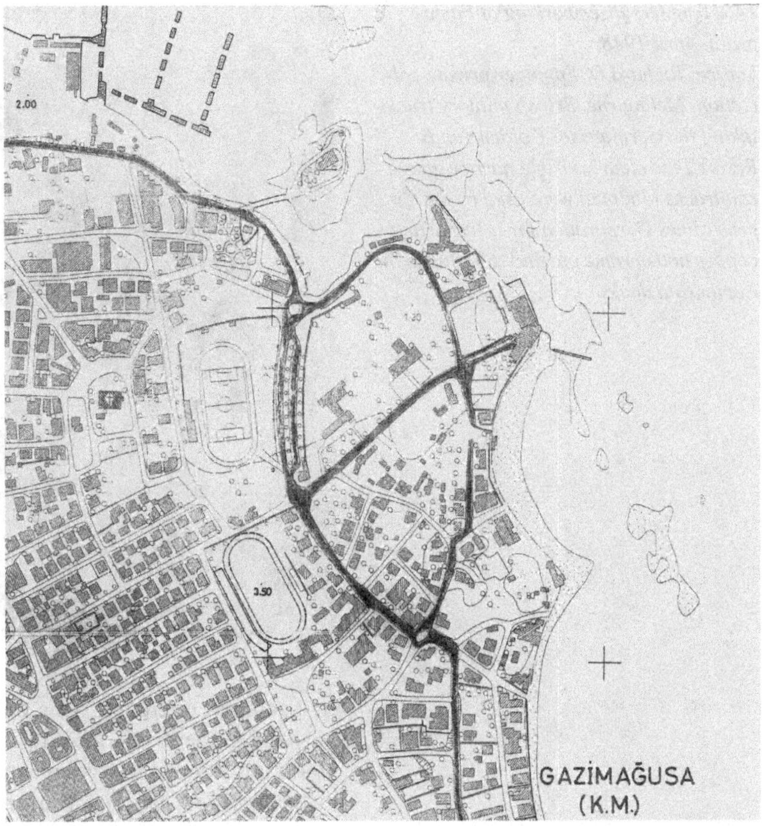

144. 'Golden Sands', detailed map. North is up. The area is between the two crosses next to the beach line. The 'arrow-head' structure in the upper part is Palm Beach Hotel, and 'Golden Sands' beach stretches to its south. The British intended to develop the area as a resort for their troops, and employed German POWs for the development

145. Golden Sands, 2005, image by DG

The relocation of the Templers to Famagusta was the outcome of a swiftly-taken decision of the British administration in Palestine on 18 April 1948. The trigger was a military operation of Jewish armed forces, resulting in taking over the two northern German colonies in Palestine *Waldheim* and *Betlehem*[6] near Nazareth, on the night of 16 April.[7] The events of the operation were violent and traumatic, with German civilian casualties. The next morning the British realized they could no longer guarantee the safety of the Templers,[8] and shipped them out of Palestine as fast as they could

146. Templers disembarking at Famagusta, April 1948.
Source: Richard O. Eppinger private collection, Melbourne. British military trucks taking the Germans to 'Golden Sands Resort'; the clearly visible narrow gauge rail tracks (762mm) were used by the Cyprus Mines Corporation for transporting copper and chrome ore and asbestos to the Famagusta docks

in a complex operation. This was also the time of beginning of hostilities between the Jews and the Arabs in Palestine, actually the first days of the 1948 war. Templer sources mention the 'whizzing bullets' in Haifa harbour as the *Empire Comfort* was boarding the evacuated Germans.[9]

The German Templers were caught between a weakening British administration, which was about to leave Palestine on 15 May 1948, and the two main populations, the Jewish and the Palestinian Arab. In the years immediately after World War II and the Holocaust, strong anti-German feelings in the Jewish community of Palestine generated hostilities directed against the Templers, culminating in the violent taking over of the two northern colonies.

The Templers came to Cyprus as refugees on 22 April 1948 and were accommodated there until October that year [and beyond, ed.].[10] The British felt they were doing the Templers a service, saving them from possible further hostilities in Palestine. The acting governor of Cyprus reluctantly accepted the German civilians, notifying all parties concerned that he expected the Germans eventually to be shipped out to Australia.[11] Templer sources mention feelings of relief shared by the evacuees on being brought to Cyprus. It was the first time in years that they were not confined to 'perimeters' (as the British termed it), since in the Palestine of 1948, they were concentrated in their own colonies behind barbed wire under guard. In Cyprus, the British did not consider them prisoners, and allowed individuals to come and go without restriction.[12] Altogether there were 378 Templers [some were non-Templers, PH] in 'Golden Sands',[13] but there is no information on how many births, if any, took place in camp. Four died in Cyprus, and three were buried in the Anglican cemetery, located in the neighbourhood of *Maraş*, not far from 'Golden Sands'.

147. Templer headstones, Famagusta British Cemetery
Photo by DG, March 2005. This is the only relic that remains of the Templer Camp. The Germans were buried side by side with British servicemen. The cemetery is a few steps from the Canakkale Memorial Cemetery; the fourth German was buried somewhere else, probably in the Franciscan Terra Sancta Church in Famagusta, today in the out-of-bounds area of Maras. The headstones, in all probability made by the internees, were of sanded and polished concrete, and the lettering was done with molten lead poured into the grooves. The stones look as new to this day

The 'Golden Sands' site contained two separate camps in the one location, with the Templers in a camp of small tents, and next to it, German POWs, mainly from Rommel's Army, captured by British forces in the battles of the Western Desert in late 1942.

The 'Golden Sands' tents for the Templers were pitched by the German POWs from the adjacent camp, located on the land side of the road that ran parallel to the beach. The Templer camp, on the seaward side of that road, accommodated about 380 Germans (including about 50 non-Templers).[14] The same group of German POWs who built the Templers' accommodation also built the Jewish refugee camps at Dekelia.[15]

The German POWs were repatriated to Germany on 3 September 1948. The Templers in the camp next door were left behind, to be released later [in stages from October 1948 to March 1949, PH]. They stood on the beach of 'Golden Sands' and waved good-bye with bed sheets to the departing ship of German POWs.[16]

148. The German POWs were repatriated to Germany on 3 September 1948. The Templers in the camp next door were left behind, to be released later. They stood on the beach of 'Golden Sands' and waved good-bye with bed sheets to the departing ship of German POWs

As for the exact location of the Templer camp, there exists only one accurate description. R. O. Eppinger, a Templer who was elected Camp Leader wrote in his diary:[17]

22.4.1948: Arrival in Famagusta in the morning, transported by the British military to 'Golden Sands' camp, situated about 5km south of Famagusta. The sick and infirm were taken by Army Red Cross vehicles and buses to Kantara in the mountains north of Famagusta.

It states clearly that the camp was located on a site where today there is a strip of hotels, stretching a few kilometres south of the Old City (see map and photos). As soon as the Templers understood that this was going to be a long stay, they opted to create a functional order, normalizing their lives in the camp as much as possible. Following their tradition of democratic community culture, as they had practiced in Palestine, they elected individuals to positions of camp leader, postmaster, treasurer, spiritual leader – assisted by religious services leaders – and established medical and educational services.

Moreover, the historical rift between Templers and Protestants (also called *Kirchlers,* 'Church-goers') that had occurred in Palestine in 1874, seemed to have healed, at least while the group remained in Cyprus. They were detained together in the same camp; Sauer reports "Sunday services were conducted in part by the Templers and in part by the Protestant church members."[18] Each group, however, did have its own spiritual leader.

Since both Jewish refugees and German Templers were resident in the Cyprus camps at the same time, the British functionary Sir Godfrey Collins, who was responsible for the Jewish refugees in Cyprus, was appointed commissioner for the German Templers as well.[19] The British decided not to create separate administrations for the two groups, but still kept the Jews and the Germans apart in separate camps, keeping the German presence secret. The Jews were north of town, and the Germans were south of town. It appears that this was deliberate British policy. Local Cypriots were not made aware of the German presence in their own town, perhaps because the British feared possible hostilities between Jews and Germans, or even between Cypriots and Germans as they, too, had strong anti-German feelings even three years after the war.[20] The Templers were also an angry group, having been expelled from their colonies, which they had regarded as their homeland, and having suffered the expropriation of their properties and the loss of generations of hard work and lifetime ventures, thus leaving them antagonistic toward the Jews and the British.

The Templers and the Jews recorded positive relationships with Cypriots. The Templers recall walking to the neighbouring Greek village, being greeted by friendly Cypriots, and listening to their music. Löbert recalls how they would go to a local cinema and when the obligatory 'God save the King' was played, the locals would whistle, stamp their feet and 'jeer' loudly in protest. "The Cypriots' feeling was that now it was their turn to be rid of the British."[21]

The Germans had some 'informal' trade relations with the locals. Hornung recalls how a German POW who was working in 'Golden Sands' for the British, created a little business by selling cement to locals:

[He] *made sure during the day that some unused bags of cement remained on the job, and at night he came back with his 'armoured cruiser' [make-shift boat the POWs made] to pick them up, [...] and pushed them through the knee-deep water for half a mile or so to a secluded spot well beyond the tents, where he sold the cement to the local Greeks.*[22]

Some Templers found employment in Cyprus while in camp. Blaich describes how she applied for and accepted a position as a housekeeper with a British family who lived in Famagusta.[23]

The Jewish camp residents, on the other hand, had a much more complex and operational relationship with the Cypriots. The first move they made upon arrival was to issue a written statement (with the help of the Jewish underground operatives who had infiltrated the camps)[24] to all Cypriots, describing their own sufferings, saying that they shared with the locals the same struggle against the British. They also made it known that they had no intention of settling in Cyprus, or depriving any Cypriots of their resources. The statement was distributed amongst the Cypriot intelligentsia.[25]

Both Templer and Jewish sources document the British attitude as mostly fair. Templer sources describe the camp commandant as a person who "had, in a way, undergone a metamorphosis, from camp boss to supervisor to friend, who even spoke German."[26] In the Jewish camps, the fact that so few (relative to 52,000 total population) died, may be attributed to the humane attitude of the British,[27] and the involvement of Jewish care agencies who were allowed to send in medical assistance, educational personnel, equipment, etc. There were social tensions in the Jewish camps described in detail by Bogner,[28] resulting from the traumatic background of the camp's population. The Templer camp was small and more homogeneous; there is no documented evidence of social tension or friction; on the contrary, in their memoirs, Templer camp veterans repeatedly mention the sense of togetherness and camaraderie. The only four deaths in the Templer camp may also be associated with the fair British attitude and the fact that the Germans succeeded in managing their lives in the best way they could, volunteering for community work, and giving much attention to the spiritual aspect of their existence.

The British granted independence to Cyprus in August 1960. The British are gone now, except for a limited presence on their 'Sovereign Bases'. But relics of the British period are to be found everywhere in Famagusta, as evidenced by public structures and the 'GR' [*Georgius Rex*] plaques and mailboxes. Hidden away in the shade of old trees in the quiet cemeteries of Famagusta are the graves of war refugees and POWs from the camps, the only remaining, mute relics of this eventful period. They stand in Famagusta as markers of human suffering and bittersweet reminders to old camp survivors, and their descendants, of the friendly Cypriots and their welcoming island.

149. Entrance to the cemetery in Famagusta

The author wishes to thank those who contributed information and personal experiences for this documentation. – Among these, in random order, are: Martin Higgins, U.K.; Manfred Löbert, Melbourne; Dubbi Meyer, Israel; Raanan Reshef, Israel; Prof. Uri Yinon, Tel Aviv University, Israel; Sara Ben-Zeev, Haifa; Horst Blaich and the Albert Blaich Family Archive, Melbourne; Klaus-Peter Hoffmann, Sydney; Neomi Izhar, Atlit Detention Camp Memorial Site archive; CZA; Dr Nahum Bogner, Yad Vashem Institute, Jerusalem; Mr. Mustafa Demirel, EMU, Famagusta; Dr Jan Asmussen, EMU, Famagusta; Prodromos Ch. Papavassiliou, Limassol; Dr Turkan Uraz, EMU, Famagusta; Selin Oktay, Izmir, Turkey; Esin Sezer, Nicosia; Dr Hüseyin M. Ateşin, EMU, Famagusta; Orhan Ozcihan, Nicosia; Ephraim Gilan, Israel.

The publishers of *'Exiled from the Holy Land'* express their deep gratitude to Dr Goldman for providing these excerpts.

Interested readers may want to peruse Dr Goldman's original work for further study at http://lib.haifa.ac.il/www/electdata/etexts/1102075.pdf

NOTES

1 *Baron General P.N. von Wrangel, (1878-1928), the 'Last Commander-in-Chief of the Russian National Army'.*

2 *The Templers are Christian members of the Temple Society, the 'Tempelgesellschaft', originating in the Württemberg Region in southwestern Germany, who emigrated to (Ottoman) Palestine during the late 1860s. (Commonly confused with* **Templars**, *an order of crusader warriors from various locations in Europe, who were active in Palestine in the 1100s– and later in Cyprus – and were also called 'Order of the Knights of the Salomon Temple'. There is no connection between the Templers and the Templars.)*

3 *Luke, Harry. 'A Portrait and Appreciation, Cyprus', London: Harap, in association with K. Rustem & Bro., Nicosia, 1957, p. 86, quotes the 'Convention of Defensive Alliance' between Great Britain and the Ottoman Empire. Luke describes in detail the increasing involvement of Great Britain in Cyprus, pp. 85-97.*

4 *Which is still done at the time of writing, in a number of 'Sovereign Bases' in Cyprus, considered British territory and operated mostly for intelligence purposes.*

5 *Gunnis, Rupert. 'Historic Cyprus, a Guide to its Towns & Villages Monasteries & Castles', Nicosia: K. Rustum & Bro., 1936, p. 22.*

6 *Not to be confused with historic* **Bethlehem** *in the Judean Mountains.*

7 *Detailed description of the events of the operation in Sauer, Paul. 'The Holy Land Called, the Story of the Temple Society', (G. Henley, trans.), Melbourne: The Temple Society, 1991, pp. 268-270; Wassermann-Deininger G., 'Here We Have No Lasting City', C. P. and Ruth Seidler, (trans. from German). Schorndorf: Author, 1995, pp. 68-74; Ben-Artzi, Y. From Germany to the Holy Land, Jerusalem: Yad Izhak Ben-Zvi, 1996 [Hebrew], pp. 12-13.*

8 *Glenk, H., in conjunction with H. Blaich and M. Haering, 'From Desert Sands to Golden Oranges: the History of the German Templer Settlement of Sarona in Palestine, 1871-1947', Victoria, BC, Canada: Trafford, 2005, p. 22; Gen. Sir A. Cunningham to the Secretary of State, telegram no. 5284 30 31, May 1st 1948, PRO file FO371/68626, explaining that "[the Germans] believe their lives to be in danger. In some cases this is undoubtedly so." This was already after the evacuation of the main group of Germans on April 22.*

9 *Sauer 1991, p. 270; Hornung, P., 'From Palestine to Cyprus', unpublished documentation, 2003, p. 1; Glenk 2005, p. 225. On that day there was already street fighting in Haifa between Jews and Arabs [DG].*

10 *Sauer 1991, pp. 272-273. This was the first group to leave camp. Other groups followed in December 1948, and January and March 1949.*

11 *Acting Governor of Cyprus to High Commissioner of Palestine, Telegram no. 262, April 29, 1948, PRO file FO371/68626, insisting that "My agreement to receive these refugees was, of course, only given in view of your assurance [...] that the arrangements were being made for onward journey to Australia".*

12 *Blaich, Irene, 'The Wennagel Story, The Fate of the Wennagel Families of Master Builders from the Black Forest, Germany, the Templer Settlements in the Holy Land and onto Australia 1699-2007' BC, Canada Trafford 2007 p.44.*

13 *Counting the numbers of persons in each departing group (see note 10 above).*

14 *Hornung 2003, p. 2; Sauer 1991, p. 271.*

15 *Bogner, N., 'The Deportation Island, Jewish Illegal Immigrant Camps on Cyprus, 1946-1948', Tel-Aviv: Am Oved Publishers, Tel-Aviv University, and the Shaul Avigur Association for Research of the Immigration Struggle, 1991 [Hebrew], p. 201. Bogner indicates a group of 1000 German POWs. Dekelia is sometimes spelled Dehkelia or Dikelya; the actual location was Xylotimvou or Xylotimbou, about five miles northwest of Larnaka.*

16 *Löbert, M. (1998, March). Templers' Stay on Cyprus in 1948, paper presented at the age 60 class reunion of Tatura camp internees, Echuca, Australia, pp. 3-4.*

17 *Eppinger, Richard. O., "Cyprus Diary", Die Warte des Tempels 267 and 268, May 1969 and June 1969 (many thanks to Martin Higgins).*

18 *Paul Sauer 1991, p. 273.*

19 *Paul Sauer 1991, p. 271.*

20 *P. Ch. Papavassiliou, personal communication, March 2005. P. Ch. P. was in a senior position in Famagusta at the time, in daily contact with the British authorities, and maintains he had no knowledge of the presence of the Germans.*

21 *Löbert 1998, p. 3.*

22 *Hornung 2003, p. 3. The British intended to develop 'Golden Sands' into a resort spot for British military personnel and named the area 'Golden Sands Holiday Resort'. The POWs were paid a small wage. See in this book.*

23 *Blaich, Irene 'The Wennagel Story' Trafford Canada, 2007, p. 51.*

24 *Gilan, E. 'From a Land of Exile to the Chosen Land, the Story of a Commander in 'Shurot Hameginim', the Haganah in Cyprus Deportation Camps', Tel Aviv: Tirosh, 2005 [Hebrew], pp. 43-61 describes in detail the involvement of the Jewish underground in the camps.*

25 *Bogner 1991, p. 49.*

26 *Hornung 2003, p. 2.*

27 *Bogner 1991, p. 218. citing Laub (1985) and Oren (1985), describing Major Maitland, the commandant of camp 65, where all the children were housed, as a 'friend of the children', a person who despised the situation of having to detain children in a camp.*

28 *Bogner 1991, pp. 219-235.*

PART THREE

Appendices

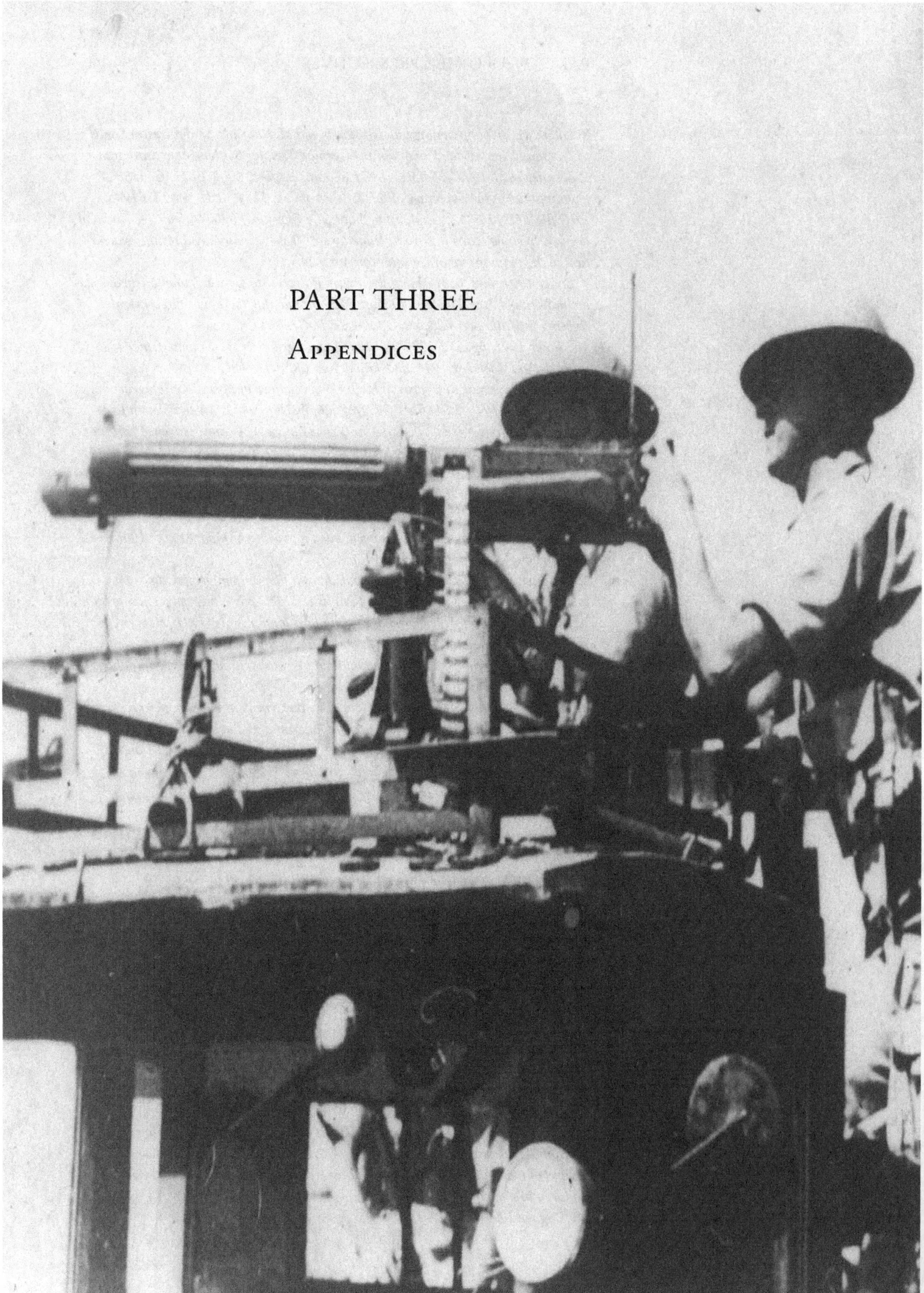

Appendix I

Siegfried Hahn (1924-)

Biographical note on Gotthilf Wagner

Born: Jaffa, Palestine, on 14 July 1887
Died: en route to Sarona, Palestine, on 22 March 1946
Father: Wilhelm Heinrich Wagner (1853-1893) died in Jaffa, Palestine
Mother: Katharina Molt (1855-1898) died in Jaffa, Palestine

Gotthilf Wagner lost his father at the age of six and his mother when he was eleven. Gotthilf and one of his three younger sisters found a new home with Georg Wagner sen. and his wife Wilhelmine, their uncle and aunt. He went to the German school in the Jaffa Templer settlement and completed his education at the American College in Beirut, Lebanon. As a twenty-year-old, he went to Germany, where he trained and worked at Deutz Engineering Works in Cologne. It was here that he met his wife-to-be, Lina Frings. On his return to Palestine, he found temporary employment with Theophil Frank in Haifa. He married Lina, who had followed him to Jaffa, on 11 December 1909. This marriage was blessed with two boys, Walter and

THE FIRST WORLD WAR BROKE OUT WHILE GOTTHILF WAS EMPLOYED AT *GEBRÜDER WAGNER*. HE WENT TO GERMANY AND ENLISTED IN THE GERMAN ARMY, WHERE HE WAS PROMOTED TO CAPTAIN AND EARNED THE IRON CROSS, SECOND AND FIRST CLASS

150. Gotthilf Wagner (1887-1946)

Kurt. The younger, Kurt, a Lieutenant, was killed in action in Tunis on 8 May 1943, leaving a wife and a young daughter. The older son Walter, with wife and children, was deported to Australia with many others in 1941.

The First World War broke out while Gotthilf was employed at *Gebrüder Wagner* (Wagner Brothers), his uncle's firm. He went to Germany and enlisted in the German army, where he was promoted to captain and earned the Iron Cross, Second and First class. In December 1920, he returned to Jaffa and to his job at Wagner Bros. He was a conscientious and hardworking man. He went back to Germany just once more in 1931 for business reasons. During those years, his energy was dedicated to the firm and he soon rose to the position of Managing Director. In 1934, Gotthilf and Lina celebrated their silver anniversary.

GOTTHILF WAS ALSO A RELIGIOUS MAN. IN 1930, HE BECAME AN ELDER IN THE SARONA/JAFFA TEMPLER COMMUNITY, A SERVICE HE PERFORMED UNTIL THE END OF HIS LIFE

Gotthilf was also a religious man. In 1930, he became an elder in the Sarona/Jaffa Templer community, a service he performed until the end of

He took his role seriously and always gave his best

his life. He took his role seriously and always gave his best. One of the six directors of the Temple Society Central Fund from 1922, he was also a director of the *Tempelbank* [Bank of the Temple Society] from 1925. As an elder, he was a member of the *Tempelrat* [Templer Council], the body responsible for electing Templer presidents, such as Philipp Wurst in 1935, after Christian Rohrer had died. In spite of all his commitments, he always found time for meeting his peers at the Lorenz restaurant or at Stephanus Frank's *Weinstube* [wine saloon].

In 1934, he became the guardian of Siegfried and Erich, the two youngest sons of his uncle Imanuel Hahn, who had died. He had a good understanding for young people and always tried to guide them on to the right path. He delighted in spending time with the boys, taking them up the *Kastel* mountain, a stretch of road on the way to Jerusalem with lots of bends. After having driven them to the top in his car, he would let them race down the hill on their scooters or bikes. On another occasion, he woke the boys at midnight to show them how the flames of a burning timber yard were lighting up the sky.

On another occasion, he woke the boys at midnight to show them how the flames of a burning timber yard were lighting up the sky

1936 – 1939, a time of political unrest in Palestine, caused much uncertainty, fear and worry. *Gebrüder Wagner* was commissioned to produce armoured cars for the British Palestine Police. This, and the manufacture and supply of irrigation equipment, which was instrumental for the devel-

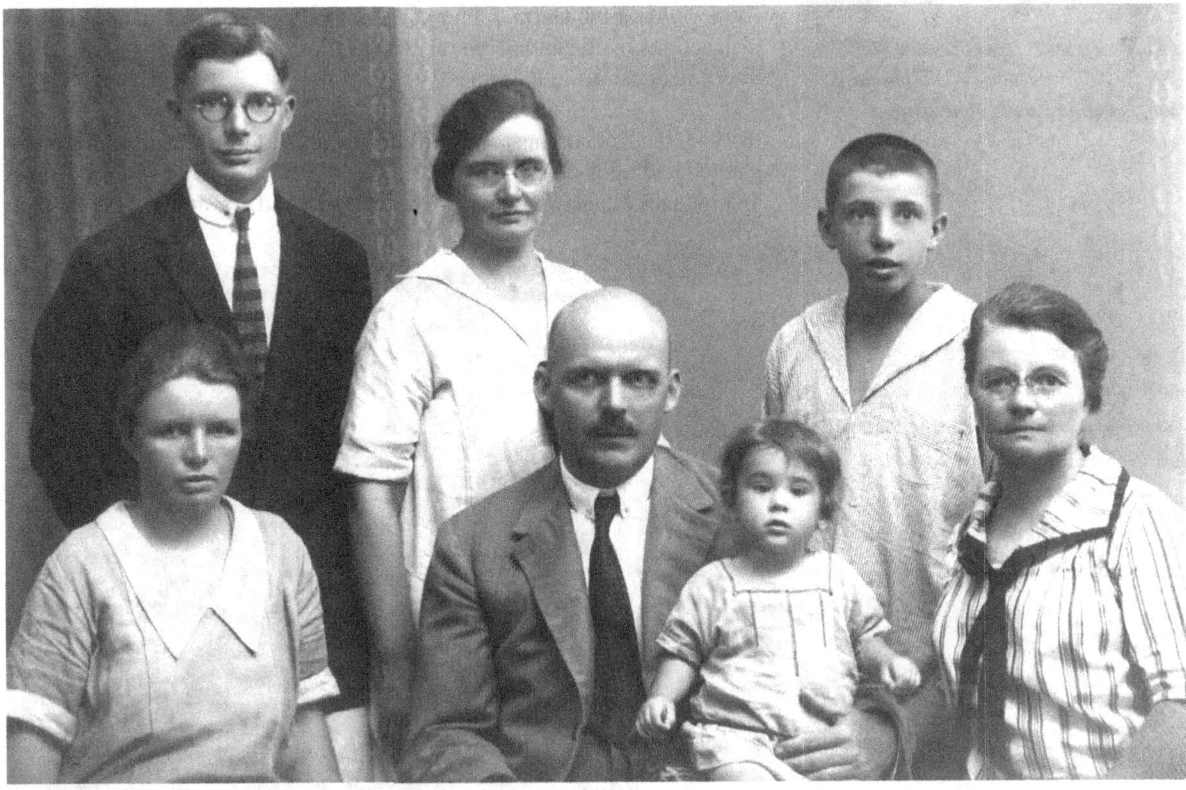

151. The Gotthilf Wagner family
Back row: Walter (son); Frida (sister); Kurt (son)
Front row: Maria (sister); Gotthilf; Erich Hahn; Lina (wife)

152. Gotthilf was an excellent businessman, negotiator and public speaker

opment of the region, earned Gotthilf Wagner an MBE [Member of the Order of the British Empire].

Gotthilf's biggest worry at the time was the City of Tel-Aviv's continual attempts to buy the land of Sarona. He was constantly haunted by the vision of Sarona being swallowed up by the city. He steadfastly believed the settlers' compensation should not be money, but land elsewhere in Palestine, or in another country.

During this period, a group of Elders was looking at a large tract of land in Lebanon, planning to buy it on behalf of the Temple Society. Gotthilf Wagner, their chief negotiator, had visited the area, Beekah Valley, at least four times before the final payment was made. The Temple Society Central Fund provided most of the money. The land was purchased in Gotthilf's name.

The outbreak of the Second World War changed everything. Many young men had left for Germany to enlist, and those left behind were interned in camps. Gotthilf was particularly shocked when the Haifa Templer community was ordered to vacate their homes and abandon the settlement. This was followed by the evacuation of the Jerusalem, Jaffa and Walhalla settlements. Gotthilf, with his wife and the two boys – Siegfried and Erich – was evacuated to Sarona, where he established his office opposite the British camp administration. He became the liaison officer between the British Authority and the German internees. His office handled all enquiries and instructions by the authorities as well as the communications between the internment camps in Palestine.

In 1943, the first attempt on Gotthilf Wagner's life was made with a bomb planted under his office window. He was wounded, but not severely. It was assumed the attack was aimed at the men who had assembled there for their

1936 – 1939, A TIME OF POLITICAL UNREST IN PALESTINE, CAUSED MUCH UNCERTAINTY, FEAR AND WORRY. *GEBRÜDER WAGNER* WAS COMMISSIONED TO PRODUCE ARMOURED CARS FOR THE BRITISH PALESTINE POLICE. THIS, AND THE MANUFACTURE AND SUPPLY OF IRRIGATION EQUIPMENT, WHICH WAS INSTRUMENTAL FOR THE DEVELOPMENT OF THE REGION, EARNED GOTTHILF WAGNER AN MBE

153. Gotthilf at home

daily roll call. Months later, however, the Jews struck again by blowing up his house in Walhalla which, fortunately, was not occupied.

In March 1946, Gotthilf Wagner, his wife and another fifteen people, the last to have remained in Sarona, were evacuated to Wilhelma. He continued to administer the lands and orange groves of Sarona from his office in Wilhelma.

One of Gotthilf Wagner's official duties was to make weekly payments to the Arab workers, who were looking after the Sarona land. He was shot and killed by a Jewish group on his second trip. This was no random shooting; no one else in the car was touched and no money was taken. It was a well-planned action to eliminate this person, the biggest obstacle to obtaining land from the German settlers.

154. War memorial service, speaker Gotthilf Wagner

Appendix 2

Arab newspaper report (*Ad-Difaa*) 25 March 1946

It is now known that Gotthilf Wagner, who was murdered by some Jews on Friday, had driven from Camp Wilhelma to pay the wages of Arab workers. It was probably the second time that he left the camp for this purpose. He knew that leaving the camp every week was fraught with danger, because the Jews had tried to kill him two years before by planting a bomb, which exploded but, miraculously, left him unscathed.

When a motor cycle followed in his tracks, his passengers were worried and somewhat afraid, but Mr Wagner insisted on keeping going. When a car deliberately stopped his progress in Livinski Road, he asked its Jewish driver to move. Then, suddenly, Jewish youths fired three shots at him at point blank range. The Jewish guard who was assigned to Mr Wagner had not made the slightest attempt to defend him. The whole thing was well thought out from A to Z and the murderers were well prepared for the ambush.

When Gotthilf Wagner was buried, there was adequate guard protection. Mr Steller was the one most affected by the murder, because he was worried about not being able to shoulder the sole responsibility for the colony with all its lands and agriculture.

Gotthilf Wagner was totally against yielding even a foot of land to the Jews and maintained this attitude to his last breath. He had pursued the land controversy as far as the Colonial Office, even up to the Privy Council. He was aware of the great Jewish demand for the land of Sarona, to which the German owners had clung in spite of bribery attempts and other difficulties. For many years, the Tel Aviv authorities had asked for a road to be built through Sarona, but Gotthilf Wagner fought against it tooth and nail. Most of the colonists were born in this country; they are familiar with the customs and habits of the population and love this land like their own lives. Thus, they parted with not a single dunum [unit of land, 1000m^2]. The Jews never tired of trying to grab parts of the German colonies, especially the lands of Sarona. They knew that Wagner was the greatest obstacle in their way. The land was the real reason for his assassination and, to get it, they did not shy away from anything, even murder, such as was committed on Gotthilf Wagner.

By courtesy of Shay Farkash

Appendix 3

Jewish newspaper report (*Haboker*) 25 March 1946

Gotthilf Wagner and his family lived in Wilhelma for the last two weeks. Before his transfer, he lived in Sarona, from where he conducted his work and supervised the lands.

From Wilhelma, he regularly drove to Sarona every Friday morning at 8am to look after his workers and pay them their wages. Some Jews knew about this. When Wagner left the camp, two men followed him on motor cycles. Steller, who was with Wagner, noticed them and alerted Wagner, asking him to turn back, but Wagner rejected this and kept going. His sister and his secretary were in the car as well. Six Germans, with an Armenian driver and an Arab guard were behind them in another car, intending to go to Jaffa.

Gotthilf Wagner was respected in the camp by the British, who allowed him to drive anywhere. When the war situation had become critical for the Germans, the Germans in Palestine had become afraid and asked the government to sell their lands and to give them British citizenship. Gotthilf Wagner, however, was against this and made a speech forbidding them to sell [even] a square foot of land.

By courtesy of Shay Farkash

Appendix 4

Palestine Post Newspaper Report 24 March 1946

Publication: The Palestine Post; Date:1946 Mar 24; Section:None; Page Nun

German Shot Dead Near T.A.

Mr. Wagner, Former Sarona Burgomaster

Palestine Post Reporter

TEL AVIV, Saturday. — The pre-war Burgomaster of the German village of Sarona, Gotthilf Wagner (59) was murdered on the outskirts of Tel Aviv yesterday morning as he drove in a weekly convoy of enemy detainees from the Wilhelma detention camp to Sarona to pay hired workers.

Friday's convoy consisted of two vehicles, in each of which sat a supernumerary policeman. Mr. Wagner's car was in the lead and as it passed Yahudieh village, one of the passengers saw a man at the side of the road look closely into the passing vehicle and then get on the pillion seat of a waiting motorcycle. The cycle then raced down the road, passed the two cars and disappeared.

Shortly after 9 o'clock, as the detainee's car turned into Rehov Litvinsky, a small car concealed behind a hillock, came out into the road and forced the Germans to slow down. As the oncoming car swerved past, two men jumped on the running boards on either side of the car in which Mr. Wagner was sitting, fired at their victim point blank, one man thrusting his hand inside the car to avoid hitting anyone else.

Payroll Untouched

Mr. Wagner died instantly from the bullet wounds in the head. His sister, a secretary and another detainee, Karl Steller, as well as a Jewish supernumerary who were also in the car, were unhurt. According to the evidence, the assassins were joined by two others in their flight. No attempt was made to touch the LP800 payroll which the dead man had been carrying.

Mr. Wagner was born in Stuttgart, Germany, and came to Palestine when a year old. His father founded an engineering works and foundry in Jaffa in 1890, and the deceased joined the firm after the first World War. He is survived by his wife and two sons who are in Germany.

The car used by the assassins to block the road at the scene of the murder had been taken from a driver of the Carmel Taxi Company earlier in the morning. It was recovered at the corner of Rehov Yehuda Halevy and Rehov Hamagid at 11.30 after the driver was released by his abductors.

By courtesy of Shay Farkash

Appendix 5

18 Feb. 1941

Auswärtiges Amt

Nicht für die Presse !

Kult E/Nf (Zv) Decker (Palä.)

Lage der Deutschen in PALÄSTINA

(Stand Februar 1941)

Nach einem Bericht des Spanischen Generalkonsuls in Jerusalem ist auf Vorstellungen, die dieser bei den britischen Behörden in Palästina erhoben hat, das Internierungslager A k k o in der ersten Novemberhälfte 1940 aufgelöst worden. Auch der Vertreter des Internationalen Roten Kreuzes in Genf, Herr Dr. Vaucher, hatte sich nach seinem Besuch im Lager für eine Verlegung desselben eingesetzt.

Die Internierten wurden nach einem neu errichteten Internierungslager in der Nähe von J a f f a verbracht. Dieses Lager ist am 24. November 1940 von dem Spanischen Generalkonsul besucht worden. Der Generalkonsul berichtet über seinen Besuch folgendes:

"Das neue Lager, das vollkommen von Stacheldraht umgeben ist, befindet sich ungefähr 2 km von Jaffa und ebenso weit vom Meer entfernt. Das Gelände, auf dem es sich befindet, ist sandig, wodurch sich Schwierigkeiten für den Sport der Internierten, wie z.B. Fußball, ergeben, den die Internierten in Akko getrieben haben.
Die Internierten sind in einigen großen, einstöckigen Pavillons aus Zement untergebracht, die in Zimmer für je 3 bis 4 Personen unterteilt sind. Obgleich die Zimmer sehr bescheiden und nur mit den notwendigsten Einrichtungsgegenständen ausgestattet sind, stellt das neue Lager bei Jaffa

doch

Pal. 3 (13.2.41 1000)

- 2 -

doch eine erhebliche Verbesserung gegenüber dem Lager Akko dar, und die Internierten sind daher mit dem Wechsel sehr zufrieden. Das neue Lager verfügt über Badeeinrichtungen mit warmem Wasser und Duschen; jedes Zimmer hat auf einem kleinen Hof, der sich hinten an die Zimmer anschließt, eine Toilette und einen Hahn mit warmem Wasser. Es besteht eine Revierstube für die leichten Fälle von Erkrankungen, während die Patienten mit schwereren Krankheiten in das Krankenhaus von Jaffa überführt werden. Der Zeitpunkt der Einschließung der Internierten wird voraussichtlich demnächst auf 20 Uhr verschoben werden, sofern die Internierten ihr Ehrenwort geben, daß sie zwischen Sonnenuntergang und 20 Uhr keinen Fluchtversuch unternehmen."

Die Anschrift des Lagers lautet:

Interniertensendung, Gebührenfrei

Name
German Internment Camp
near J a f f a
c./o. A.J.G., C.J.D. Jerusalem.

\+ +

\+

By courtesy of Lore Decker

Auswärtiges Amt Not for publication
[German Foreign Office]

Situation of the Germans in PALESTINE

(as at February 1941)

According to a report by the Spanish Consul-General in Jerusalem, who has made representations to the British authorities in Palestine in this matter, the **Acre** internment camp was dissolved during the first half of November 1940. The representative of the International Red Cross, Dr Vaucher, also recommended relocation of the same after his visit.

The internees were taken to a newly established camp in the vicinity of **Jaffa**. This camp was inspected by the Spanish Consul-General on 24 November 1940. The Consul-General reports about his visit as follows:

"The new camp, which is totally surrounded by barbed wire, is situated about 2km from Jaffa and the same distance from the sea. The terrain is sandy, which presents difficulties for the internees' sporting activities like football, which they had pursued in Acre.

The internees are accommodated in several large, single storey, concrete pavilions which are subdivided into rooms for 3 to 4 persons each. Although the rooms are very modest and only most basically furnished, the Jaffa camp constitutes a considerable improvement versus the camp in Acre, and the internees are therefore very happy with the change. The new camp offers bathroom facilities with hot water and showers; in a small courtyard adjacent to the back, each room has a toilet with a hot water tap. There is a sickbay for light cases of disease, while seriously sick patients are transferred to the Jaffa Hospital. The lockup time is soon expected to be postponed to 20:00, on condition that the internees give their word of honour not to undertake attempts to escape between sunset and 20:00."

Camp address:

Internee post, no stamps required
Name
German Internee Camp
near Jaffa
c/o A.J.G., C.J.D. Jerusalem

Appendix 6

Auswärtiges Amt

Berlin, den 16. September 1941

Kult E/Nf (Zv) Palästina
Decker

Nach einer leider erst jetzt beim Auswärtigen Amt eingegangenen telegrafischen Nachricht der Schutzmacht sind ca. 700 Reichsdeutsche aus Palästina am 31. Juli 1941 über Aegypten nach Australien abtransportiert worden.

Das Auswärtige Amt hat sofort telegrafisch Rückfrage bei der Schutzmacht gehalten und um beschleunigte Übersendung von Listen gebeten, um festzustellen, welche Deutschen von diesem Abtransport betroffen wurden und ob es sich etwa nur um Männer handelt. Weiter ist ein Delegierter des Internationalen Roten Kreuzes, der z.Zt. in Ankara weilt und von dort nach Palästina weiterreist, um nähere Ermittlungen gebeten worden. Das Internationale Rote Kreuz hat ebenfalls seinen Delegierten in Aegypten um entsprechende Auskünfte ersucht.

Es wird auch ermittelt werden, ob hierdurch der von deutscher Seite seit längerer Zeit betriebene Austausch von Frauen und Kindern und deren Heimschaffung nach Deutschland hinfällig geworden ist.

Vermutlich sind diese Palästina-Deutschen in dem im australischen Staate Victoria gelegenen Internierungslager T a t u r a - etwa 180 km nördlich von Melbourne - in dem gegenwärtig ca. 700 Reichsdeutsche interniert sind, untergebracht worden. Das Lager ist in mehrere Abteilungen unterteilt. In ihnen befinden sich Reichsdeutsche, die bei Kriegsausbruch in Australien ansässig waren und solche, die von England dorthin überführt wurden. Unterbringung, Verpflegung und Behandlung haben im großen und ganzen bisher zu besonderen Klagen keinen Anlaß gegeben.

Über das weitere Schicksal der Palästina-Deutschen werden die Angehörigen baldmöglichst unterrichtet.

DER REICHSMINISTER DES AUSWÄRTIGEN
Im Auftrag
Rundt

By courtesy of Lore Decker

Auswärtiges Amt

[German Foreign Office] Berlin, 16 September 1941

According to an unfortunately late telegram of the Mandate Power, ca 700 German nationals were deported from Palestine to Australia via Egypt on 31 July 1941.

The *Auswärtige Amt* immediately wired the Mandate Government to ask for the prompt dispatch of lists to ascertain which Germans were affected by this deportation and whether perhaps only men were concerned. Moreover, a delegate of the International Red Cross, who presently resides in Ankara and plans to go to Palestine, was asked to further investigate the matter. The IRC has also asked its delegate in Egypt for relevant information.

In addition, it is to be investigated whether the exchange programs for women and children and their repatriation to Germany (which had been pursued for some time by the German side) would now be cancelled.

We understand these Palestine Germans were taken to the Tatura detention camp in the Australian state of Victoria – about 180km north of Melbourne – where presently 700 Germans are interned. The camp is subdivided into several compounds. Some contain Germans who had lived in Australia at the outbreak of war and those who were transported there by Great Britain. In general, their accommodation, their food and their treatment have not given rise to serious complaints so far.

The next-of-kin will be informed about the ongoing fate of the Palestine Germans as soon as possible.

REICH MINISTER FOR THE *AUSWÄRTIGE AMT*

Signed .....

List of Photographs

LIST OF PHOTOGRAPHS

Source of Photographs

There are many people and archives who contributed photographic images for this book. We like to thank them all.
The first number refers to the number of the photograph and the second number refers to the page number in the book.
Note: More than one family or archive are in possession of the same photographs.

Archive of the Temple Society Australia, Bentleigh, Australia: 3:x; 5:3; 38:43; 51:56; 53:57; 55:58; 58:59; 73:68; 81:74; 83:77; 86:89; 87:89;
Archive Collection of Nahalal. Israel: 112:109; 116:140; 140:181;
Australian War Memorial, Canberra, Australia: 20:32; 21:32;
Albrecht, Aberle family collection: 44:53;
Albert Blaich Family Archive - Australia, Victoria: 37:42;
Blaich, Irene private collection: 28:37; 79:72; 113:116; 114:120; 117:145; 142:186;
Caxton World Atlas: 1:i; 11:12; 13:17; 63:62;
Eppinger, Richard O. private collection: 2:iii; 12:14; 40:44; 44:53; 49:55; 50:55; 52:56; 54:57; 57:59; 59:60; 60:60; 61:61; 64:62; 65:63; 66:63; 70:66; 75:68; 80:72; 84:84; 85:88; 96:98; 98:99; 100:99; 102:100;
Goldman, Danny private collection, Israel: 4:3; 118:147; 119:147; 120:148; 121:148; 122:149; 123:150; 124:152; 125:152; 126:152; 127:154; 128:154; 129:155; 130:155; 131:156; 132:157; 133:159; 134:162; 135:163; 136:163; 137:167; 138:173; 141:185; 143:188; 144:1889; 145:189; 146:190; 147:191; 148:191; 149:194;
Graze, Theo private collection: 82:75;
Hahn, Siegfried private collection: 41:46; 42:47; 43:51; 47:54; 48:55; 56:58; 62:61; 67:64; 71:66; 72:67; 74:68; 76:69; 88:91; 89:92; 90:93; 91:93; 97:98; 99:99; 101:100; 103:100; 104:101; 105:101; 106:103; 107:104; 108:104; 109:104; 150:198; 151:199; 152:200; 153:200; 154:201;
Haering, Manfred private collection: 8:10; 18:25;
Higgins, Martin private collection, UK:4:3;
Klink, Alfred private collection: 115:139;
Kolb, Horst private collection: 68:64; 94:97; 110:105; 111:106;
Kroh Family collection: 93:95;
Postcard Australian: 14:22; 15:23; 16:24; 17:24; 19:31;
Ruff, Helmut private collection: 69:65; 92:95;
Sauer, Paul private collection, Germany: 7:8;
Schnerring, Ingrid private collection: 6:4;
Schwarzbauer Family collection: 9:11; 10:11; 22:33; 23:33;
Steller, Bringfriede private collection: 24:35 78:71;
Thornton-Smith (Temby) private collection: 46:54;
Tilbury, Alan, UK: 139:181;
Wagner, Ewald private collection: 26:37; 27:37; 29:37; 30:38; 31:39; 32:40; 33:40; 34:41; 45:53;39:44;35:41;36:41; 95:97.

Note: *All photographic images of this book are stored on the "Albert Blaich Family Archive-Australia" computer data base, 24 John Street, Bayswater, Victoria 3153, Australia.*

About the Author

Horst Blaich was born on 1 November 1932 in Haifa, Palestine. His parents, Albert and Herta nee Katz, were both born in the Palestine Templer settlements. During WWII Horst, his mother and brother were interned in the Waldheim Camp by the British Mandate Authority. He was exchanged to Germany in November 1942. After the war Horst completed an apprenticeship as a colour photo lithographer (Graphic Arts) then emigrated to Australia and settled in Bayswater, Victoria.

In the early 1950s he was active in the Templer *Jugendgruppe* (Younger Set of the Temple Society Australia), publishing the JG newsletter and organised the annual *Sommerfest.*

Horst furthered his education and skills by completing an Advanced Printing Technology Course and then proceeded to study management and Industrial Engineering. As a member of the Institute of Industrial Engineering he served several years on their committee.

For years he was the production manager of P. C. Grosser & Co, a large Printing and Packaging Company with over 300 employees. During this time he spent several months in Chicago USA, studying the latest trends in lithographic printing with the Lithographic Technical Institute. He trained apprentices and developed an in-company training course with exceptional results.

Horst was interested in productivity improvement and quality control, especially in the concept of Quality Circles, a group problem-solving method with employee participation. He undertook a study tour of Japan to learn of that country's phenomenal productivity boom. In 1982 Horst successfully installed Quality Circles at W. D. & H. O. Wills (Australia) a major company of the AMATIL Group in Melbourne.

As an industrial engineer with long-standing productivity management experience, Horst continued to demonstrate the benefits of Quality Circles. Horst was one of the 'pioneers' in the Quality Circle concept in Australia. In 1982 he was instrumental in forming the Melbourne Chapter (organisation) of the IQAC the first such chapter outside the USA. As president of the Chapter Horst organised the first Quality Circle conferences in Australia. After five years, he became the inaugural president of the independent Australian Quality Circle Association.

In 1985 Horst formed his own company, Horst Blaich Pty Ltd, Total Quality Management Consultants and Publishers. Horst has worked successfully for and with major organisations in Australia, including government authorities, such as the defence department, the manufacturing sector and various service industries. In conjunction with Donald

Dewar, of the USA, he published a 'Team Leader Manual' on statistical problem solving techniques for employee participative teamwork.

Horst has a keen interest in family history and has lectured and trained people in the science of genealogy for over 30 years. He served as Genealogical Advisor to the Church of Jesus Christ of Latter Day Saints for many years on a voluntary basis and trained the staff in over one hundred Family History Centres throughout Australia. Horst served in many leadership positions and as a Bishop in the Church.

Horst has been married to Irene for over fifty years and they have five children and twelve grandchildren.

He is now retired and is deeply involved in family history and, as its founder, maintains his *'Albert Blaich Family Archive-Australia'* with a large Templer family computer database. He supplied valuable information and photographic images of the old Templer buildings and families to the Sarona Restoration Team under the control of the Tel Aviv municipal council in Israel. He also supplied many historical Templer images to Danny Goldman for his doctorate studies and Danny said that: "Without Horst's help and images I would not have succeeded in this task." Horst also donated many large photographs of Templer scenes to the Eretz-Israel Museum in Tel Aviv, which initiated the successful *'Chronicle of a Utopia - The Templers in the Holy Land, 1868-1948'* exhibition and book of the same name, 2006.

Horst has initiated and organised the Temple Society Australia - Heritage Group and is leading the group in modern archival and historical research. The Albert Blaich Family Archive - Australia is an invaluable treasure for researchers and historians in Israel, Germany and Australia. In recent years, Horst made many presentations of Templer themes in Australia and Germany. He also organised a permanent Templer Gallery with photographic exhibitions in the German-spoken "Tabulam & Templer Homes for the Aged" in Bayswater.

Horst is responsible for editing the TSA Heritage Pages in the monthly Templer Record and publishing the Templer Record Supplement booklets.

Index of Names and Places

Other books on the Temple Society and their settlements in Palestine are listed below. For German publications please contact Tempelgesellschaft in Deutschland (TGD), Felix Dahn Strasse 39, 70597 Stuttgart-Degerloch, Germany, E-Mail info@tempelgesellschaft.de internet: www.tempelgesellschaft.de ; or Temple Society Australia, Regional Office, 152 Tucker Road, Bentleigh 3204, Victoria, Australia. E-Mail: tsa@templesociety.org.au internet: www.templers.org

The Architecture of the Templer Colonies in Eretz-Israel, 1868-1948, and their Settlements in the United States, 1860-1925, by Dan Goldman. The Union Institute and University, Cincinnati, Ohio USA, 2003
Available as a CD from the Heritage Group, Temple Society Australia

The Holy Land Called - The Story of the Temple Society by Paul Sauer. Temple Society Australia 1991
ISBN 0 9597489 3 8

Memories of Palestine - Narratives about the Templer Communities 1869-1948, ISBN 0 9587229 8 6, TSA Heritage Group, Temple Society Australia, 2005

From Desert Sands to Golden Oranges - The history of the German Templer Settlement of Sarona in Palestine 1871-1947, by Helmut Glenk in conjunction with Horst Blaich and Manfred Haering. Sarona is known today as Hakirya in the heart of Tel Aviv, Israel. Trafford Publishing 2005, ISBN 141203506 6 Canada. E-Mail: orders@trafford.com Internet: www.trafford.com/robots/04-1334.html

Chronicle of a Utopia - The Templers in the Holy Land, 1868-1948, by Sara Turel, Eretz-Israel Museum Tel Aviv, Israel 2006

The Case of the German Templers in Eretz-Israel, by Yossi Ben-Artzi, TSA Heritage Group - Temple Society Australia 2006, ISBN 0 9577837 2 8

Shattered Dreams at Kilimanjaro - An historical account of German settlers from Palestine who started a new life in German East Africa during the late 19th and early 20th centuries, by Helmut Glenk in conjunction with Horst Blaich and Peer Gatter. Trafford Publishing 2007. ISBN 142513922 1

The Wennagel Story - The Fate of the Wennagel Families of Masterbuilders from the Black Forest, Germany, the Templer settlements in the Holy Land and on to Australia. From 1699 – 2007, by Irene Blaich and Horst Blaich. Trafford Publishing, 2007, ISBN 142512629 4